# The Making of a European Constitution

## Judges and Law Beyond Constitutive Power

Not only addressing European constitutional jurisprudence, but also the strategies and philosophies that judges and lawyers bring to bear when creating it, *The Making of a European Constitution* investigates and promotes the sustainability of a theory or praxis of 'procedural' constitutionalism.

Building upon European and American critical legal scholarship, Michelle Everson and Julia Eisner argue that constitutional adjudication has never been a neutral matter of mere judicial 'identification' of the values, norms and procedures that each society seeks to concretise in its own body of constitutional law. Instead, a 'mythology' of comprehensive national constitutional settlement has obscured the primary legal constitutional conundrum that is created by the requirement that a judiciary must always adapt its constitutional jurisprudence to the evolving values that are to be found within any society; but must, at the same time, maintain the integrity and autonomy of the law itself.

European judges and lawyers, having been denied recourse to all forms of constitutional mythology, provide us with an alternative model of constitutionalism; one that does not require a founding myth of constitutional settlement, and one which both secures the autonomy of law, as well as ensures dialogue between law and society. This occurs, however, not through grand theories of 'constitutional adjudication' but rather, as *The Making of a European Constitution* documents, through practical process.

**Michelle Everson** is Professor of Law at Birkbeck College University of London.

**Julia Eisner** has worked extensively as an academic assistant, specialising in empirical, interview-based research.

# The Making of a European Constitution

## Judges and Law Beyond Constitutive Power

Michelle Everson and Julia Eisner

Routledge-Cavendish
Taylor & Francis Group
a GlassHouse book

First published 2007
by Routledge-Cavendish
2 Park Square, Milton Park, Abingdon, OX14 4RN, UK

Simultaneously published in the USA and Canada
by Routledge-Cavendish
270 Madison Avenue, New York, NY 10016

A Glasshouse book

*Routledge-Cavendish is an imprint of the Taylor & Francis Group, an informa business*



Typeset in Sabon by Exeter Premedia Services Pvt Ltd., Chennai, India
Printed and bound in Great Britain by Antony Rowe Ltd, Chippenham, Wiltshire



*British Library Cataloguing in Publication Data*
A catalogue record for this book is available from the British Library

*Library of Congress Cataloging in Publication Data*
Everson, Michelle.
The making of a European Constitution : judges and law beyond constitutive power / Michelle Everson and Julia Eisner.
p.cm.
ISBN 978-0-415-43905-3 (hardback : alk. paper) – ISBN 978-0-203-93980-2 (e-book) 1. Constitutional law–European Union countries. 2. European Union. I. Eisner, Julia. II. Title.
KJE4445.E98 2007
342.24–dc22
2007008686

ISBN 10 (hb): 0-415-43905-1
ISBN 13 (hb): 978-0-415-43905-3

ISBN 10 (e-book): 0-203-93980-8
ISBN 13 (e-book): 978-0-203-93980-2

# Contents

# Acknowledgements

This book was completed within the ambit of the fifth framework project on Citizenship and Democratic Legitimacy in the European Union (CIDEL), funded by the European Commission and co-ordinated by the Centre for European Studies at the University of Oslo (ARENA). We are grateful to the Commission for financing, which allowed us to conduct empirical research. We are also indebted to all colleagues within CIDEL, and especially at ARENA, for their academic support and insightful critiques and commentaries. In particular, thanks are due to Erik Oddvar Eriksen, John Erik Fossum and Christian Joerges. In addition, we are also indebted to Chris Engert for editing that went far beyond the call of duty.

# Table of cases

Introduction

# The transfigured constitution

## I. The failure of the constitutional moment

The course of constitution-making within Europe has never run less smoothly. At the time of writing, French and Dutch electorates have inflicted a brutal blow upon the aspirations of European sentimentalists everywhere, rejecting the adoption of the draft constitutional treaty for Europe. As a consequence, the putative 'European Constitution' – so carefully drawn up by the European Constitutional Convention and so firmly approved by an Intergovernmental Conference – now languishes in limbo, a seemingly unloved and unlovable document, and simple testament to the failure of European parliamentarians and governments to force a true constitutive moment within Europe.

Why did this happen? What caused the peoples of Europe to reject such a carefully prepared appeal to their constitutional instincts? The answer to this question is especially revealing: popular rejection of the draft treaty cannot be traced to a single source of public discomfiture with or about the specific aims of European integration. Instead, voices of constitutional dissent are clearly discordant with one another, as well as with the current process of European integration as a whole, indicating that the lack of agreement about the future European *telos* is not, simply, a temporary check on integrationist ambitions, but, rather, a pathological feature of European politics.

At the level of the identification of a joint political will to create or entrench Europe as a 'Union', the death-knell has been sounded for constitutional aspirations. A European polity does not exist. For all of the European Convention's efforts to forge a common European desire for and interest in 'closer European union', the publics of Europe remain inexorably divided, not simply along national, but, vitally, also along ideological lines. For every 'European federalist', who is possessed of a firm will to join within a European political community, we can also identify a malcontent, to whom the notion of a constituted Europe is anathema, either since he or she possesses a preference for the maintenance of national community, or, importantly, since he or she has already committed him/herself far beyond the European ideal, in order to embrace more globally conceived conceptions of community.

In terms of traditional constitutional theory, such overwhelming discord and disjunction amongst Europeans amounts to one highly uncomfortable fact: the political effort to create a European constitution has been comprehensively frustrated. It has ground to a standstill because European publics have failed to join together as a constitutive power, or *constituent pouvoir*, with a common will powerful enough to endorse the efforts of a European Convention to draft a constitutional text of enduring ideological and governing power. Further, the brave, if perhaps naïve, endeavour of European elites to open up the process of the concretisation of the governing institutions of the EU to review and endorsement by the peoples of Europe has backfired in a historically significant manner. It has intensified rather than overcome division and discord amongst individual Europeans, thus retarding the establishment of the unitary European political community from which a clear and common constitutive power might be derived. If the making of a European constitution is primarily a matter of an inspirational political process, whereby individual Europeans come or are brought together to identify and to endorse the shared set of common and entrenched values that will create and guide the institutions of European governance, then our European Union must surely remain without a constitutional text for the foreseeable future.

## II. The power of law beyond the constitutional moment

Yet, the failure of the constitutional convention process is also far from being the end of the European constitutional story. More particularly, and with a specific eye to the evolution of the European legal order, the European Constitutional Convention and the International Governmental Conference (IGC) on the draft constitutional treaty might be argued to appear less in the guise of momentous, if counterproductive, attempts to force the pace of political constitution-making within Europe, and more in the character of momentary distractions from the real-world and nitty-gritty business of the judicial establishment and elaboration of a specific form of constitutionalism for Europe. Speaking historically, processes of European integration have often been driven by law, rather than politics, such that one former Advocate General of the European Court of Justice (ECJ), when interviewed for this volume, might comfortably assert the utter irrelevance of the convention process:

> If the French or the British or whoever it is, or the Dutch, are voting against it, that's not a disaster for me. More important for me is constitutionalism. And we have constitutionalism.

'Constitutionalism', a legal process of the extrapolation of the values and institutions, which will determine the course of our joint European life, proceeds apace, untroubled by all failed political efforts to establish a European polity. To this exact extent, then, the unexpected strength of public frustration with the draft treaty, as well as glee at the failure of the Constitutional Convention and ralification process, might be readily explained. Not only were Europe's self-nominating governing elite assuming a politically constitutive mantle for a public who felt, by stark contrast, that their popular sentiments had been subverted rather than represented; instead, they were also doing so in an on-going context of European integration, within which a supranational European legal order had already long set about creating the long-term values and institutions that characterise Europe, imposing them upon a European public without any thought for popular legitimation.

For European lawyers at least, negative popular referenda in Holland and in France have had little impact upon a daily legal task of giving life to a European constitution. European lawyers confidently declared that Europe was (in part at least) already in possession of a European constitution as early as the 1980s. Increasingly, national lawyers overwhelmingly concur. The European legal order *already* constitutes a constitutional framework, within which the ECJ, with its seat in Luxembourg, has consistently usurped the traditional role of a constitutional court, and under which, national law and national politics have slowly been subordinated to a 'federal type structure' that is governed by a 'supreme' European legal order.

In popular imagination, which has, perhaps, cast its eye over historical instances of constitution-making, such a situation cannot but seem to be curious and alienating. Within the western tradition of popular self-determination, constitutions, supreme courts and sovereign political communities (including federal political communities) are generally established following tumultuous political conflict, or even revolutions – whether glorious, bloodthirsty or velvet in nature – at the conclusion of which, 'we, the people' join together to establish common goals and values, and to direct institutions of government, including the law, in pursuit of those aims. The Philadelphia Convention, establishing the self-evident truths of the US Constitution, thus still holds the power to capture and inspire the public mind, standing as a beacon to the ability of a once-colonial populace to throw off the legal fetters of an oppressive power and to furnish itself with a measure of national self-determination.

Within the European setting, however, historical paths of constitution-making would seem to have been reversed. Once-proud and self-determining nations succumb to the progressive powers of legal edict. Lawyers and their legal order furnish revolutionary impetus: swords and guns are put aside in favour of the more muted, but equally effective, revolutionary fervour of judicial and legal pronouncement. Europe's law is supreme since its lawyers have declared it to be so, and because national lawyers have acquiesced in such pronouncements. 'We, the peoples of Europe', by contrast, are no longer the authors, but have instead become the passive subjects of a new and usurping European constitutional tradition.

Alienation is layered upon alienation. Europeans are not only disregarded by their own political elites. Instead, they are also dictated to by their own legal servants. This apparent fact gives rise to one overwhelming concern about the legitimacy of current processes of constitution-making within the European Union and, accordingly, furnishes a simple explanation for the primary investigation undertaken within this book. The political effort to impose a written constitutional document upon the peoples of Europe was, perhaps, lacking in legitimacy: how could the national and European parliamentarians and bureaucrats gathered together within the European Convention have simply usurped the constitutive prerogatives of European peoples? Yet, this effort was also easily rebuffed: the peoples of Europe have rejected the draft constitutional treaty. At the same time, however, the legal process of constitution-making within Europe continues unabated, apparently unchecked by negative public sentiment. Accordingly, vital questions must now be posed to lawyers throughout Europe with a renewed urgency: for whom are you making a constitution, where does your constitutive authority derive from and how are you accountable or responsible to the peoples who are the subjects of your constitution?

## III. Law in the making of the European constitution

Both national and European lawyers play their important part in the creation of a constitutional order within Europe. At national level, member state judiciaries have allowed European law to encroach upon their own established jurisdictions, often setting the political preferences of their member state governments aside – and sometimes even uprooting age-old national constitutional principles and traditions – all in the service of the strictures and individual rights found within European law. At European level, the ECJ has taken on a mythical character; its notoriety within legal history has been resoundingly assured by its proven ability to transform a once-simple order of international law – addressed to the member states and lacking in immediate relevance for individual Europeans – into an all-pervasive fact of European life, which can be relied upon by all European citizens, in order to assert their European rights above politically legitimated national legislation. Equally, however, the ECJ also plays a daily and vital role in the shaping and the controlling of the character and relative governing powers of European institutions, such as the European Parliament, European Commission and Council.

Academic lawyers have evolved very many theories to explain and to justify the unusual and unusually potent role that national and European lawyers have played in entrenching the European legal order throughout the continent. Thus, to give only one example, it can be argued that the assertion of the dominance and legitimacy of the European legal order is always only conditional in nature, since European law is derived from and, therefore, dependent upon the constitutive power and approbation of national constitutional orders for its existence. Equally, however, non-legal academics have also sought to cast the apparent expansionism of the European legal order in a less pejorative light. The European legal order is not in the business of usurping (national and European) political competences. Instead, or so European political science argues, European law is still subject to political checks and guidance, because member state governments, or the 'Masters of the Treaties', are always free to rein back, or even overturn, European legal developments during the process of the revision of European treaties (i.e., at IGCs).

However, powerful as such arguments may be in academic terms, they are nonetheless also limited in one very important respect: founded either in grand ideological schemes, which seek to explain how the European Union as a whole is legitimated, or, alternatively, derived solely from the internal grammar and logic of law and legal development, they fail to offer non-lawyers a direct insight into the mind of the law. A telling question remains unanswered: why should a European public trust in a European constitutionalism, or the ability of European law to compensate for the lack of a constitutional moment and to establish the values and institutions which do and will dominate European life? In other words, if constitutions are generally held to encapsulate the common values of the publics that they serve, extra-legal opinion is surely entitled to ask how the lawyers, who are creating a European constitution 'outside' conventional political process, sift through a multitude of competing European ideologies, establish authoritative constitutional values, and, subsequently, reconnect with the popular sentiments and aspirations that are prevalent within European society. The European legal order, encompassing national and European law, is said to be unique. Its emergence has challenged all our common preconceptions about the nature of law within constituted societies. European law was not created by the peoples of Europe; nor is it directly governed a European political community. Seen in this light, the onus upon law and lawyers is thus surely a heightened one of self-justification and extra-legal explanation. Where do the values promulgated by a European legal order derive from? Is Europe's law a simple reflection of the personal opinions and prejudices of Europe's lawyers, or does it have its roots in a deeper form of legitimation? Given the absence of a European constitution, how does Europe's 'ethereal' or abstract law reconnect with the concerns, interests and values of a European public?

This book seeks to answer these vital questions. More particularly, it seeks to examine interconnections between judicial/legal pronouncement and political processes of constitution-making, as well as the wider relationships that are maintained between modern (post-national) law and modern (post-national) societies. In tackling these questions, however, the study also diverges in its approach from many current academic analyses of constitution-building within Europe. First, a lesser, tangential, emphasis is placed upon the current political effort to furnish the EU with a constitution. Second, re-locating the primary focus of analysis upon the role of law in constitutional progress, the study is concerned less with grand interdisciplinary theories, which seek to explain the whole of European integration, and more with the identification of a legal narrative of constitution-building, which focuses upon the establishment of the immediate 'societal' legitimacy of a European legal order. Third, and as a direct consequence, the study also departs from established approaches to the theorising of constitutional development, arguing that the story of the emergence of a legally driven constitution-building process within Europe cannot be usefully explained with reference to entrenched frameworks of state and constitutional theory, but must, instead, be analysed through the lenses of legal and social theory.

## IV. Seeing into the mind of European law

'Seeing into the mind of law and lawyers' is not an easy task. In particular, and as a part of its integral vocation to remain 'apart' from the society that it serves, law is created by its own semantic and grammatical structure. The necessary social impartiality of law – its ability to retain independence when adjudicating between diverse and conflicting interests within a single society – demands that law and lawyers pursue their own logics of legal development. Accordingly, law is an ethereal and abstract construct, a transcendental framework with its own veil of 'formal' legal reasoning, which both protects law from partisan embroilment within the competing values or 'value irrationalism' present within a non-legal environment, *and* safeguards a wider society, ensuring that lawyers remain true to the cause of law, promoting *its*, rather their own personal, ethics and morality. At the same time, however, law is *also* a part of society, a mechanism of social interventionism and integration, which is beholden to extra-legal aims and values and which has measurable impacts within a real-world of societal organisation.

Law exists at the very heart of a contradiction. On the one hand, it is and must preserve its status as an autonomous institution, set apart from the real-world of social interaction. On the other hand, however, it is also a social institution, having tangible relationships with and material impacts upon an extra-legal environment. At the level of the effort to understand the part that lawyers have played and continue to play within the making of a European constitution, this contradictory status has a number of consequences. First, and most importantly, the genesis of legal constitutional development within Europe cannot simply be laid bare by doctrinal or purely legal investigation of the case law and pronouncements of European and national courts. These are the simple external manifestations of internal lawyerly dedication to a theology of legal evolution, which might only be understood within its own transcendental terms. Instead, the self-referential veil of legal reasoning can only be drawn aside, the real impetus for constitutionally expansionist judicial decision-making only be teased out from behind an established canon of legal self-justification, where judges and lawyers are ejected from their courtrooms and law libraries. The underlying justificatory narrative for the judicial and legal act of constitution-building within Europe can only be found where law and lawyers are denied recourse to traditional legal dogma, to be subject, instead, to carefully prepared structural interrogation, which peels back the layers of formalist self-illusion to slowly, if tentatively, reveal the true manner in which the law and lawyers conceive of their relationship with a real-world.

To this end, this current study turns away from traditional doctrinal legal analysis to instead embrace and deploy socio-legal methodologies that seek to pry behind the façade of formal law, in order to identify the exact manner in which lawyers and law engage with the facts of an extra-legal environment. How do lawyers and judges confront social facts? How do lawyers and judges choose which non-legal interests, concerns or values to privilege within a legal semantic? How, more importantly, do judges and lawyers seek to reconcile extra-legal interests, concerns and values within a self-contained body of abstract legal doctrine?

At the level of national law, structured interviews are accordingly conducted with judges and lawyers of the High Court of England and Wales in an effort to reveal the reasons why member state jurists have been so complicit in the rolling back of national jurisdictions and have likewise played their integral part within the acceptance of the supremacy of the European legal order. Why have national judges dispensed with national self-interest? Why have they allowed their constitutional orders, given constitutive power by the individual peoples of Europe, to be encroached upon by a supranational legal order, which itself seems to have little or no constitutive authority? The famous Article 234 EC 'preliminary reference mechanism' establishes an interface between national and European legal orders. Why, at this interface – establishing the exclusive right of the ECJ to rule on the meaning of European law – have national judiciaries acquiesced in the process whereby individual European legal right has been asserted above national political community? Equally, however, at European level, complementary questions can be and are posed. Taking a data-set made up primarily of former judges of the ECJ, and focusing the analysis upon the pivotal European 'constitutional' principle of 'the balance of powers', the effort is one of ascertaining why European judges feel confident in asserting the constitutional authority of European law. Which are the means that European judges deploy in order to justify their readily apparent stance that European society has developed to the degree that its lawyers can confidently declare the ever increasing breadth of their own jurisdiction? Equally, how does or can European law justify decisions, apportioning prerogatives and competences within its own jurisdiction; decisions that determine who, amongst a cacophony of competing European and national institutions, governments and publics wields the real power of decision within a European Union?

## V. From constitutional to legal theory

This structural unveiling of constitutional legal narrative within Europe, however, also has its theoretical consequences. The traditional division that is made between political processes of constitution-building and legal processes of constitutional adjudication is a powerful one. Law, we are often reminded, has no part to play in the initial determination of the values and institutions that will govern any given individual society. Instead, the primary legal constitutional function is one of execution of the constitution and its preservation in the face of any illegitimate assault by 'constitutionally deviant' political forces. First comes the constitution, then comes the law: traditional constitutional theory accordingly focuses on the faithfulness or otherwise of a constitutional judiciary to a founding constitution, as well as the means whereby such faithfulness can be assured. Which interpretational rules should a constitutional judiciary apply in order to divine the meaning of a constitution in any given context? How can we be sure that judges and lawyers will not subvert the constitution to their own or others' political aims? These questions are asked in all constitutional jurisdictions, and also find their echo within recent European constitutionalisation debates with, for example, the European Constitutional Convention seeking to establish written constitutional guarantees for the professional competence and independence of a European judiciary. The substance of Europe's politically conceived constitution, it seems, would most appropriately be safeguarded by a professionally irreproachable and apolitical cadre of European lawyers.

The independence and, above all, the professionalism of Europe's lawyers is also a factor within the following analysis. However, given the lack of a founding (political) constitutive act within the EU, as well as an underlying aim to unveil the thinking behind a legal process of European constitution-building, this analysis cannot but step beyond constitutional theory in its endeavours to examine the European legal order's narratives of constitutional self-justification. Constitutional theory can help us to understand how lawyers treat a constitutive act, or a formal constitution. What it cannot do, however, is explain how lawyers justify their own actions in substituting for the constitutive act and formal constitution. The political process of constitution-building within European has failed; law continues to compensate for that failure, ordering and mediating between diverse interests, values and ideologies within a 'federal-type' constitutional framework. However, the legal act of ordering and mediation, and, above all, its legitimacy, can only be revealed and tested within bodies of social and legal theory, which investigate the far broader relationships that are established between law and the extra-legal environment in which it is embedded.

Social and legal theory is thus concerned far less with intricate, if abstract, questions of how law might identify and apply the values encapsulated within constitutional norms, and far more with the fundamental, but nitty-gritty question of how law maintains its own impartiality, or autonomous character, but, likewise, responds appropriately to a real-world and its very immediate social and political demands. What is law's *proprium*? Law, so social and legal theory reminds us, is forever caught on the horns of a dilemma. Law is not of this world, but is, instead, a transcendental force of self-referential reasoning. At the same time, however, law's underlying claim to dispense of social, as well as legal, legitimacy determines that it must engage with a world outside law, in order to bring its abstract formulations into line with an actual realm of social and political contestation. The 'constitution' might well claim its own pre-eminence above law, or, indeed, above social and political process. Nonetheless, we are all aware that this pre-eminence is constantly tested by far more immediate and tangible processes of legal and social interaction, which, in their turn, cannot be legitimated with simple recourse to the imagined norms of constitutional tradition.

As such, social and legal theory offers us a far greater opportunity to assess the hidden narrative of legal constitution-building within Europe, testing its legitimacy in the light of the ability of Europe's legal system to order and mediate effectively between the tangible, yet often conflicting, interests and values of European publics. To return to our starting point: political processes of constitution-building within Europe have failed *precisely* because European publics have been unable to identify and establish a constitutive will, a common ideology, or set of shared values and an agreed upon goal of integration, which might be used to direct the institutions of European governance, including a European 'constitutional law'. Yet, Europe is a social and political reality, to which Europe's legal order does and – if we are not simply to dispense with the European experiment or, alternatively, descend into meaningless political violence – *must* respond.

Europe presents us with a real-world of social and political integration. Likewise, this is a real-world, which is characterised by the presence of very many and very diverse political, social and economic values and interests. Similarly, the European legal order exists and, with its founding roots within national (liberal) constitutional traditions, exists *precisely* in order to mediate conflict between interests and to give voice to 'legitimate' values. Seen in this real-world light, the on-going process of legal constitution-building within Europe might, accordingly, be considered less an assault upon the value-laden integrity of European publics, and more the continuance of a 'civilising' European tradition beyond national boundaries, whereby conflict is diffused and 'just' social organisation established with reference to an authoritative framework of law. Yet, in order to make good this claim, the legal process of constitution-building within Europe must likewise be subject to probing investigation: taking a legal narrative of constitution-building as the focus for analysis, which are the mechanisms that ensure the authority and legitimacy of a constitutional and constitutionalising European legal order? Similarly, stripping the question down to more immediate terms: given continuing deep-seated conflict on the meaning and value of European integration, how can and do European lawyers mediate – daily and authoritatively – between divergent social and political positions, deciding which value or which interest will prevail in each concrete case before them?

## VI. The transfigured constitution: a force for legal and social good?

The problems posed by European integration are not, perhaps, unique: after all, and all equalising constitutional traditions apart, all societies continue to be marked by deep-seated conflict between the values espoused and interests promoted by social actors. Accordingly, exacting study of the mechanics of legal constitution-making within Europe gains in general significance; not, however, since European law is *sui generis* in nature, but rather since functionally imperative European processes have – uniquely – denuded and stripped away all totalising constitutional myths to reveal, instead, a real-world of inexorable societal contestation, as well as the true – and very fragile – nature of the legal process that governs contestation.

The current degree of alienation felt by European publics towards a European legal order that is no longer anchored within notions of service to an established political community is wholly understandable. Nonetheless, Europe's law is not simply an alien force, responding to novel and unknown problems of human governance. Instead, the European legal order has grown out of national complexes of law and responds, at European level, to social conflicts and problems of social organisation, which are also present within member state societies. The oft-touted *sui generis* nature of Europe's law must, as a consequence, be cast in more carefully differentiated terms. Certainly, the underlying legal narrative of constitution-building within Europe contrasts starkly with traditional constitutional narratives with all their appeals to elusive and illusionary notions of joint and indivisible national community. Nonetheless, this narrative is also a generalised and generalisable one, applicable to all modern societies, whether those societies are national, post-national, supranational or international in nature. To the extent that processes of European integration have simply stripped away all myth and all illusionary narratives of constitutional and legal perfection to reveal true social process, they have also revealed the true face of law, as well as its underlying and inspirational modern mission of structuring societal integration within a real, rather than imagined, world.

Public alienation in the face of a constitutional and constitutionalising European legal order might, thus, also be considered misplaced. To the exact, but *only*, degree that European law can furnish us with a narrative that justifies its constitutional and constitutionalising functions, it appears less in the guise of a repressive and destructive instrument of ideological (federalist) domination, and more in the character of a modern and responsive instrument of societal governance. In the absence of abstract, pre-conceived schemes of human governance, the legal order within Europe is forced to articulate real-world schemes of legal legitimacy or self-justification. A revealed real-world possesses its own tangible demands for 'justice'. In order to establish its own authority, legal narrative must accordingly both preserve its own internal integrity, and be socially responsive. It must reply reflexively to the conflicting political and social demands found within a realm of real, rather than posited, social organisation, mediating between those demands without, however, ever sacrificing its own legal impartiality. This modern legal task is undoubtedly an onerous, possibly even an impossible one. Nonetheless, where all totalising axioms and myths of social equalisation are stripped away, and law is forced to face a reality of societal contestation – which, by the same token, allows for the political articulation of social concerns and values that are otherwise repressed and disregarded within governing (constitutional) myths – legal acts of social ordering and mediation may also take on a truly universal character that transcends, rather than destroys our historical constitutional traditions.

Political efforts to force a constitutional moment within Europe have failed. Yet, it is perhaps a blessing that they have done so. Our traditional (politically constituted) constitutions are undoubtedly flawed, being founded within an inspirational but ultimately spurious universalism, which itself derives from the illusionary notion that the concretisation of one set of social values and institutions can or does represent the whole of human nature. The result is (sadly) the creation of a myth and a betrayal of real-world social process; an exclusionary act, which denies the validity of emerging interests, concerns and values that conflict with the revolutionary, but entrenched, aims of the founding constitutive act. The true inspirational quality found within messy, but realist, processes of European integration is one of transfigured universalism. Europe currently transcends the limitations of its member states, with their national myths, national constitutions and national laws. Founded within legal principles of (national) non-discrimination and responding piecemeal to real-world functional demands, the European Union has also escaped the confines of ideological pre-determination, allowing a real-world of social and political organisation to continue to articulate its real-world (sometimes yet-to-emerge) demands for social and political justice. Seen in this light, the final and formal constituting of a closed

European governing order would also be anathema to transfigured universalist European ideals, an exclusionary reversal of the historical effort to ensure that *all* may actually share within a joint European existence.

To the extent that legal processes of constitution-building within Europe are also a part of a historical movement, which (though necessarily imperfect) has seen all European and national institutions of governance, as well as European publics, implicated within the (largely accidental) effort to transcend the limited and illusionary universalism of nation states and national constitutional settlements, such processes should never be too readily dismissed as illegitimate and alienating legal acts. Instead, to the degree that an underlying European legal narrative of constitution-building preserves the integrity of law (legal autonomy and impartiality), facilitates the social responsiveness of law (legal reflexivity) and, further, sustains and orders societal contestation (legal universalism) within Europe, the constitutional activities and aspirations of European judges and lawyers are not a part of the end of the constitutional story. Instead, they are a blueprint for legal process within the next chapter of the constitutional story; a constitutional story which is now witness to the transfiguration of the notion of the constitution. The Constitutional Convention may have failed in its political efforts to constitute Europe. Nonetheless, European law may yet hold the key to a brighter constitutional future.

Chapter 1

# Constitutional mo(u)rning

## I. The constitution is dead

This book begins with a radical message: the conclusion of a constitutional treaty by the European Union would not have ushered in a glorious new age of constitutions and constitution-making. Instead, the still on-going, but increasingly uncertain, effort to present Europe with its own constitutional treaty, together with the context of continuing European integration within which it is embedded, is only one step further down a road of contemporary social, political, legal and normative development, which cannot but end in a radical reformulation of our modern perceptions of constitutional provenance, constitutional application and constitutional change. This radical message is not, however, specific to European developments; nor is it limited to the telling, but conceptually restricted, observation that whatever Europe's recent proposed constitutional treaty was, it was not a 'Constitution'.[1] Instead, the guiding contention is nothing more, nor less, than the assertion that the axiom of liberal constitutional settlement that was determinative in the formation of a modern, civilised and civilising, *res publica* or state is now too blunt an instrument to capture and control contemporary patterns of governing and governance, too antiquated a myth to nurture and sustain complex, questionable and questioning polities in all their myriad and contested national, supranational, post-national and transnational constellations.

The emphasis of this book upon European processes of 'constituting' and 'constitutionalisation' is therefore best understood, not as an introspective European act of examination, explanation and analysis of particular post-national assaults on the leading paradigms of modernity, but, rather, as an effort to deploy Europe as a mirror to global processes of disaggregation and disintegration within notions of the constituted polity and, further, to construe the European Union as a laboratory within which many of our new, often highly experimental, forms of societal organisation are now being formed. In particular, however, Europe proves its full analogous worth, as its core assault on statal organisation, its factual, though often accidental, undermining of the axiomatic certainties of national polities and constitutions, is accompanied by tentative and stumbling endeavours to retain many of the normative qualities of the liberal (nation) state and its concomitantly liberal constitutional settlement within its own 'organic'[2] organisational web of legal and institutional evolution – or within what might and will be termed (European) constitutionalism.

## II. The constitution is dead; long live the constitution!

Accordingly, the radical nature of this guiding assertion does not necessarily lie in any positive rejection of the substantive values that are congruent with liberal constitutional settlement, but, rather, within an overdue empirical verification of the inherent fallacies and mythologies of the constituted state, or modern *res publica*. Our contemporary constitutions are complex and wondrous beings. Their vocations to encapsulate and normatively instantiate the 'deeper' guiding governing principles, not just of one polity at one time, but of whole societies and groups of societies in all their evolutionary diversity – from their revolutionary (constitutive) beginnings, to their contested efforts to supply universal (substantive) justice, and to their (process-based) political maturity[3] – cannot but mean that a single modern constitution will serve (as, indeed, many have served) many concrete purposes in very many different ways at very many different times.[4] To give but a few examples: the constitutional function of the protection of the individual from the sovereign power may be contrasted with that of the incorporation of the individual within the sovereign power; the constitutional definition of political process or apportionment of the sovereign power between individuals and groups of individuals may be compared with the constitutional promise of primacy for unitary political process, and further contrasted with the constitutional re-assertion of individuality against political process, as well as with less tangible constitutional functions, such as the furnishing of the focal point for a national constitutional identity.[5] Nonetheless, amongst such a cacophony of real-world and poetic constitutional purpose, the liberal constitutional settlement seems also to proffer us a central and constant modern axiom of logic-serving polity identification and empowerment; and it is precisely this axiom that Europe so neatly, if wholly unthinkingly, undermines.

The logical genius of modernity and its liberal constitutional settlement is thus, perhaps, best identified in the post-revolutionary constitutive act that both confirmed the pre-eminence of human individuality ('rights of man and of the citizen') and secured the *ancien* sovereign, at the same time transfiguring that once authoritarian sovereign into an expression of the collective political will of an indivisible and finite (national) polity, made up (of inspirational necessity) of individuals. In other words, the modern revolutionary republic, in all its constitutional fervour, was to transcend the achievements of an ancient *res publica*, not only incorporating Judaic-Christian notions of individual empowerment within a republican political collective, but also, and all the while, maintaining the real-world functional advantage of the pre-modern monarchical sovereign in the character of the modern political collective.

In the ancient *polis*, '[Roman] citizens were men bound to one another by the personal bond of fellow-membership of one body [the Republic]' (Salmond 1902: 49), to such an extreme degree that the citizen's individuality was wholly and damagingly submersed within the political collective (Riesenberg 1992). Equally, at the dawn of individualistic modernity, and all Church promoted notions of *salus populi* notwithstanding (Gough 1955: 53),[6] Europe was still left with the task of identifying an institutional mechanism of collective political expression forceful enough to discipline the functionally imperative, yet wholly despotic,[7] pre-modern sovereign. By contrast, the post-revolutionary constitutionalist process whereby the sovereign (republican) state was created, the status of the individual was legally defined (rights of man), and the relationship of the individual with the state (rights of the citizen) was established, furnished the forum in which philosophical attempts to reconcile autonomy and sovereignty could be formally translated into and enshrined within constitutional law. The normative battle to balance competing notions of individual and empowering autonomy with collective (political) sovereignty was thus resolved, in axiomatic constitutional theory at least, in favour of a construction that not only confirmed individual autonomy, but also simultaneously placed the individual at the heart of a sovereign collective power that might legitimately curtail individual empowerment.

This is, of course, a somewhat crude exposition of the several centuries of philosophical struggle that were invested in our modern constitutional settlement. It is also, however, a picture of constitutional settlement that might quickly be subject to equally broadly drawn *critiques* of real-world pragmatism: what price the claim that individual autonomy and collective empowerment had been reconciled by a normative document or ideal, when the history of social development has far too often witnessed special interest groups hijacking sovereign powers and binding no-longer autonomous individuals to political and social goals that are not necessarily to their liking?[8] Nonetheless, crude as such a sketch of the axiom of constitutional settlement might be, it is still sufficiently well drawn both to give us a taste of its inspirational qualities and to furnish an explanation for the fact that realist *critiques* made of the notion of settlement have very little relevance within a world of state-based constitutional theory.

The simple logical construction that both identifies individuals as the source of sovereign power, and at the same time curbs individuality is, in all its circularity, a vital social mechanism, facilitating of the impossible; to wit, the governance of complex societies, as irreconcilable real-world disputes are neutered and channelled into seemingly impartial and wholly authoritative processes of constitutional interpretation, adjudication and application.

Settlement creates the appearance of permanent accord between actors and interests within society. Granted, the complex machinations of constitutional theory – for example, arguments as to whether neutral constitutional interpretation is best served by 'originalism' or by 'textual immanence'[9] – may appear to be little more than 'theological games' in 'atheistically' realist circles.[10] However, for as long as the practice of such games continues, at logical level, to belie the constant revolution, or state of nature that would otherwise attend upon the shotgun philosophical marriage of individualism, contractualism and sovereignty, realist *critiques* nonetheless do not speak to, but, instead, aim to the left of axiomatic constitutional discourse. The underlying point, of course, is not one of whether constitutional settlement has solved the irreconcilable conundrums of social organisation in a 'real-world', but one of whether it furnishes a logically coherent (and emotionally appealing) institutional edifice behind which we can get on with the necessary business of governing ourselves and our societies.[11]

This final statement is clearly reductionist: after all, much of current constitutional theory and philosophy is also inevitably engaged in bridging the gap between realism and abstract thought, in building bridges between facts and norms, or between 'facticity' and 'validity'.[12] Nonetheless, in a paradoxically 'real-world' of constitutional dogma, doctrine and nation states, the logical axiom of constitutional settlement has long held sway high above inconvenient social, political and (highly importantly so) economic reality, or had, at least, held sway until the evolutionary arrival of post-national institutions of governance, such as the 'once' European Communities and the 'forever' European Union.

Thus, the full measure of the almost accidental revolution of European integration is, perhaps, not merely to be found in the highly disorienting processes of societal disjunction between such once-stable bedfellows, say, as markets and states (Joerges 1996b), administrations and governments,[13] or majoritarian democracy and the business of government; such messy divorces seem only to mirror processes long underway behind the edifice of the liberal constitutional settlement (Everson 2004). Instead, revolutionary potentiality is perhaps best manifest in the wholly laudable but slightly hysterical and ultimately failed (within the terms of traditional doctrinal discourse), efforts of national and European constitutional dogma to square the circle, or to respond coherently to the challenges of European legal supremacy, supranationally enforceable European rights and the technocratic (supranational) or intergovernmental assault upon the national political collective. The notional of the 'open constitution' '*Die offene Verfassung*', or the conceptual endeavour of, amongst others, the conservative German constitutional justice (Paul Kirchof 1998)[14] to rationalise the logically irrational, or to explain how a national constitution can be both 'open' and 'closed', might not only dispose of final, comprehensive and constitutive sovereignty, but also be subject to the limitations imposed by other autonomous and equally

sovereign normative orders, is, without doubt, both a figurative indication and a confirmation of the true apocalyptic nature of European integration – its concomitant sounding of the death knell of the real-world potency of the logically perfect, though factually fallacious, state-building constitutional settlement.

The constitution is dead; long live the constitution! The ripping out of the sovereign heart of the axiom of constitutional settlement is, however, all the more striking for the fact that it neither derives from real intent, nor represents the real-life murder of a flesh and blood being; we mourn instead the death, not of an idea, nor yet of an ideal, but of mere logical perfectionism. Tears shed for Cock Robin are, then, perhaps misplaced. Furthermore, the paradoxical impulse to constitutional murder, or 'constituicide', seems never to have been 'destructive', but was, instead, 'liberal' in its genesis. Thus, one of the central European players in the accidental death of constitutional settlement is surely that most liberal of European principles, the notion of (national) 'non-discrimination'. The attack from within the constitutional settlement that individual and enforceable European rights have entailed, an attack which has seen individuals assert their rights above political collectives, and beyond the sphere of individuality pre-ordained by national settlements, can thus be argued to be a mere overdue response to the abiding flaw in liberal constitutional settlement, or the inevitable real-world particularisation of the axiomatic 'universality' that finite (national) settlement entails.

From its first real-world historical manifestation in a French revolutionary constitution, the abiding universalist aim to achieve full inclusion within Marx's 'symbolic republic' has long been undermined, not simply by the crass distinction made between the rights of man and those of the citizen, which set the justificatory stage for the exclusion of various groups from the body politic (Marx's 'slaves'), but also and, by contrast, by the finite limits to universality created by settlement itself. Certainly, no pre-political limits were set on membership within the Republic,[15] so that all who shared revolutionary French philosophical ideals could become fellow members within that body; nonetheless, the very constituting of the Republic also drew an exclusionary particularist line between those within and those without the sovereign power. In simple practical terms, territoriality, as a guiding principle, ensured that the demarcation between the citizens of the republic and its slaves would, as a matter of course, be furnished by nationality. Seen in this light, Europe's principle of (national) non-discrimination, enforceable in law and extending within the notion of 'supranationality' to include a political ideal that sovereign national polities should always be constrained in exercising their sovereign powers by the interests and values of other sovereign polities, represents Europe's greatest normative achievement.[16] Yet, it also presents us with its greatest normative challenge, as liberal universalism is extended to a neo-Kantian conclusion, all the while unravelling liberal constitutional settlement.

That the process of European integration is congenitally conditioned by liberal values, at one with those found within the constitutional settlement, is without doubt: after all, even in the most functionalist of analyses of European integration which place a central emphasis on the policy-enhancing pooling of national political or administrative powers, the ultimate aim remains one of empowering the national political community in practice as well as in theory.[17] Equally, as a largely law-driven process, European integration is indelibly marked by liberal notions of a rule of law, which privilege all the traditional liberal legal traits of process, certainty and formality. Likewise, stumbling endeavours to give greater voice to the peoples (rather than the governments) of Europe, as well as to develop and secure substantive social values throughout Europe, indicate that the European Union is also in thrall to all the complex substantive concerns of late liberal constitutional settlement, or the empowerment of a nascent European political community and the striking of a just balance between (politically defined) social solidarity and (legally secured) individual autonomy (the social constitutional settlement).

By this universal and pragmatically liberal token, we are accordingly presented with a logical conundrum: on the one hand, the process of European integration is destructive of normative constitutional settlement; on the other, that selfsame process is far from anti-constitutional in nature. In its universalist aims, its structured procedures, and in its pragmatic efforts to address the abiding themes of political primacy versus individual empowerment, or to establish equilibrium between political community (and, at least to a degree, democracy) and personal autonomy (legally enforceable rights), the integration process is programmed and conditioned by the very values, processes and social and political contexts (and problems) that mark traditional constitutional debate.

Abstracting to pure theory, though still absent constitutional settlement, liberal processes and patterns of European integration might thus be argued to represent a highly unusual and uncomfortable situation of permanent, but constitutionally conditioned, 'revolution'. The failure to identify one, uncontested *pouvoir constituent*, the failure to conjoin contractualism and a sovereign power within settled constitutional union, certainly forecloses all simple interpretational and adjudicational recourse to axioms of 'neutral', or uncontested, normative order, and further suggests a polity in constant political turmoil. Yet, at the normative and real-world levels of ideals, processes and substantive values, European integration is not about unlimited and violent political contestation between the various and varied poles of a traditionally bloodthirsty revolutionary polity, but instead presents us with an on-going effort to re-establish normative and real-world order *beyond* settlement. This, then, is Europe's 'constitutional morning'; stripped of its normatively finite moment of constitutive settlement, the concept of the constitution still stands as an idealistic, process-based and substantive beacon for societal organisation.

Seen in this light, many on-going debates about Europe's proposed constitution, and, indeed, the very work of the European Constitutional Convention and its various concomitant Intergovernmental Conferences,[18] might accordingly be argued to have slightly missed the point. We are not witnessing a momentous constitutive moment within Europe, which will furnish us with normative finality, or with an axiomatic hook upon which to hang all our future constitutionally authoritative pronouncements on the shape and nature of a settled European polity. In stark contrast, we are witnessing (an equally momentous) end to the constitutive moment and one further step down a very difficult road of constitutional experimentalism; namely, a constitutional experimentalism which entails an incremental effort to identify the institutions and processes that will ensure normative and real-world order in a necessarily revolutionary polity.[19]

As such, this book deviates slightly from a current norm of enquiry into constitution-making and change within Europe. Not only does it draw a far wider net than that of enquiry into the substance and form of any proposed new European constitution, it also invests far less faith in the formal political processes of substantive constitutional debate. Instead, its major emphasis is placed upon the notion that the whole of the process of European integration must be understood as representing a 'constitutional mo(u)rning', in which experimentalism, largely though not exclusively, of the legal variety, plays a vital role in identifying the 'deep' structures and processes that might maintain social order, civility and individual autonomy beyond 'constituicide'. The primary issue is thus one of the identification of the mechanisms that substitute for the constitutive moment and for constitutional settlement, of evaluation of the on-going (institutional and legal) processes, doctrines and practices that make up for the missing axiom of the normatively finite republican polity. The search is on for the mechanisms which translate 'fact into norm', and which characterise an authoritative 'European constitutionalism'.

## III. 'Bringing the law back in': from constitutional theory to legal and social theory

Clearly, the sobriquet of 'constitutionalism', in the sense used here, extends slightly beyond its more common role of identifying the contextual methodologies applied to the study of constitutions by scholars such as Stephen Holmes or Bruce Ackerman.[20] Undoubtedly, a new European constitutionalism is also about the evolution of an analytical academic tool that places the normative law of a constitution in the rationalising context of its relationship with the ideas and political power that are current within the entirety of a given historical society. However, this book does not seek to argue that Europe's constitutional mo(u)rning can be shorn of its internal normative meaning and viewed through the simplifying lenses, say, of a historical institutionalism, which seeks to explain constitutional development and change within Europe through simple relativising study of the fluctuating powers and ideals of national governments, supranational institutions (European Commission) and intergovernmental bodies (European Council).[21]

This book is not a work of historical methodology, nor is it based primarily within political science disciplines. In sharp contrast, the effort is legally normative in nature, viewing European constitutional experimentalisation, or European constitutionalism, as an intrinsic claim to the existence of a constitution beyond axiomatic constitutional settlement, which is justified by, and *only* by, the continuous process whereby real-world facts and social evolution are subsumed within normative legal and institutional frameworks of analysis to be transfigured from simple happenings into instances of authoritative ordering. At the same time, however, the act of 'bringing the law back in' cannot allow itself the luxury of normative reductionism. The entire process of European integration and the specific character of European constitutional mo(u)rning is not only a confirmation of the fact that our current axiomatic frameworks of normative analysis (i.e., those founded within the notion of constitutional settlement) are too limited and too crude to be able to capture the nuances of societal evolution fully;[22] instead, it is also an immediate challenge to the entire concept that law, or legal principle, might ever function as a stable instrument of normative pre-determination.

At a very simple argumentative level, the demise of the traditional constitution and the end of the constitutive act has also had severe consequences for law as an entire discipline. Beyond all intricacies of constitutional interpretation and adjudication, the death of constitutional settlement in Europe has thus deprived modern positive law of its most functional day-to-day illusion: the notion that the irrational 'natural' character of pre-modern legal authority has seamlessly been replaced by its 'political' legitimation through direct derivation (of law) from the modern constitutional settlement.[23] Certainly, settlement has always masked continuing underlying controversy on the authoritative nature of law, and this is the bread and butter of constitutional theory: to what degree, for example, can constitutional judges deploy the will of the original framers of a constitution to limit the future political will of a constituted polity?

Nonetheless, the notion of constitutional settlement, in staking out the jurisdiction in which individual acts of adjudication and interpretation occur, and in ascribing comprehensive sovereignty to one finite polity within that jurisdiction, has, of itself, ensured that the polity's judiciary would always be free to call on the devices and desires of the concept of 'non-divisible sovereignty' to give authority to its acts of interpretation and adjudication, irrespective of the nature of the decision taken. Within an unsettled European polity, it is precisely this traditional illusion of legal authority, which is lacking. In an order characterised by the continuing co-existence of equally sovereign normative legal orders, each and every decision taken by the European

Court of Justice (ECJ) to define the exact reach of an individual European right within national legal orders, as well as any national judgment applying or not applying that right, represents an act of legal reasoning and application at the very limits of jurisdiction, which is simultaneously and paradoxically authoritative within the sovereign legal order of decision, while, at the same time, lacking authority within the European polity as a whole.[24]

This paradox of authoritative non-authoritative decision-making has a number of vital consequences, not least of which is the fact that almost all legal decision-making within Europe is constitutional in nature, at least to the degree that it involves the definition of jurisdictional limits between sovereign normative orders.[25] More immediately, however, it also determines that the legal systems of Europe (both national and European) are often engaged in acts of double (self-) justification: judicial interpretation and adjudication within the paradigm of European constitutionalism is, therefore, not simply about reaching 'the right decision' or about translating 'the right facts into the correct order-giving norms', it is also about sustaining the authority of law. Thus, the crisis of adjudication within Europe is not only of a far higher quality than that found within traditional constitutional theory debate (Kennedy 1997), but is also of such a nature as to determine that traditional constitutional theory is not an adequate methodological or normative mechanism within which to capture the emergent and experimental notion of European constitutionalism.[26]

Accordingly, although it addresses very many common themes, this book is not a work of constitutional theory. More particularly, it cannot afford to limit itself to a philosophical analysis of how, as an illuminating example, European law *might* sensibly balance collective political sovereignty against individual autonomy, and likewise determine the limits to constitutional pre-determination. Instead, the challenge that the process of European integration has posed to law necessitates that this book adopt an analysis founded in legal and social theory, and further demands that European constitutionalism itself be conceived of in terms of the real-world relationship established between law and society. Non-authoritative law-giving at the limits of sovereign jurisdiction is not just a mere matter of the sudden unsettling exposure of the political preferences and social peccadilloes of European and national judiciaries. Similarly, it is not simply a wound in the fabric of constitutional adjudication and interpretation that can be quickly masked by abstract theories of constitutional interpretation or by the ascription of a 'constitutive' nature to a hierarchically construed ECJ (Kahn 1995).[27] Instead, it cannot but entail the efforts of law, both national and European, to step beyond its own pre-determined framework of normative legitimacy to re-root itself and its own authority within a wider European society. It is in this light that all normative reductionism must be eschewed. Undoubtedly, European constitutionalism beyond constitutional settlement can only be recognised as such where the facts of European constitutional evolution are constantly translated and re-translated into lasting norms that secure (just) social order; nonetheless, the normative act of fact-translation must also be rooted in tangible and socially reflexive processes of legal (self-) justification.

## IV. *Rechtsverfassungsrecht*: between facts and norms in European constitutionalism

The ready conclusion that Europe is a 'revolutionary' polity governed by (paradoxically) authoritative (in the logic of each legal system) non-authoritative (within the European polity as a whole) law is disturbing at a number of levels. In a real-world of complex social processes, for example, the simple conclusion that Europe possesses no final normative authority, with the result that its polity cannot *but* be seen as a mass of competing groups, individuals, values and interests, inevitably belies the possible success of the current and urgent efforts to re-cast Europe as a socially just, rather than simply economically driven, polity: the social 'rights' inserted within the (largely defunct) draft constitutional treaty, as well as more social process-based efforts to ensure social equality,[28] are, in this light, empty shells of sound and fury, since their lack of final normative authority determines that real-world decisions on distribution will simply be driven by the most powerful social interests. Equally, from the viewpoint of law and legal coherence, the notion that authoritative dogmatic legal reasoning can be confronted with situations in which its normative authority cannot but be doubted threatens collapse in the entire legal paradigm, as the existence of 'legal indeterminacy', or the notion that law can mean many different things at many different times, is transformed from the subject matter of limited discussions between a few legal theorists into a potentially de-stabilising fact of European legal life.[29]

Nonetheless, dramatic as such conclusions are, they are not new. Here, Europe can be viewed as a mirror on a world in which legal indeterminacy and continuous (social and political) revolution have always been recognised at national level.[30] The European Union's uniqueness does not stem from the fact that its societal organisation is far from perfect, but from the fact that it has so clearly destroyed the established illusions of perfection. At national level, the unpalatable analytical consequences of withdrawal from axioms of normative perfection have also often been highlighted. In one memorable analysis, the curious operation of accepting the truth of legal and constitutional acts of deconstruction, whilst all the while holding true to the ideals of constructivist liberal theory, has been likened to standing at the edge of an abyss and groping wildly for the safety rail (Wiethölter 2003).[31] At the same time, however, debate at national level has also struggled to find this safety rail, and, as a consequence, has bequeathed us a vocabulary and a series of methodologies within which we can begin to sketch out the empirical contours and normative powers of our new European constitutionalism.

In part, such vocabularies are very old, indeed. From Max Weber's struggle to reconcile the necessary formalism of normative orders founded within the stabilising rule of law with inherently socialising tendencies of legal 'materialisation' found both within a rule of law and within society as a whole,[32] to Harald Laski's full frontal de-bunking of the myths of sovereignty and the location of the genesis of social order in political utility rather than in pre-determined axiom (1935), as well as the tentative efforts of 'sociological jurisprudential' to sketch out some form of connection between social and legal development (Sinzheimer 1977; Ehrlich 1987), social and legal theory was to spend much of the first part of the twentieth century engaged in the problematical effort of solving the essential paradox of law, or in maintaining the normative coherence of the legal order, whilst all the while locating it firmly within a wider societal setting of social legitimacy. However, old as such debates may be, they are also still highly contemporary as the century-old effort to marry facts and norms, or to maintain the internal normative coherence of law and simultaneously open it up to social influence, finds its echo in recent constitutional theory as the rationalising powers of a Richard Posner demand that 'theory' open itself up to 'fact' (1998), and the socially sensitive antennae of a Cass Sunstein build (perhaps unwittingly) on Gadamer's principles of interpretation, to exhort the justices of the US Supreme Court to reframe their jurisprudence in the light of social reality, or to include 'social facts' within their 'closed' hermeneutical frameworks of analysis (1993).[33] More particularly, however, the relevance of social and legal theory to a debate on European constitutionalism is fully revealed, as we reconsider the contribution that both have made to the very creation of union in Europe.

'Bringing the 1980s back in' (Joerges and Everson 2004): in an old story that bears much repeating (Majone 1994, 2005: 197), a vital pre-condition of our current efforts to effect 'closer union between the peoples of Europe' was the withdrawal from the 'command and control' paradigm of the national welfare state, or the 'socialised' constitutional settlement;[34] a withdrawal prompted, in no small part, by the recognition that such a state, and its law, could not, in fact, furnish its purported normative promise. Social and legal theory, of course, played their own major part in the paradoxical dismantling of their own circle-squaring axiom of politically determined and legally secured social justice, as various corners of academic debate noted that politically legitimated 'interventionist law' was: (1) in danger of undermining the very paradigm of liberal settlement, as regulation spread its wildfires into all areas of society, both private and public, and the concomitant 'colonisation of the lifeworld' threatened to bring about the collapse of individual autonomy (Habermas 1996a); (2) in itself becoming an atrophying force, destructive of social justice, as the advanced proceduralism of the modern welfare state translated demands for social emancipation into empty legal maxims of, say, 'the equality of bargaining power', which merely masked the realities of unchanging economic organisation (Unger 1976: 192–222); and was (3) simply ineffective, and far too crude an instrument to transpose detailed programmes of social renovation into a real-world made up of complex social relations.[35]

At a practical level of judicial politics, such theoretical self-destruction and uncertainty might surely be argued to have bolstered many courts and legal systems (national and European) in their preparedness to step outside the established paradigms of politically legitimated law-making in order to give greater force to normative orders founded in abstract (liberal) rights or even more abstract programmes of economic renewal.[36] However, at a level of legal and social theory, it has also left us with much unfinished business. More particularly, it has once again confronted law in Europe with the onerous task of 're-socialising' law, or re-navigating a path through the formal-material legal paradox, to identify new modes of incorporating social reality and, importantly, the demands for justice which such a reality entails, within a necessarily socially distant law, without once compromising its own legitimacy.[37]

At one level, such a conclusion returns the analysis firmly to the theoretical preoccupations that dogged scholarly legal debates within the Weimar Republic. More particularly, law has turned full circle as the objections raised by the German political and constitutional theorist, Hermann Heller, about Hans Kelsen's pure theory of law and derivation of legal norms can no longer be assumed to have simply been incorporated within an eternal and durable welfare state or social constitutional settlement (Heller 1928a).[38] Heller's demands that law be founded and constantly re-founded in real-world structures, or within an 'operational reality' (*Wirksamkeit*), as opposed to being 'scientifically' derived from one constitutive norm,[39] can thus no longer simply be assumed to have been satisfied by a final constitutional settlement; a social constitutional settlement, which, although founded within an abstract *Grundnorm* of its own – the welfare or social state – still fully privileges the continuous formation and reformation of society, through its redistributional activities and consequent continual re-constituting of the underlying social basis, or the operational ability of individuals within the state to play their full part within inclusive political process.[40] At yet another level, however, this conclusion also takes us further back, and once again forward, in the history of legal theory, as instability in the welfare state and social constitutional settlement equally underlines the incomplete nature of Heller's struggles to overcome the formal-materialisation paradox that was first identified by Max Weber, and which continues to challenge modern jurisprudential theories and methodologies to this day.

To Heller, 'indeterminacy' in law was the motor for the just and reality-proximate constituting and reconstituting of society (Dyzenhaus 1999: 204). The lack, or, more precisely stated, *only the lack* of settled and undisputed legal content would allow for continuous ethical and moral legal appraisal, re-appraisal and constituting of *Wirksamkeit*.[41] Operational reality could only be given normative force by law as an 'achieved' societal constitution if the law were unconstrained and might constantly adapt itself to social reality and the inherent justice demands that such social reality reveals and entails.[42] At the same time, however, and all indeterminacy apart, law should remain an authoritative constant, an organising beacon around which potentially violent political forces could congregate and coalesce, in full and shared respect for legal adjudicational authority.[43]

Leaving aside all discussion on potential distinctions between constitutional substance and constitutional procedures (a distinction largely dismissed by Heller), the paradoxical demand for authoritative law-giving rooted in legal indeterminacy led Heller to focus his writings on the search for, inevitably enigmatic, 'ethically' and 'morally informed' legal principles of dynamic interpretation.[44] Equally, however, this paradoxical demand also relocates our discussion firmly within the parameters of Max Weber's paradigm of a formally rational law, whose authority would always, and perversely so, be undermined by its own inherent materialisation tendencies, or search for wider social legitimacy (Weber 1969). In other words, and in Weber's terms, Heller, along with other, more practically inclined, proponents of juridical materialisation within the Weimar Republic (for example, Hugo Sinzheimer, as well as his historical precursor, Eugen Ehrlich), were tempting the Gods. They were dancing on the grave of the rule of law – or legal ability to give effective authoritative voice to *Wirksamkeit* – as they undermined normatively pre-determined or 'scientific' law-internal legitimacy (formal rationality), all the while flirting with legal destruction in their search for a wider but elusive social legitimacy for law.

To the degree that the moral and ethical principles of dynamic but authoritative adjudication could not be rationally identified *within* the legal system itself, the rule of law would forever be haunted by the spectre of socially created irrationality (value-irrationalism). Thus, the underlying paradox remained: furthermore, it returned with renewed force as the focus for legal theoretical study in the 1980s, as the welfare state and social constitutional settlement began to lose their socially organising force, and not least so, since processes of European integration were increasingly placing their functional operation in doubt.[45]

*Rechtsverfassungsrecht* (Wiethölter 2003): the effort of one German jurist and legal theorist to identify legitimate legal order within a law that constantly and concomitantly constitutionalises both itself and wider society through the socially sensitive construction of (normative) reality, cannot thus be described as a coherent theory of legal, let alone, constitutional, legitimation and interpretation. Instead, the sobriquet,[46] 'self-constitutionalising/socially constitutive law' is, at best, an open-ended programme which brings together the study of real-world legal application with the host of theories and methodologies that are still seeking to find a legitimacy for modern law in its normatively sensitive and socially reflexive efforts to ground itself both in philosophical ideal and in social reality. Between facts and norms, stretching from the extremes of philosophical analysis to the *minutiae* of sociological enquiry, including strands of thought as diverse as systems theory, economic analysis, or simple legal-sociological muddling, *Rechtsverfassungsrecht* finds one of its most immanent spheres of application in a European constitutionalism, which, *explicitly* lacking in constitutional settlement, but in the light of both an ideal and an impetus for liberal and social justice, is experimentally seeking to normativise fact in Europe, or furnish a coherent order in which the danger of traditionally violent revolution recedes in the face of accepted and acceptable modes of legal mediation between the legitimate but competing justice demands made by individuals and social/political collectivities.

This, then, forms the primary core for the empirical and methodological analysis within this book. Europe's constitutionalism cannot be identified in a limited review of the normative nature of any proposed European constitution; nor is it yet shaped or moulded by any clear adherence to any limited set of putatively 'common' European values. Instead, re-learning an old lesson,[47] Europe's constitutionalism, its *Rechtsverfassungsrecht*, is to be found in a study and open-ended sociological-theoretical analysis of the attitudes and operations of European lawyers and law. How, at the very limits to authoritative jurisdiction, does non-authoritative law set about establishing its self-constitutionalising/socially constituting order? How does law translate facts into norms? How can law balance and stabilise the competing claims, values and interests of Europe's revolutionary polity? Constitutions are traditionally closed and self-contained instruments of logical reasoning. Cast asunder and exposed to social reality, they are fragile. How can law, under these circumstances, re-establish its constitutional authority?

## V. Bringing politics back in: liberal deliberation and the limits to democracy

In a very real sense, then, European constitutionalism is all about identifying the contours of a new and radical legal proceduralism. The establishment of liberal or social justice is, paradoxically, auxiliary to a core constitutionalist aim of furnishing the European polity with a normative framework within which social order and social justice might be secured and re-secured. To re-iterate: constitutionalism beyond the constitutional settlement cannot logically be about the curtailing of the creative powers of a revolutionary polity through the imposition of pre-determined normative schemes of governance and values.[48] Instead, the initial aim is one of keeping violent revolution in check. Absent settlement, European law (at the non-authoritative interface between authoritative legal orders) is indeterminate; a series of empty shells around which revolutionary national, supranational, public and private interests cluster in the effort to determine the substance of European integration. European constitutionalism, therefore, is all about the normative-laden procedures of integration – the provision of stable mechanisms whereby social reality is transformed into stabilising (just) norms. European constitutionalism should be understood to be procedural in nature; but not in the empty sense of the furnishing of self-contained maxims of justice, behind which a very different social reality might lurk (Unger 1976). Instead, it is procedural in the sense of its aspiration to 'civilise' revolution, in order to give continuing voice to social reality and social justice.

With this, constitutionalism, or *Rechtsverfassungsrecht*, speaks to the vital and unending interrelationship between law, social reality (social justice) and politics. Post-settlement, constitutional aspiration is procedural, but inspirational. Alternatively, 'politics' matter: politics, and not law, are the primary expression of social reality and social justice. To give full vent to the fury of a pluralist *critique* (Laski 1935): to the degree that settlement and all pre-determined normative schemes of governance (i.e., law) deny reality, they are always illegitimate, the false façades of social atrophy, behind which a multitude of vested interests gather and dictate. Beyond settlement, creative political revolution allows social reality to re-assert its justice-giving voice. Beyond settlement, politics gives voice to creative revolution. Beyond settlement, constitutionalism provides the distinction between creative and destructive revolution, furnishing the procedural framework in which politics, rather than political violence (including the political violence of false constitutional settlement) is determinative, and also gives voice to social reality. The impulse remains universal in its fullest sense – no social voice might fall victim to false settlement or constitutional sentiment[49] – and, as such, plunges this book into the heart of one of the greatest analytical problems of European integration. Europe's 'democratic deficit', its necessary failure to give proper (constituted) political voice to its polity, is a phrase heard so often as to rob it of its full analytically apocalyptical importance.[50] In short, however, just as the process of European integration represents an undermining potential within law, thereby thrusting the fact of the existence of legal indeterminacy onto centre stage, it also entails an assault on our most fundamental modern understandings of how civilising constraints might be placed on politics.

European integration has heralded the passing of majoritarian politics, or conventionally legitimated democracy, not simply because it has introduced elements of technocratic rule within its supranational governance structures, but because it has dispensed with *demos* and thus has equally dispensed with the very foundation for legitimising political representation. In the (post-settlement) non-authoritative gulf between sovereign (democratic) orders, there is simply no room for an imputed political collectivity, and thus no home for any legitimising democracy founded on majoritarian political process.[51] In other words, whilst politics might remain central to the organisation of our society within Europe, politics itself seems to have been denied recourse to its central mechanism of self-legitimation – the forming of democratic majorities.

Political and social theory has thus witnessed many efforts, every bit as intense as those seen within law, to bridge this gap between the fact of political process that is taking place within Europe and the normative desire that this political process be legitimated, or be given some character that raises politics above the level of political violence. Undoubtedly, many such efforts seem to be paradoxically apolitical in nature; and here notions of technocratic governance with all their emphasis upon the protection of the polity from the undemocratic impulses of a leading political class spring immediately to mind (Majone 1996). However, others take the maintenance of politics as their central organising principle, drawing on well-worked Habermasian themes in their efforts to locate political legitimacy, not in the majorities formed in the wake of political process, but in process itself, and, more particularly, from the notion, most clearly enunciated in *Facticity and Validity*, that 'deliberative' communication within political process, rather than any final form of decision-making, establishes the core of political legitimacy.[52] In this light, 'arguing, rather than bargaining' (Fossum 2004: 226) characterises the act of legitimate political process; gone are the interest compromises that tended to characterise the building of majorities, to be replaced with the 'quality' of political discourse. In view of this qualitative democratic impulse, recent academic writing on Europe and European democracy has witnessed a turn away from notions of political representation (majoritarianism) towards notions of deliberative democracy, which are increasingly seen as having a central role to play in giving some form of normative validity to political interaction within Europe (Chalmers 2003).

Clearly, in its privileging of the processual over the (majoritarian) axiomatic in the matter of establishing political legitimacy, the notion of deliberative democracy seems to echo the efforts of this book to locate both the study and the structures of European constitutionalism within a radical proceduralism that gives appropriate voice to politics, and, as such, proves to be a major methodological plank within the following analysis. However, a very major *caveat* must be added. The forms of deliberative 'democracy' applied within the setting of the European Union seem, of necessity, to differ from Habermasian conceptions; and not least because the discourse ethics and communicative democracy relied upon by Jürgen Habermas are themselves also established within and dependent upon constitutional settlement, and not just upon the primary 'reflexive' constitutive role played by political discourse.[53] Instead, in the light of Europe's revolutionary polity, deliberative conceptions of politics seem to have retained an experimental air, still largely being deployed to aid in the analytical effort to capture the nature of an emergent European polity, and, as a consequence, are still struggling to locate their own moment of normative transition.

At one level, such experimentalism is to be seen in the very modest claims made for 'deliberation' by various theorists of European integration. Thus, for example, evaluations of the European polity embedded within the ancient discipline of the conflicts of law – that is to say, in notions of deliberative supranationalism that argue that political legitimacy within the European polity stems from the ability of still autonomous national polities to take each others' interests into account in their own decision-making – do not dwell on the democracy-enhancing functions of deliberation, but instead regard deliberation merely as a useful tool to structure international debate (Joerges and Neyer 1997; Joerges and Everson 2005).[54] At yet another level, theories of deliberative democracy applied in relation to the European Union, at least in their inspirational inception (Cohen and Sabel 1997), seem even to court a degree of 'illiberality' in their endeavours to give immediate voice to all interests within a revolutionary European polity. In this analysis, and drawing heavily on the works of the US theorist Joshua Cohen, the basic point of concern is not a Habermasian one of preserving a liberal lifeworld through deliberatively constrained political process, rather than through the simple primacy of rights, but is, instead, one of giving universal voice to interests within a lifeworld which may or may not choose to organise themselves along liberal lines (Cohen 2002).[55]

These approaches have proven extraordinarily useful within a European arena, but have not, perhaps, been properly understood. Their underlying achievement is still, surely, analytical; they are, at best, only experimental at normative level. Such theories only seek to give us a glimpse of how politics and democracy *might* exist beyond constitutional settlement; how groups of individuals and different polities that are not bound together as fellow-travellers within one republic *might* yet be organised together within one sustained and civil political process. 'Deliberation', in these analyses, is not a perfect Habermasian theoretical construct which preserves both liberal autonomy and political process, but is instead an analytical attempt to address and capture democratic politics beyond settlement, both in its external (inter-polity) and internal (pluralist) facets. What forms of organising norms can we identify to civilise relations between polities at the non-authoritative limits to authoritative jurisdiction? What forms of organising norms can we identify to civilise relations between groups within one unsettled polity, or 'polyarchy' (Cohen and Sabel 1997) – for example, the European Union as a whole – which do not necessarily hold fast to the same substantive (liberal?) values? Seen in this light, the examination of the self-legitimising potential of 'deliberative communication' is, perhaps, misplaced.

Certainly, if one views the now defunct draft constitutional treaty as a normative project to constitute Europe, it is undoubtedly correct to examine the workings and machinations of the European Convention for their deliberative quality; and, of course, if necessary, to criticise such a Convention for failing to identify a clear constitutive moment.[56] On the other hand, detailed examination and *critique* of the quality of deliberative communication in on-going processes of European integration does slightly miss the point. As deliberative theorists themselves concede (Cohen and Sable 1997), at normative level, the endeavour is one of 'democratic experimentalism', rather than one of logical perfectionism. Deliberative communication in these vitally important analytical perspectives is not a self-justificatory theoretical fulcrum upon which the whole of the legitimacy of democratic politics might be hung. Instead, it is an analytical and experimental model within which we might begin to conceive of post-settlement democracy; a model that opens up new political channels of communication, which must, in their experimental turn, be linked with normativising processes of legitimation.[57]

## VI. Constitutional morphogenesis

The *caveat* in this book's methodological reliance upon notions of 'deliberative democracy', or 'deliberative politics', is thus revealed. Both the courting of potential 'illiberality', as well as the potential downgrading of 'democracy', indicate that these theories share much in common with *Rechtsverfassungsrecht*. In examining political process beyond settlement, these approaches are fully sensitive to reality, but are also teetering on the brink of an abyss. Democratic experimentalism within deliberative polyarchy may fumble for common modes to identify deliberation (Cohen and Sabel 1997), but its inherent potential for substantive illiberality will always undermine any claim that some form of universal common will, or desire to secure a 'good' social order, exists.[58] Likewise, deliberative supranationalism's central functionalist reliance on 'rationalising scientific' – sometimes technocratic (Joerges and Neyer 1997; Everson 1998b)[59] – norms in order to discipline political debate will always raise doubts about the model's ability to furnish final moral authority in times of conflict between incommensurate political interests.[60]

This, of course, is not a criticism, but is, instead, a qualification. Thus, deliberative theories are engaged in exactly the selfsame process of experimentation in the matter of translating facts into norms, as is European constitutionalism. As a consequence, even though this book places great analytical faith in deliberative processes of democracy, more particularly, in their ability to furnish socially distanced law with a post-settlement mirror on a social political reality in all its self-defining normative traits,[61] it cannot simply relax in some false hope that deliberative democracy, or the functional dedication of law to the support of deliberative democracy, will simply solve the post-settlement crisis of constitutional legitimation. Instead, deliberative politics and deliberative democracy are prized for their analytical qualities; their ability to offer a glimpse of the existence of politics, political organisation and even (experimental) democracy beyond the paradigm of constitutional settlement.

Analytically speaking, this book accordingly possesses a dual organising theme. The effort to civilise politics beyond the constitutional settlement, to maintain and discipline the revolutionary polity with non-authoritative (authoritative) law, might best be methodologically described as a rejection of notions of 'paradigm shift' (Kuhn 1970). Arguing within a Habermasian mode, the future would be described as follows: the old paradigm of national constitutional settlement has, for a variety of functional and idealistic reasons, been eroded by social forces; it should, accordingly, now be transformed into a new paradigm of European constitutional settlement, sensitive enough to meet the intricate demands of a new European polity (Habermas 2001). In contrast, however, by arguing, in a conscious act of constitutional mo(u)rning, that the European Union's primary contribution to constitutional debate is not its re-founding of Europe, but is, instead, its struggle to give normative meaning to 'an ever closer union between the peoples of Europe' in a post constitutional settlement environment that retains many features of national organisation (including liberal principles of social organisation), the analysis firmly rejects a transformation of our state constitutional settlements into a new paradigm of a European Constitution. Instead, in an act of 'morphogenesis' (Krippendorff 1984: 45), the study demands that we open up our existing understanding of the law, politics and constitutions (as well as relations between the three), so as to enable us to capture, both factually and normatively, the realities that have always lurked behind the traditional constitutional settlement, as well as the very particular reality and normative force of the process of European integration and constitutionalisation.

Morphogenesis entails the opening up of perspectives (of patterns of legal observation of social reality) beyond the false constraining features of pre-emptive normative axioms, in order to allow for the legal appreciation of the 'social' in all its complex forms (including its normatively conceived forms). Accordingly, an analytical notion of constitutional morphogenesis gives further structure to the dual attempt to avoid the abyss: the interrelated and experimental efforts of law and political philosophy (political science) to normativise European integration and to give character and meaning to European constitutionalism (*Rechtsverfassungsrecht*).

Concentrating first on notions of constitutional process, the study seeks to capture the empirical legal realities of constitutional morphogenesis, investigating the (self-legitimatising) attitudes and efforts of lawyers at the non-authoritative gap between authoritative constitutional orders (Article 234) to found Europe's law (national and European) within the real-world of European integration, and to translate such realities into a normative narrative of European constitutionalism (see below, Chapters 3 and 4). Focusing second on constitutional principle, the study also undertakes empirical investigation into the workings of the organising European 'principle' of 'institutional balance'; seemingly, the notion (legal and political) that furnishes the vital institutional fulcrum of dialogue between the various national, supranational, political and institutional actors within the process of European integration (Jacqué 1990). Expanding the notion of institutional balance to include a new set of European actors, a self-nominating and self-organising private European polity, within the analysis, the study seeks to test the empirical political realities of constitutional morphogenesis, examining whether politics in a process of European integration, or dialogue between a multitude of public, private, national and supranational actors, interests and values, has or can be legally translated into a normatively sustaining or sustained process of (democratic) deliberation that both acts to reveal social reality and keeps political violence in check (Chapters 5 and 6).

Beyond the analytical, however, the distinction between (constitutional) law and politics is a necessarily false one. Learning a Habermasian lesson, albeit greatly magnified through the looking-glass of European integration, validity can only be distilled from facticity, and a bridge can only be built between fact and norm, when the two are brought into a doubly sustaining reflexive relationship. Just as law can only glimpse social reality through political process, political process can only give normative force to reality through law. In the analytical light of constitutional morphogenesis, and under academic conditions of constitutional (normative) experimentation within both law and politics, the most important thing that can be said of emergent European constitutionalism is that it is neither the preserve of law, nor of politics. Thus, the message to legal and political science (political philosophy) is that neither can claim to be able to capture the realities and normative force of European constitutionalism without reference to the other.

## VII. Bringing politics back in: an 'illiberal' conclusion

Although this book's call to 'constitutional mo(u)rning' is potentially revolutionary, its initial conclusions cannot but be tentative. In legal terms, the effort 'to bring the Eighties back in', to open up the study of European constitutionalism to social reality, is, perhaps, radical in its efforts to relocate the study of constitutions away from reliance on constitutional theory and to re-root analysis within legal and social theory. In academic terms, however, it remains a part of a far from finished movement. The multitude of approaches and methodologies followed, the tortuous on-going (perhaps never to be realised) efforts to maintain liberal sentiment in the face of illiberal reality, the concomitant problems presented by uncertainty within liberal philosophy, all, perhaps inevitably, add up to a process of academic muddling that cannot, for the moment, offer much more than a series of minor procedural legal mechanisms to maintain some daily form of civil constitutional morphogenesis within the process of European integration. Those seeking some form of final, minutely tuned, theoretical resolution to the problems posed by the lack of constitutional settlement will be disappointed.

Nonetheless, it is submitted that such muddling efforts are fully justified; and not least for the reason that it is to be hoped that the adepts of critical and liberal philosophy can, through reciprocal *critique*, refine them. Instead, the restatement and *critique* of current constitutionalisation efforts in Europe within broader legal and social theory also lead to a second, somewhat more radical, conclusion. Thus, in its final prospective essay (Chapter 7), this book also concludes with a *critique* of proposed efforts to give Europe a formal constitution, which is occasioned by concern with and about the consequences of the effort to force a 'constitutive moment' within Europe. Bruce Ackerman has spoken powerfully of the 'arrogance' of the Philadelphia Convention, and of the arrogance to be found in the Federalist Papers (1984). In this analysis, the inspirational words 'we the people' take on a more sinister hue as the vision of a few bewigged individuals, laying claim to a moral force that was not their own – in order to raise the US Constitution above a realm of 'normal' politics and to bind future generations to a 'foreign' will and imposed order – inevitably gives rise to a continuing, though wholly understated, 'counter-majoritarian difficulty', or to the notion that politics can be restrained by a myth.

What is troubling in this analysis, however, is not so much Ackerman's individuation of the arrogance of the historical Convention, but rather his final acceptance that the fact that myth has become reality is a defining characteristic of a US national identity in which he feels positive pride. By this token, the one final difficult question that might be asked of this book is as follows: why is it so concerned to maintain the unsettled nature of European constitutionalism? Why not simply reject the tortuous constitutionalist muddling that constitutional mo(u)rning entails and argue, with Habermas, that Europe must be constitutionally settled? Why not accept that, for all current normative muddles, the future of the European constitution will lie in the subsequent acceptance (politically and socially driven acceptance) that we, 'the members of a European Convention' have constituted Europe?

The answer to this question, however, sounds somewhat illiberal. The very process of historical airbrushing that this emotional identification with a specifically 'European' culture-engendering document will necessarily entail is both an act of treason against European history and an act of betrayal to those cultures and identities (both internal and external to Europe) with which Europe has unfinished business. This, however, should not be understood as a crude statement of any desire to retain the closed ethnic, cultural and emotional identities of existing European nations. Instead, it is an appeal to retain the inspirational (if not necessarily wholly liberal) universality of the project of European integration, to allow Europeans at all times to take a cold, hard look at the realities of the exclusionary tendencies of constitutional settlement and make reparation to the individuals, groups and nations which Europe (and perhaps liberalism in general) has damaged and will continue to damage in the future, through the maintenance, not of normative coherence, but of 'difference' (*la difference*) within a European polity.

## Notes

1 Certainly, applying a formalist legal eye to Europe's statement of brave constitutional intent (or failed constitutional treaty) is a highly sobering experience, revealing, as it does, that Europe has singularly failed to solve its own peculiar constitutive dilemma, which locates the genesis for constitutive constitutional action within the already constituted orders of member states, but fails, in the final analysis, to identify any undisputed sovereign who might authoritatively mediate between autonomous (national and European) normative orders; to wit, in German terminology, the continuing, constitutionally fatal, absence of a final '*Kompetenz-Kompetenz*'. See, for an overall comment on the logical problems of the internationalisation of constitutionalism, Grimm (2004).

2 Note, however, that the notion of 'organic' legal organisation and development is a highly problematic one within the terms of the analysis, see Chapters 2 (III), 4 (III.3) and 6 (IV).

3 A promise seemingly ending only with reconstituting 'revolution': in other words, the constitution endures as long as society itself; it can only be cast asunder by positive and imperative acts of political violence. See, for the enduring problem of the binding nature of constitutions and consideration of the appropriate nature of the concretising of revolution within the constitution, the various essays in Preuß (1994a).

4 In contrast to conventional constitutional theory terms, the point here is not a normative one of whether, at any one time, interpretative theories of the original intent (of the framers of the constitution) should dominate above interpretative theories of natural or substantive justice, or *triadic vice versa*, but is, instead, an empirical one founded on the simple fact that such varied theories have, at different times, and for different reasons (political, social or legal), been applied in order to give meaning to one single text.

5 The lack of tangibility in constitutional functions is, perhaps, best expressed not by notions of 'constitutional patriotism', which, in themselves, claim a rationalist origin in the philosophical concordance of the polity with the values expressed in and by the constitution, but in 'constitutional narratives', or the on-going constitutive appeal of contemporary constitutions to histories (better stated 'poetries') of revolutionary and colonial struggle (Hanafin 2001).

6 Though philosophically inchoate, the idea that the people retained an original God-given power of oversight over earthly rulers neatly furnished the Church with the right to direct kingly rulers on earth.

7 Constrained, only, in Hobbes' memorable phrase, by his 'Christian conscience'.

8 A *critique* that might, somewhat controversially, be made of the supposed 1945 welfarist 'constitutional moment' within the UK. See Everson (2003b).

9 As recently noted, an argument at least as old as the *Federalist Papers*, yet one that continues to rage in academic and legal circles, see Posner (1998: 2).

10 For the latest in a long line of determined critique of 'self-contained' or hermeneutically sealed constitutional theory, see Kennedy (1994) and Kennedy (1997).

11 And indeed, one of the best explanations of the irrelevance of realist theory in these terms is (implicitly and paradoxically) given within the guru of realism's highly convincing efforts to deconstruct the work of the master of constitutional mysticism (Kennedy 1979). In a final analysis, it did not matter whether

Blackstone's description of the UK constitution was a myth or not. Instead, what mattered was his ability to dominate perceptions of the constitution for two hundred years. His antiquarianism was only overcome by Dicey.

12 Viewing Habermas as a philosopher rather than as a social theorist. See, for efforts to bridge the gap between facts and norms, Habermas (1992). For recent confirmation that Habermas now considers himself to be a philosopher rather than social theorist, Habermas (2005a).

13 To unfairly apply a final, potentially polity destroying logic to Majone's characterisation of the EU as a fourth branch of government (Majone 1994). To conclude that Majone's rationalising schemes of governance would lead to a destruction of the polity is an overly simplistic argument: as Majone's latest work confirms, disjunction between political process and administration serves the aim of the preservation of a liberal polity that is founded in a broadly conceived sphere of private autonomy, see Majone (2005).

14 Although this conservatism is surely, even if famously, overstated by Joseph Weiler (1995). See, for examination of the shortcomings in Weiler's analysis of the German constitutional court's jurisprudence, Chapter 2 below.

15 Along the line of a German constitutional settlement that restricted membership of the German body politic to those sharing in the imputed characteristic of 'German-ness' (Riesenberg 1992).

16 And this is the core normative message of certain theories of deliberative supranationalism (Joerges and Neyer 1997). Interestingly, Giandomenico Majone (2005: 195) also identifies a philosophically inspirational element within processes of European integration in just this respect: 'The experience of the EU shows that a rule-based system of cooperation and dispute settlement can not only civilise relations among sovereign states by eliminating the excesses of narrowly conceived national interest but, by protecting the rights of citizens even against their own government'. Granted, Majone does tend to an extreme of liberalism, in which individual rights of autonomy are prized above political process. Nonetheless, his is one and the same inspirational programme – European integration processes have lessened the ability of the nation state, or national *res publica*, to create its own 'slaves' (commenting on Rousseau's treatment of the subject, p.194), both internal and external to the body politic.

17 That is, an expansive notion of 'functionalism', which also includes technocratic integration theories, encompassing writers such as Haas (1964), Ipsen (1972) and Majone (1994). In both technocratic and functionalist accounts of European integration, a recurring theme is one of the maintenance of the 'real' political power of the national polity as European national administrative powers are pooled to enhance overall policy implementation.

18 The draft constitutional treaty, finally voted upon in French and Dutch referenda, had been modified by member state governments following conclusion of the convention process. Intergovernmental Conferences, meetings between European heads of state, are assumed to possess their own constitutional significance within the European setting.

19 In other words, without settlement, the revolution continues; however, see, for the inverse conception of a revolutionary polity, Preuß (1994b). In the latter view, the goals of the revolutionary polity are legitimately concretised in the final revolutionary act, that of conclusion of the revolutionary constitution. Revolutionary aims are thus perpetuated inside rather than outside the constitution, see Chapter 3 below.

20 On the distinction between constitutional theory and constitutionalism, see Posner, (1998). The methodologies chosen by Ackerman and Holmes are undoubtedly effective analytical tools for understanding constitutional development.

Nonetheless, with its emphasis upon legal theory, or the struggle of law as a whole to adapt itself to social evolution, this book augments traditional 'constitutionalism' studies, moving beyond historical context to seek to understand a 'constant' within legal evolution – translation of fact into norm.

21 See, for a US-based effort to transform constitutional theory in these terms, Griffin (1999). However, see, also, Chapter 2 (II) for the methodological usefulness of historical institutionalism within this volume.

22 See, for the peculiar problems that attend on the act of 'bringing the law back in', Joerges (1996a).

23 In other words, the Kelsen-derived notion that the constitutive act furnishes a political *Grundnorm* for law.

24 In other words, since European law lacks a *Grundnorm*, there is no one hierarchically construed rule, which can mediate between the various national and European legal orders, see Chapter 3 (III). Accordingly, any claim to adjudicate for the whole of the European polity is a non-authoritative claim.

25 This is the real issue behind the recognition that the ECJ was always a constitutional court and one of the major motivating factors for the emphasis of this book on processes and developments taking place far beyond the European convention in its efforts to analyse the nascent European constitution. Simply stated, quite crass economic decisions to allow say, the movement of alcoholic products across community borders, are constitutional in nature since they entail adjustment between autonomous normative orders. See below, Chapter 2 (II.3).

26 Again, simply stated, interpretive or, say, immanent adjudication on the basis of a constitutional text relates only to that text, and offers no aid within the exercise of co-ordinating constitutional adjudication *between* various constitutional texts.

27 Kahn neatly demonstrates that most if not all modern US constitutional theory attempts to rebut realistic critique rely heavily upon the constitutive character of the US Supreme Court, or its unrivalled position at the centre of the US Constitution; a position surely secured both by history and by less tangible 'constitutional emotions', such as loyalty to the Court, or by constitutional patriotism. By contrast, the ECJ, as a German Constitutional Court has often reminded us, has no unparalleled claim to normative or emotional primacy.

28 For example, the Open Method of Co-ordination, or the process whereby national authorities and interest groups within the EU engage in mutual learning and bench-marking through the exchange of best practices.

29 High profile clashes between national, supranational and national judges over the meaning of provisions of national, European and international law (or, indeed, the breadth of each jurisdiction) cannot but raise social doubts about the legitimacy of law as a whole.

30 English pluralist thought is a case in point here. Harald Laski's response to Labour Party efforts to create the 'just' post-welfare state through a call to the organising power of sovereign social power founded in the myth of 'the common good' is particularly telling: The claim to justice was misplaced, '[P]rofoundly mistaken for the simple reason that there is no general will in the Community at all. We never encounter any will that can be denominated good by definition'. Furthermore, collective will was always mistaken because, 'A number of minds does not become one mind any more than a wood is a tree or a hive a bee. The will of the state is the will of certain persons exercising certain powers' (Laski 1935).

31 Conceding in a somewhat bemusing formulation, that whilst Derrida may very well be right, Habermas is nonetheless more appealing.

32 In other words, the existence of a necessary demand for 'social justice' within law, or a law that is rooted in real-world facts (in the vocabulary of more

modern constitutional theory, the existence of 'social facts' (Sunstein 1993)). Weber (1969) is the first to apply the 'materialisation' sobriquet to the legal order.

33 For a more explicit analysis of the relevance of Gadamer within modern 'constitutional theory', see Flood (1991).

34 In other words a 'materialised' view of the constitution, founded in its ability to give normative force to real-world demands for redistributive justice.

35 In essence, the roots of the UK evolution of a socio-legal methodology.

36 In other words, the 1980s witnessed a change within the prevailing legal *Grundnorm*, away from a final constitutive legal authority based within the national political settlement to a final constitutive legal authority founded within economic theory. Nonetheless, as Chapter 2 (II. 1) argues, the accusation of radicality must be tempered. The ECJ may well also have accidentally embarked upon its radical deregulatory activities as a part of its mission to protect (formal) European law from political influence.

37 For full details of the struggle of the ECJ to tackle the formalisation–materialisation paradox within judicial processes of European integration, see Chapter 2 (II).

38 For comprehensive discussion on the conflicts between Hermann Heller and Hans Kelsen, as well as on Heller generally, see Dyzenhaus (1999).

39 The vital point is not only one that Kelsen's 'scientific' derivation of norms is flawed in itself by virtue of legal indeterminacy, but also one that Rousseau's (*a priori*) *pouvoir constituent* is a chimera, unable to give proper expression to a real-world body politic, or to the structures of *Wirksamkeit* that the polity continuously creates and recreates for itself (Heller 1934). A predetermined *Grundnorm* is not sufficiently sensitive to social realities thrown up by social evolution (for example, the evolution of a disadvantaged industrial class). The only just or moral law is an indeterminate law, which constantly responds to realities created by society and to the social justice demands that such realities (inherently) entail.

40 In other words, the law of the welfare state entails continual reconstitution of society as individual opportunities for action are assured in real as well as theoretical terms, ensuring dynamic individual input into political process.

41 As Dyzenhaus notes, the term is difficult to render in English. *Wirksamkeit* thus contains an operational element – it is not merely a reflection of reality, but of the shared work that society and law undertake to give positive form to reality. In other words, the term entails a degree of dynamic *self*-expression: hence, 'operational reality', or the concept of 'societal constitution', inevitably also embodies inherent normative elements, or the 'justice demands' that a particular society, responding to its own evolutionary realities, pursues within its achieved (legal) structures.

42 See note 55 – *Wiksamkeit* also entails the plea for justice.

43 The point is one reproduced throughout Heller's writings (Heller 1934; Heller 1927; Heller 1928b). Heller's *Wirksamkeit* therefore also builds upon Weber's use of the term – a usage that stressed the pivotal role played by law in giving secure expression to social reality, or constituting social reality. For detailed and careful explanation of the development of the term, see only Dyzenhaus (1999).

44 In a final analysis, Heller's moral and ethical legal principles are distilled from shared pre-political characteristics within the given society of his time: morality and ethical concordance within a society facilitates the creation of appropriate moral and ethical stances within law. Granted, Heller's incipient communitarianism has very little in common with nationalistic conceptions of cultural predetermination, being explicitly dismissive of the notion of the *pouvoir constituent*, and being built instead upon a class analysis, which stressed the importance of

a spiritual commonality, or the shared and effective desire to overcome the real-world functional and social differentiations that were evolving within an advanced industrial society (in particular, Heller (1928b)). Nonetheless, and updating the underlying vocabulary, but importantly retaining the dynamic elements within Heller's analysis, the notion of 'social homogeneity within communities of fate' is an inappropriate source of ethical and moral principle within a modern real-world, in which the particular operational significance and problem of (industrial) class cleavages (or the effort to overcome them) has been added to (or superseded?) by the specific operational significance of ethnic, gendered, religious, etc., cleavages. Heterogeneity, not homogeneity is the modern *Wirksamkeit* – or a heterogeneous reality, which both contains its own operational problems and gives rise to its own (inherent) justice demands. See below, note 55.

45 Majone is explicit: the true problem in Keysian notions of economic redistribution was that they required the segregation of national economies. By the same token, once national economies were integrated, the functional operations of the welfare state would no longer be a given (2005: 197).

46 Sadly, another phrase that is impossible to render properly in English.

47 Joseph Weiler (1994) was undoubtedly right to identify the normative power of Europe, not simply within its positive law, but also within the network of legal relations maintained between legal orders in Europe.

48 Again returning to Heller, Rousseau's *pouvoir constituent* is not only a chimera; but rather also a barrier to legal and constitutional materialisation as pre-determined normative 'givens' frustrate efforts to adapt law to social reality.

49 Referring again to Europe's greatest achievement, its principle of national non-discrimination and its related efforts to open up the symbolic republic to its slaves.

50 And here, analyses criticising say, the German Constitutional Court for its apparent emphasis on the need for Europe to establish an *ethnos* (culturally pre-political polity) as a pre-condition for European democracy are wholly misplaced. What has marked the efforts of that Court, by contrast, and in particular its *Brunner* judgment (*Brunner* [1994]), has been its preparedness to glance into the abyss, to ask itself whether a *demos* can *ever* be established in the absence of constitutional settlement (see Chapter 2 (IV.2)).

51 Again, the point is largely made for analytical rather than normative reasons. There is no desire within this analysis to get caught up in the interminable discussion on whether Europe can or cannot ever create its own *demos*: see, for the latest rejection of the European *demos* Majone (2005). Instead, the point is a simple one: Europe's failure to identify a *pouvoir constituent* within an overarching political collectivity made up of all Europeans has equally denied it recourse to a focal point for representative and majoritarian politics. In this analysis, the European Parliament might well represent one element of the will of Europeans. It cannot, however, represent *the* European will (however mythical) since the *demos* from which it would educe, has not been formed.

52 The Habermasian view on political legitimacy being also self-consciously procedural in nature; a proceduralist impulse confirmed by Robert Alexy (1994).

53 A political discourse that, in turn, determines the breadth of political rights and the exact concomitant room afforded a sphere of private autonomy within the polity. See, only, Alexy (1994) for an incisive explanation of the later works of Jürgen Habermas. This construction of course at once confirms that whilst Habermas is very much a part of the latter day effort to relate law to its social environment and to avoid the crass constructivism of axiomatic pre-determined normative settlement, he is still without doubt tied in to notions of constitutional settlement. To be sure, the unusual (in terms of traditional state theory) privileging

of political discourse above civil rights within the constitution, as well as the reflexive relationship established between rights and politics, is an indication of unrivalled subtleties in the analysis: normative hierarchical dominance of civic rights above political discourse would only give axiomatic rather than 'real' substance to the sphere of liberal autonomy; likewise the establishment of a continuing reflexive relationship between law and politics lessens the danger of blind legal faith in the pre-political predominance of the constitutional settlement. Nonetheless, as Alexy points out, and Habermas himself tangentially confirms in his writings on European constitutional settlement ((2001); the point being that Europeans must make the 'painful transition' from 'kinship' to higher liberal constitutional settlement), the notion of 'settlement' still contains an inspirational moral force (constitutional patriotism) and imbues the proceduralism inherent to deliberative democracy with a settled substantive content. One unchanging (non-reflexive) force within the Habermasian settlement thus remains adherence to normative preconditions for deliberative discourse; or philosophical concordance with the abstract and objective nature of the political citizen. In this, the Habermasian construction surely shares in the 'flaw' of the revolutionary French Republic or Kantian ideals of 'universal' political community. It can thus be argued that is not fully universal in nature – inclusion within the *res publica* still requires inclusion within the constitutional settlement and still demands (imputed) philosophical concordance with the ideals of the constitution. If the revolution is thus instantiated, the republic may yet be in possession of slaves. See, however, for recent alterations in Habermas' philosophical stance, and for a greater emphasis upon the importance of the subjective self within political process, Habermas (2005a).

54 Note, however, that notions of supranational deliberation, as developed by Christian Joerges, continue, in a final analysis to rely very strongly upon Habermasian constructions of the legitimate polity. In other words, Habermasian forms of deliberation must continue to obtain within the nation state. Deliberation, in this analysis, takes on two guises: an 'experimental' character one at supranational level, as relations between national polities are 'civilised' through application of deliberative standards; and a comprehensive legitimising nature at national level, as national political community continues to be the primary locus for the construction of material justice. The conflicts of law mechanism ensures that no violence can be done to any one national process of deliberation.

55 In other words, such works stem from a contemporaneous effort to solve the problem of *res publica*, to extend universality and incorporate the republic's slaves within the symbolic city. How can a universal republic play host to citizens who are not fully at one with the republic's ideals? Equally – and restating the issue with modernising reference to Heller's conceptions of social evolution and political community – where once political violence might also have been kept in check with reference to the social homogeneity of the political community (1928b), a modern social *Wirksamkeit* can no longer be overlooked. European societies are plural in nature and play host to a multitude of pre- and post-liberal identities (both communitarian and self-constituting (e.g. gender identities)). To the degree that relations between plural groups within Europe are generally managed 'peaceably', the *praxis* of European societies would seem to have outpaced the theories of their founding. To this degree, then, the final 'flaw' in the French revolutionary republic, or in Kantian notions of universal political community, is calling out for legal resolution – a *Wirksamkeit* founded in heterogeneity (see note 44).

56 Now a position accepted by Habermas himself, with a measure of auto-critique: the urgency of establishment of a European counterweight to US imperialism could not compensate for myriad failings in the constitutive act (2005b).

57 The worst academic mistake, of course, would be to take the notion of deliberation, without due regard for all Habermasian intricacies, and apply it slapdash to on-going processes of European integration, *à la* 'they have deliberated, therefore Europe is democratic'.

58 'Good' by axiomatic definition? Thus, for logical example, what price common (universal) modes of expression *between* self-defining groups, if persons within those groups are denied voice?

59 In explanation, supranational deliberation (at least beyond the deliberation maintained within the national sphere, which is still comprehensively Habermasian in nature), appears to share the 'civilising' techniques of more technocratic approaches to European governance. Deliberation is (experimentally) assured with reference to standards, such as 'proportionality', or 'state of the art' decision-making.

60 At least at the level of a fundamental clash between the justice demands of two national polities.

61 See, in particular, Chapters 4 and 6.

Chapter 2

# Retelling the legal integration story

> It is safe to say with the benefit of hindsight, that had the Court followed the Governments, Community law would have remained an abstract skeleton, and a great number of Treaty violations would have remained undisclosed and unredressed.
>
> Eric Stein (1981: 6)

## I. Introduction: law's proprium and the inadequacy of interdisciplinarity

The story of European integration is one that is told *ad nauseam*, and from a variety of perspectives. With the possible exception of sociology, or social theory,[1] the process of integration has proven to be a beacon for broad swathes of social science research, holding historians, lawyers, political scientists, economists and political theorists in its thrall, as unforeseen and unexpected processes of transnational co-operation, the disaggregation of state functions and, latterly, attempted (if not successful) supranational constitutional consolidation have challenged, and likewise rejuvenated, tired disciplinary discourse. Simply stated, processes of European integration have questioned the seemingly once-entrenched economic, political and social structures of the post-war nation state. As the cause of supranational integration has advanced, it has unveiled the deep-seated and long-standing fissures that have always been present within the modern state; fissures that shed doubt upon the ability of conventional governments to integrate and to govern economic, social and political interests within the individual nation-state setting. At the same time, and as a direct result, traditional academic discourse has been called upon to re-address not only its own premises and methodologies, but also its own (ideological) provenance.

With this, scholarly European discourses of functionalism, neo-functionalism, 'exit, voice and loyalty', intergovernmentalism, economic constitutionalism, the 'association of functional integration' (*Zweckverband der funktionellen Integration*) and 'technocratic governance', are thus not simply to be understood as well-meaning efforts by individual disciplines to furnish

Europeans with apt descriptors of the nature, workings and purpose of their Community and/or Union.[2] Instead, and vitally so, the act of telling the European integration story is also an academic business, and, on occasion, an academic extravaganza; an internal process of re-appraisal and re-definition of the carefully chiselled out, long-cherished, but now practically disintegrating axioms and methodologies prevalent within lecture halls of the continent and beyond. The impetus is clear, at least in broad brush-stroke terms: unbearable contradiction between common (European) post-war pursuit of wealth and security and individual (national) sculpting of social democracy – a contradiction giving rise to notions of 'democratic deficit' and 'welfare deficit' within Europe – not only feeds the dual causes of the establishment of supranational governance and statal disaggregation, but also drives a stake through the heart of all-encompassing reference frameworks for academic discourse and appraisal. What price the social democratic settlement, founded in the axiom of the state/constitution-endowed triad of civic, political and social rights if the individual national citizen is also a European citizen, legally primed with the potential means to tear nationally consolidated solidarity apart? Equally, lawyers remain as challenged as political scientists and theorists: what is the value of Kelsen's *Grundnorm*, or the notion that the national *demos* legitimates its own law through its own constitutive act, if national constitutions must be bent, however haltingly, to the demands and to the strictures of supranational legal integration?

The result is academic confusion and challenge: should political scientists and theorists desist from their once traditional normative role of maintaining integration between economic, political social spheres (Offe 1981), in order to adopt the individualistic maximisation strictures of economy, efficiency and effectiveness instead? Should lawyers, in the absence of clear political legitimation for constitutive law, retreat into their ancient, pre-constitutional, formalism, substituting the 'mystic' power of 'the law itself' for the much vaunted post-war legitimising power of democratic settlement?

Confusion and challenge, however, are also masters of opportunity. For the brave normative few, new theoretical horizons are also opened up by the potential offered to bridle the integration paradox, to rein in the supranational/national contradiction: functionalism, neo-functionalism, intergovernmentalism, economic constitutionalism, etc., in all their dual normative-descriptive characters, are thus contemporaneous endeavours to categorise and also to de-limit 'integrative disintegration', maybe not in the service of the maintenance of national settlement, but, at the very least, in pursuit of the securing of the basic values of democracy, individual right and solidarity that national settlement entails.[3] For the pedestrian many, the apparent novelty and undeniable intricacies of practical integration processes are likewise rewards in themselves. For once, the devil truly is to be found in the details, and shattered governance axioms and methodologies open up new vistas for detailed empirical research in an effort to ascertain the exact nature of the practices, processes and purported normative frameworks that have taken their place. Finally, however, for the select methodological *cognoscenti*, confusion and trial transmute into core disciplinary opportunities as the challenges of integration are deemed to be no longer treatable within the confines of, say, the law, political science, or economic theory, but are instead necessitating of the wholesale re-orientation and re-dedication of academic discourse, with lawyers, political scientists, economists and theorists of every ilk now dependent, the one upon the other, for each of their hard-won insights into the integration process (Joerges 1996a).

Given that interdisciplinarity has much in common with the founding assertion of this book – that constitutions and constitutionalism generally, and European constitutionalism in particular, can no longer be adequately grasped or evaluated in simple terms of traditional constitutional theory[4] – this retelling of the tale of European integration, together with its explanation for the growing impetus for an appropriate understanding of European constitutionalisation, cannot but be framed in interdisciplinary terms. The core constitutional importance of European integration, it argues, is that it has revealed the indeterminacy of constitutional settlement; the inability of any isolated constitutional theory to account for the inevitable evolution of law beyond the devices and desires of its founding collective polity. Just as a succession of European lawyers, political scientists and theorists have grasped that no one discipline can claim primacy in the matter of describing and evaluating an uncertain and conditional process of European integration, this book also argues that the explicit death of constitutional axiom occasioned by European integration forces constitutional study away from its traditional constitutional theory anchor, and towards a foundation within legal and social theory.

However, in its specific brief to retell the story of European legal integration and, in particular, to re-examine and re-evaluate the supposedly 'purposive' or 'activist' jurisprudence of the European Court of Justice (ECJ), the following analysis nonetheless deviates to a significant degree from more common understandings of interdisciplinarity. To quote Jo Shaw (1995), in a reflection approved of by Slaughter and Mattli (1998: 206):

> What is slowly emerging, out of a number of disciplines and out of interdisciplinary work is a body of commentary which examines European legal process and legal institutions in their broader social, economic and political context, rather than regarding legal processes as an object of study in themselves.[5]

And indeed, this sentiment can neither be doubted nor decried – but that is only in so far as it goes. Certainly, 'pure' formal legal methodology might rightly be regarded as a 'true', but distinctly subordinate, brother of, say, a theory of constitutional interpretation, so that its usefulness or potency cannot outlive the death of its mentoring (constitutional) axiom.[6] Nonetheless, even as law, and particularly constitutional law, is faced with the disintegration of its modern foundational bedrock – its safe anchoring within the legitimising political forces of the (closed) national constitutional settlement – it is also, and necessarily so, increasingly called upon to give a more exact account of *its internal* methodologies and operations. Law, and particularly, 'constitutional law' cannot exist without a legitimising power of its own.

Certainly, interdisciplinarity is a key in this process of accounting: where the talk is of the death of constitutional settlement, constitutional pronouncement and law can no longer be removed from the reality of economic, political or social processes, but must instead be immanent to them. However, the simple act of putting the law in social, political or economic 'context' can never, and must never, detract (at least, from the lawyer's point of view) from the intrinsic and self-contained character of law, or, indeed, of constitutionalism. If law, or the concept of constitution, is to retain its integral and legitimising character, or its ability to translate fact into norm, then interdisciplinarity cannot satisfy itself with the banal extrapolation of the political opportunities possessed by and the political constraints placed upon, say, an 'activist' ECJ, in its pursuit of the constitutionalisation of Europe (Burley and Mattli 1993). Instead, the awkward dual task faced by this interdisciplinary 'legal' constitutional study is one of identifying the internal discourse of European law, its own legitimising narrative, as well as sketching out the mutual relationships – or, in systems theory terms, the patterns of observation (Luhmann 1993: 440) – maintained between law and its social, political and economic environments. Beyond axiom, what are the legitimate legal methodologies that facilitate the incorporation of the facts of an ever-changing legal-external environment within law and their translation into a legitimising norm? How has European law constitutionalised, or given enduring normative force to the ever changing face and factual process of European integration?

Seen from this perspective, then, the oft-told story of European legal integration bears one more telling. Not from the viewpoint of the judge as a politically motivated activist, or, indeed, as an automaton agent of formalist application. But, instead, from the perspective of the judge or lawyer as a tied representative of a system of law, which is subject to its own normative imperatives, yet embedded within an external political, social and economic environment to which it must respond.

## II. The court and its academic interlocutors

In a complex world of judicial, political, social and economic interaction within the integration of Europe, one fact cannot be doubted: as Eric Stein notes in the introductory citation to this chapter, European law in general, and the ECJ in particular, has played a pivotal integrative role. Had the Court not declared the Treaty of Rome to be 'directly effective' and supreme, political inertia at national government level would have consigned the integration process to a footnote in history – a minor effort to create a largely ineffective trading block. Beyond this particular certainty, however, many questions have yet to be answered. As early as 1981, for example, Stein was confident in asserting that judicial efforts to further the cause of European integration had already resulted in the fashioning of a 'constitutional framework for a federal type Europe' (1981: 1). Nonetheless, both the 'federal' and 'constitutional' elements within this construction remain in doubt to this day. Equally, and more importantly, uncertainty also continues to prevail with regard to the motivations and impetus behind the supposedly most significant example of 'judicial activism' ever seen outside the 'New Deal' supporting activities of the US Supreme Court.[7] Why did the ECJ take action to sweep aside barriers created by political self-interest and integral national considerations? What motivated European justices to act independently of their own national legal cultures and to create a body of supranational jurisprudence, seemingly beholden only to an integrative European ideal?

Generally speaking, there are as many answers to this question as there are theories that describe and delimit the (legitimate) shape of the European polity; and indeed, it is this close interconnection between academic descriptors of the European polity and the scholarly explanations given for the actions of the ECJ that prompts this study to begin to move beyond the accepted wisdom to re-examine and retell the European legal integration story with a closer eye to the law-internal narratives and imperatives of European legal evolution, as well as to the relationship of European law with its extra-legal environment. Thus, whether the 'activist' ECJ is deemed to be a politically motivated actor, which promotes a veiled assault on national interests by supranational ideals under the totalising veil of legal formalism (Burley and Mattli 1993: 72),[8] whether it is held to be a mere agent of member state principals, forever institutionally prone to stray away from member state direction, but always constrained by national powers to rein back the integration process (Talberg 2000), or whether it is simply denoted an overtly economically liberal or rational court that is seeking to preserve a scheme of market freedoms and economic law that protects the European market from transient political interests – the result is the same. Interdisciplinary efforts to describe and explain the actions of the European Court, or to examine the marriage of law and politics, are flawed at the outset by a very particular normative-factual confusion: to wit, the endeavour to mould the actions of the Court to fit a pre-existing scheme or ideal of the legitimate nature of a finite European polity. Thus, the needs of a neo-functional Community must be served by a neo-functional Court, careless of national self-interest and dedicated to the veiled pursuit of supranational benefit (Burley and Mattli 1993: 72). Equally, an intergovernmentalist

Community and Union must preserve the 'principal' position of its founding member states and be governed, in its law, by an 'agent' Court whose over-eager jurisprudence might always be reined back in subsequent political (intergovernmental) dealings (Garrett 1992). Finally, a rational European Community, founded within the liberal precepts of a market-preserving or technocratically oriented fourth branch of government, must be overseen by a rational and technical ECJ.

To a lawyer and, in particular, to this study, the inherited weaknesses within such accounts are immediately apparent. Thus, any appellation of the ECJ as a neo-functionalist, agent or rational court not only cavalierly ignores any role that the law itself, or its internal normative mission, might have played within the process of European integration, but it is also fatally dismissive of the realities of that process. For example, the legitimate desire that Europe act, as a neo-functional association, or, in its German variant, as a *Zweckverband der funktionellen Integration* (Ipsen 1972),[9] is no guarantee that is does or will actually do so. Accordingly, to ascribe a neo-functionalist legitimacy to a 'supreme' ECJ and to view its actions under that lens is to pre-empt the analysis and wilfully disregard alternative motivations and explanations for judicial operation. The same holds equally true for intergovernmentalist approaches, which view the European Court as a principal of the member states, or for the simple categorisation of the ECJ Justices as neo-liberal or technocratic actors. The governing theme is regressive: European integration has proven to be unexpected, conditional and unforeseeable. Any effort to explain and, at the same time, to legitimise the actions of its governing court, with reference to theories that contain pre-determined visions of the legitimate shape of the European polity, is bound to prove to be inconsistent.

What, then, might be considered to be a useful 'interdisciplinary' methodology, which is appropriate for research into the actions of the ECJ? Is there some form of analysis that might be deployed to circumnavigate the pre-emptive pitfalls and redundancies of normative-descriptive analysis? Certainly, one possibility that springs to mind must surely be a methodological limitation of the analysis to empirical integration realities and a rejection of any misguided effort to seek both the motivations for, and the legitimacy that lie behind, judicial operation within any one methodological framework. And indeed, here, study of the European Court and European legal evolution as a whole does offer a rich seam of explanatory study, especially in the realm of a rational choice historical institutionalism (RCHI) and institutionalist analysis which uncannily seems to echo and augment older and more general strands of legal theoretical research (McCowan 2003). Thus, RCHI, as applicable to European integration processes, may be argued to build upon Duncan Kennedy's insightful, if somewhat wistful, finding that 'activist' jurists are not simply free to insert their political ambitions within the prevailing body of jurisprudence, since a firm and established body of precedent – together with all the social and sociological pressures to remain (at least nominally) faithful to that precedent – not only furnishes the grammar for judicial pronouncement but, at the same time, also acts as a grammatical and semantic constraint upon political judicial self-expression (Kennedy 1986).[10]

In other words, once having pronounced and created its own body of precedent, the ECJ is locked into a distinct jurisprudential course from which it can only depart to a limited degree on very few occasions and with no small doctrinal jumping through of hoops. European RCHI, however, also goes further: where judges and the law are constrained in the paths of their reasoning, powerful extra-legal actors might seize upon their opportunities to plan strategic litigation to inveigle the law and its captive justices into decision-making that is advantageous to them (Wincott 1995; McCowan 2003).[11]

Is, then, such an operative conception of the evolution of the law of the European Communities and Union, a telling of the integration story that is remarkable for its lack of normative pre-emption, a suitable methodology for the purposes of this study? Answer: yes and no. Rational choice historical institutionalism, and its specific emphasis upon the manner in which private litigants and public actors such as the European Parliament have deployed law to force the pace of the integration process, is certainly a useful tool within the canon of methodologies and theories applied by this volume, and is, in particular, vastly preferential to its neo-functionalist or principal–agent counterparts, in that it makes a vital (if perhaps unconscious) connection with an established body of twentieth century social and legal theory that is strangely ignored by much current scholarship. However, RCHI cannot furnish us with the whole of the story.[12] Instead, just as it connects with historical US critical legal scholarship, it likewise shares some of its weaknesses: in particular, it offers us an insight into, and a firm understanding of, the groaning mechanics of a legal self-legitimation, which is strictly disciplined by constraining precedent. At the same time, however, it exhibits scant regard for, or, indeed, belief in, any deeper normative impulse for legal self-legitimation.[13] Alternatively, RCHI pays little attention to the *Rechtsverfassungsrecht* impetus (Wiethölter 1985),[14] which sees law attempt to identify facts that *should* be translated into norms, in line with the justice and legitimacy demands of its extra-legal and law-internal environments.

Specifically, with its constitutional orientation, the following study cannot hope to evade the tricky interface between normative prescription and factual description. Just as it must avoid factual pre-emption in the application of normative imperatives, so, too, must it circumnavigate the potential error of the ranking of factual precedence above normative design. The particular matter for investigation is whether and, if so, how, European law might or does, in the absence of pre-determined governing axioms, but in pace with factual happenings, evolve and, at the same time, legitimise its own evolution. The study is both external and internal to law, and likewise cannot be guided by any one external theory of social legal legitimation, such as, for example, the notion that courts generally, and the ECJ in particular, are respected as instances of 'triadic dispute settlement', which furnish a neutral arbiter in cases of social conflict (Shapiro 1976: 577–578). 'Social acceptance' is certainly a factor within the legal process of self-legitimising of fact-norm translation, or *Rechtsverfassungsrecht*, but only to the degree that no institution of governance would survive for very long in a hostile environment: just as triadically conceived studies of the workings of courts seem curiously to disregard the work of the law's own legitimising (and formalising) 'saints', the 'Savignys' or the 'von Jherings',[15] the methodological approach, as a whole, fails to connect with the core defining feature of law, its internal self-legitimising discourse, much less finds the points of connection between such a discourse and the demands of law's social environment for legal legitimacy.[16]

Law's *proprium*, its demand for self-legitimation and its mission to translate fact into norm, cannot be satisfied by any form of interdisciplinary study, which fails to place the question of law at the heart of its methodological framework. Law is and must be reality-proximate: to the exact degree that it must always adjust itself to the justice demands that a real-world embodies, it must also be viewed with reference to political, economic and social realities. However, it may not be made subordinate to economic, political or sociological methodologies. In a real-world of European integration, the struggle to maintain the legitimate nature of European law, and to translate European fact into European norm, is not one that can be fully understood within the pre-determined orientations of 'foreign' disciplines, no matter how sensitive they are to one another, and no matter how sensitive they are to law. In short, the study of the process of European fact–norm translation is one which demands careful observation of European legal process – or the historical interrelationship between European law and its political, social and economic environments; observation, furthermore, which must always take care not to lose sight of abstract normative consideration, but, at the same time, must not pre-empt factual development.

## III. The market and the law: an unforeseen and accidental constitutionalism and its legal challenges

On then to the story: in the beginning, there was the market. But there again, there was no market, and therein lies the core *leitmotif* of European legal evolution, from the judicial creation of a market through to halting legal efforts to give form to evermore clearly defined processes of European political union. Whilst interest in the role of European law generally, and in the ECJ in particular, was only to explode following the intense economically integrative judicial activity of the early 1980s, as well as the passage of the Single European Act (Slaughter and Mattli 1998), creative European legal evolution had begun long before, most famously in the *van Gend & Loos* and the

*Costa* v *ENEL* jurisprudence of the 1960s.[17] At that time, functionalist visions of the creation of a politically integrated community within Europe by means of the gradual harmonisation of European economic activity had been comprehensively frustrated by the complex construction of much of the economic and market regulation prevalent throughout Europe, or by a state corporatism, which always combined and thus confused simple market failure regulation with re-distributive social and economic provision. Because national market regulation also entailed re-distributive goals, political agreement on the approximation of national economic regulation was inevitably elusive.[18]

Under such circumstances, it fell to the lot of the ECJ, as well as to European Law as a whole, to intervene in order to begin the process of giving effect to the overall aim and purpose of the Treaty of Rome through the direct legal creation of a common market. Looking back through the lenses of 40 years of European legal development, and with the luxury of much hindsight, it is, perhaps, all too easy to ascribe a political motivation to the young Court: after all, it is clear to us, and was, perhaps, also clear to the founding 'saints' of European integration,[19] that meddling with markets could not but bring 'politics' in its wake. Nevertheless, to any court of the 1960s, and to a law which was still, to a large degree, a novice in the face of the impulses of legislative interventionism, or legal materialisation, the act of the creation of a market might have appeared as politically neutral a legal activity as, say, the regulation of the day-to-day relations of private contractual parties. Certainly, corporatism and/or the political effort to imbue legislative provisions with social or material justice was undoubtedly also present within the regulatory law of the 1960s, and did, indeed, at national level, contribute to the factual frustration of the economic integration programme laid down by the Rome Treaty. Nonetheless, law, and, in particular, its judicial variant, was likewise poorly practised in its comprehension and application.[20] Accordingly, there are firm grounds for the assertion that the establishment of a judicial framework for a European market was an accidental, rather than intentional, launching of European law into an incidental process of disintegrative assault on the historically integrated social, economic and political functions of the nation state, and a complimentary task of supranational constitution-building.

In brief, the evolution of European constitutionalism, or the art of matching the norms of European legal development to the facts of European integration, is very much a story of the unforeseen legal unravelling of the social, economic and political complexes maintained within the economic regulation of the sovereign (corporate) state. It is a story of the unexpected challenges posed to law in the form and shape of residual demands made for political and social justice, and their airing at European legal level. And, finally, it is also a story of constant adjustment and re-adjustment of claims to legal primacy; a story of shifts back and forth between the legitimising powers of national and European jurisdictions.

The more detailed description of market-driven legal integration and European constitutionalism furnished below cannot hope to give a comprehensive overview of the landmark judgments that have characterised 40 years of legal evolution. Even less can it hope to give any conclusive account of the *Rechtsverfassungsrecht* of European legal evolution, or the existence or otherwise of a self-legitimising process of fact–norm translation within European law. Instead, the analysis concentrates upon a few representative, though sometimes seemingly esoteric, examples of European legal evolution, and seeks, with the aid of social and legal theory, to draw out the possible internal discourses of European *Rechtsverfassungsrecht*, as well as its potential interconnections (or lack of them) with its economic, social and political environment.

### III.1. The market created: an act of formalist constitution

As noted above, *van Gend & Loos* [1963] and *Costa* v *ENEL* [1964], mark the beginnings not only of the 'negative' integration of the European market by means of the judicial pronouncement of the inapplicability of national law, but also of the evolution of European law in its constitutional guise. At one fell swoop, the ECJ established the right of individual Europeans to call upon the predominantly market-oriented provisions of the Rome Treaty before their own national courts (*van Gend & Loos*), proclaimed the primacy of primary treaty rules giving effect to the functioning of a common market (*van Gend & Loos* and *Costa* v *ENEL*), and, in a rapidly evolving grammar and semantic of European legal application, staked out a claim to the constitutional governance of the European Communities. Novel legal terms, such as 'direct effect' and 'supremacy', were thus bravely launched upon a European legal stage.

In one of the more loquacious phrases of an early, somewhat dry, piece of European jurisprudential prose, *van Gend* established the right of European individuals to enforce Community law directly within national courts by means of the reference procedure laid down in Article 177 of the Rome Treaty [now, Article 234 EC]:

> The conclusion to be drawn from this is that the Community constitutes a new legal order of international law for the benefit of which the states have limited their sovereign right, albeit within limited fields and the subjects of which comprise not only member states, but also their nationals. Independently of the legislation of member states, Community law therefore not only imposes obligations on individuals but is also intended to confer upon them rights which become part of their legal heritage (paragraph 7).

To this unexpected and startling elevation of the individual European to the status of a subject of European law was added the notion of the supremacy of European law, albeit in the noticeable absence of a supremacy clause within the Treaty of Rome:

> By contrast with ordinary treaties, the EEC Treaty has created its own legal system, which, on the entry into force of the Treaty became an integral part of the legal systems of the member states and which their courts are bound to apply (*Costa* v *ENEL*, paragraph 425).

And, if this were not shocking enough, the point is hammered home:

> By creating a Community of unlimited duration, having its own institutions, its own personality, its own legal capacity ... and, more particularly, real powers stemming from a limitation of sovereignty or transfer of powers to the Community, the member states have limited their sovereign rights (albeit in limited fields) and have thus created a body of law which binds both their nationals and themselves (paragraph 425).

Knowingly or not, the Court had appropriated to itself the language and tools of a constitutional jurisdiction, creating its own legal subjects in the figure of the individual European, and devising for itself a scheme for the protection of that individual subject, valid above applicable law in (lesser?) national jurisdictions. At the same time, however, the Court had also introduced European legal discourse as a whole to the unexpected consequences of 'legal indeterminacy', or to the fact that provisions of law can have very many meanings. More particularly, European law was revealed not to be a monolithic construction that would always be interpreted in the light of the supposedly determinate principles of international or civil law. Instead, a 'new legal order of international law' would be subject to its own interpretational canon.

Engaging in brief explanation: the Court need not have decided as it did, and indeed, many opposing arguments were brought before it by national governments, and not least by its own *juge memoire*, Advocate General Roemer.[21] First, international treaty law did not conceive of individual nationals as direct subjects of international law. Instead, the ECJ was required to create 'a new order of international law' in order to give direct effect to European legal provisions within national jurisdictions. Equally, a simple reading of the 'words on the page' of the Rome Treaty, at least beyond its Preamble, did not seem to indicate that European law should have direct effect: nowhere was the talk one of the individual 'rights' of European citizens – these rights were instead imputed to Europeans by the Court. Finally, in a twist of reasoning so beloved of civil lawyers and so impenetrable to their common law counterparts, a 'schematic' interpretation of treaty provisions, or their inter-relationship with one another, revealed alternate enforcement mechanisms for European law within the Rome Treaty: more particularly, the Commission right of enforcement under Article 169 [now 226 EC], whose primary positioning within the Treaty could be argued to suggest that individual actions pursued before national courts under Article 177 Rome Treaty [now Article 234 EC] should only have a subsidiary status and should not be deployed to enforce European law against the wishes of the member states.

Seen in this light, the Court's identification of the principles of direct effect and supremacy might, indeed, be argued to take on an activist hue, and not least, a neo-functionalist activist hue.[22] Legal indeterminacy was read into a new body of European law with the aid of a Preamble, in which the member states committed themselves to the creation of a common market. Teleological reasoning would take the place of its more pedestrian semantic and schematic counterparts. Furthermore, teleological reasoning would be extended far beyond its normal civil law limitations (so carefully elaborated by Savigny (1779–1861) and von Jhering (1818–1892)). It would no longer entail restricted pursuit of the legislative goals laid down in individual provisions of the Rome Treaty, but would instead expand to encompass a 'purposive' function of the pursuit of the completion of the comprehensive project of the common market.

With this, of course, neo-functionalist theories, as well as the precepts of the *Zwechverband funktioneller Integration*, would seem to be proven. A rationalist supranationalist impulse had seized the Court, propelling it beyond the immediate legislative intent of the member states, to engage in supranational market-making – an activity seemingly legitimated, in its turn, by visions of the existing European polity as a(n) (limited) association dedicated to a European (market) integration project: '[L]aw functions both as a mask and as a shield. It hides and protects the promotion of one particular set of objectives against contending objectives in the purely political sphere' (Burley and Mattli 1993).

The law was not political in the sense that it had directly intervened within political process: after all, the transfer of sovereign national functions occurred within a limited economic sphere, such that lawyers, at least, might continue to assume that the core social and economic functions of the nation state would remain intact. Nonetheless, or so it might be suggested, the Court had stepped beyond the realms of formalist reasoning, by rejecting traditional canons of international legal interpretation in order to give purposive judicial preference to a political goal – clearly supported by the Commission – of market integration.

Or had it? Certainly, the language remains one of formalism. This is the case not merely in relation to the constitutionally highly significant doctrinal concept of *effet utile*: the notion that no rights must be without a remedy, which, on the internationalist stage of the European treaties, was transmuted into a process of the empowerment of the individual above the legislative strictures of politically constituted national polities.[23] It is also the case in relation to the language of *effet nécessaire* – significantly, the legal semantics of the extension of teleological reasoning beyond the securing of the legislative intent that lurks behind individual provisions of positive law, in order to encompass the pursuit of the entire market-building project, also possessed their own doctrinal appellation.[24] But, the question remains: is this language simply a 'mask and shield' for neo-functionalism? Answer: no, or, at least, potentially no.

This assertion, however, immediately relates to the comprehensive problem of indeterminacy, or to the deeper causes of, and challenges posed by, legal indeterminacy. Legal indeterminacy is thus revealed in all its social significance: the problem of legal indeterminacy is not restricted to the simple fact that legal provisions can mean many different things to many different people. The issue of the inability of positive law ever to furnish a definitive expression of social or political intent is not (only) a banal matter of individual instances of the subversion of legislative intent by politically motivated judges and courts. Instead, legal indeterminacy is a defining characteristic, not only of law, but also of its external social environment.

To return to the formulations introduced by Hermann Heller (*Wirksamkeit*) (Chapter 1 (IV)): as society evolves it creates its own operational realities, as well as its own social or political justice demands. By this token, a determinate law is also, or is potentially so, a reactionary law, a barrier to the recognition of social evolution by law and to the necessary adjustment of law to the particular political and social justice demands, which that social evolution entails. At the same time, however, indeterminate law, a force for progressive social good, must also maintain its own 'determinate' authority, or ethical and moral coherence. Indeterminacy of law is, therefore, better understood not simply as a semantic problem, but, instead, as an enduring and deep-seated challenge, giving rise to on-going legal efforts to ensure that 'legitimate' models of social organisation are not perverted in their operation by politicised judges, but at the same time posing an on-going demand that legal norm be adapted to dynamic social development.

Alternatively and curtly stated, law is forever caught on the horns of a dilemma, constantly called upon to respond to social reality, but, at the same time, required to maintain its own law-internal authority. Seen in this light, the 'alternative' formalism of the ECJ – its calls to *effet utile* and *effet nécessaire* – represents much more than a simple analysis of 'the words on the page'; and its does so *precisely* because the Court was searching for those formalist frames of reference that might lead it through a morass of competing jurisdictions and conflicting political goals to identify the deeper inter-meshing between law and the social models which, in its perception at least, governed the law-external environment.

If this argument is accepted, the Court's formalism is not a tool that masks federalist governance impulses from an unwitting European public, but is, instead, a bulwark against functionalist politicising impulses. Nor, moreover, is it a mask for simple neo-functionalist strengthening of the supranational community. Instead, formalism, as practised within the *van Gend* and *ENEL* jurisprudence, is a legal internal operation, which recalls older models of societal and legal constitution, and which safeguards European law from potential political embroilment within the conflict between national and supranational interests. Locating the analysis within a social and legal theoretical frame of reference, and noting the absence of politically constituted sovereignty at European level, the ECJ's formalism can be argued to entail a call to pre-statal legal traditions, which are all the while legitimated, not by a functional, neo-functional, or even neo-liberal perception of a legitimate (economic) European polity, but by a 'classical' *law-internal* perception of the legitimate relations that must be maintained between law, markets and society; a perception which is constitutive of the extra-statal (extra-constitutional, in the formal sense) relations established between law and a law-external environment, and which is, at the same time, self-legitimating of internal legal evolution.

'Supremacy', in stark contrast to 'sovereignty', is an instrument of legal medievalism or, at the very least, a pre-modern legal and pre-political legal mechanism that creates a relationship between supranational and national law, not by means of a rational hierarchy of norms – although Article 177 Rome Treaty [now Article 234 EC] did give it the means of rational legal expression – but with recourse to the 'common legal heritage' of European legal systems, or their 'integral' and 'organic' interconnection (that is, their pre-political character).[25] Meanwhile, the legal formalism of Europe's law (national and supranational law acting in common) is, or so it may be argued, the self-legitimating model of classical legal formalism, or formal legal rationality, identified, rationalised and promoted by, amongst others, Max Weber.

To turn initially to notions of 'supremacy': absent a 'sovereign' European Treaty, the ECJ's authority would remain conditional upon the actions and reactions of national jurisdictions. And accordingly, the legal impulse, offer to treat, or *invitatio ad offerendum*, sent out by the ECJ to its national counterparts can be argued to be that of an offer to join within a self-legitimating process of legal re-entrenchment. Formal rationality would be the guiding force for law within Europe. Alternatively, the ECJ requested national courts to return to and accept a legal formalism, within which European law would be anchored as the valid law of the market throughout the continent, economic exchange expectations would be secured by means of legal certainty in the exercise of individual economic rights (Weber 1969), and private economic autonomy would be assured by the setting aside of national legislative provisions potentially injurious to free European market exchange.

To be sure, in its results at least, this form of formalism might coalesce with neo-functionalist aims and purposes. Its internal self-legitimation, however, may yet be argued to be furnished, not by specific judicial political commitment to neo-functionalist goals, but by the happy coincidence between law's ancient and politically neutral self-legitimation discourse of secured (contractual) exchange between autonomous (pre-political) actors with classical (and latterly, neo-liberal) perceptions of 'free' and 'just' market evolution (Everson 2005). The ECJ was turning the clock back on the interventionist law of the welfare state. It was returning to a rational legal paradigm built upon and derived from neutral norms of contractual exchange. Europe's laws, both national and European, could establish their 'organic' interconnection with reference to the pre-modern role of law and its pre-political commitment to legal certainty and individual economic freedom. Formal rationality in law would act as a vital operational fulcrum, both allowing for the creation of a European marketplace, and, at the same time, opening up a self-legitimating discourse between European legal orders, whereby the rationalising powers of formalism would not only substitute for the hierarchical power of sovereignty, but would also supply the vital integrative force within Europe's law.

Seen in this light, formalist interplay between *effet nécessaire* and *effet utile* was not a mask for judicial politics, but instead played host to the contemporaneous juridical construction and legal legitimation of a European market. Equally, in a world of concrete legal norms, the ECJ had thus embarked upon a process of the privatisation of European constitutionalism – the re-anchoring of constitutive rights within the 'law of the land', or rather, the pre-political law of a market, which might be pursued in common by all European legal orders beyond their own politically constituted (national constitutional) legitimation.[26] Finally, however, in seeking to 'ensure that the system created worked and the task spelled out in the Treaty was furthered, even if legislative provision had not been made' (Slynn 1984: 416), the Court had also inevitably trapped itself within a constitutive normative process of European market-building with its own social and economic realities, to which a formally constructed European law was, in turn, remarkably ill-equipped to respond.

### III.2. The market evolving: from 'transcendental nonsense' to economic rationality and back again

If it might be doubted that the European law of the 1960s was locked into its own self-legitimating model of legal formalism which was predicated upon the immanence of autonomy-securing law to a supposed social reality of a legislatively unfettered and judicially secured private economic exchange logic, the evolution of European economic law throughout the 1980s would nonetheless appear to confirm the presence of formalism and formal rationality within European jurisprudence, at the least to the degree that, fully in accordance with RCHI observations, the ECJ seemed now to be locked into a (deregulatory) line of precedent that brooked no peace with the politically legitimated realities of economic organisation at national level. Certainly, intergovernmental alteration to the structures of the European Communities, in particular, the ending of the national veto over secondary market regulation in the Single European Act (1987), also played its own significant part in the unravelling of corporatist national complexes of political-social economic regulation.[27] Nonetheless, the presence of the formalist Court was a constant and determinative factor within the deregulatory process of negative European integration.

In this regard, then, a seemingly obscure, but vital exemplar of the formalist application of the inherently liberalising character of European primary law is furnished by the case of the *Verband der deutschen Sachversicherer* [1987]. As noted above, the accompanying *leitmotif* of European market integration through the negative judicial imposition of the largely deregulatory provisions of primary European law has been the unravelling of national post-war interventionist efforts to combine goals of social regulation (providing welfare or political voice within the economy) with standard market regulation goals (guarding against market failure). This process of 'integrative disintegration', which was to bear witness to the advancement of the constitutive structures of a European market only at the cost of the casting asunder of corporatist complexes of economic regulation maintained at national level, was one that was to spread its influence far and wide throughout European goods and services markets (Majone 1996), and, in particular, was also to reach the restrictive practices of the German fire insurance market.

In *Verband der deutschen Sachversicherer*, the long established German regulatory practice of tolerating private rate-setting cartels within the fire insurance market was accordingly, and inevitably so, to fall victim to the application of the primary provisions of European competition law [now Articles 81 and 82]. Corporatism remained the enemy of private exchange logic. Accordingly, the practice of guarding against market failures caused by too volatile a degree of competition with the aid of collusive agreements between insurers was deemed to infringe upon European principles of national non-discrimination, thus creating barriers to market entry to the disadvantage of non-German fire insurers.

The particular point of interest in this case, however, is not that it might be taken in support of a neo-liberal reading of the ECJ's politics, although, admittedly, the case did have the initial deregulatory effect of sweeping away all fire market failure regulation within the Federal Republic. Nor is the case to be distinguished simply since it illustrates the potential transmutation of European law into an 'Economic Constitution', constitutive of the external limits of the market by means of the creation of individual economic rights, and jealously guarding of internal market freedoms through the application of competition law provisions.[28] Instead, and within the purview of this analysis, the central point of interest raised by the judgment is furnished by the terms, or rather the 'non terms', in which the Court formulated its decision:

> Community law does not ... make the implementation of Articles 85 and 86 [now, Articles 81 and 82 EC] of the EEC Treaty dependent upon the manner in which the supervision of certain areas of economic activity is organised by national legislation. (paragraph 23)

The vital point to note is not simply that the ECJ might, or might not, have updated and refined its 'private' constitutionalism, thus joining with the proponents of the legitimising function of the concept of the 'Economic Constitution' to give a true and rational shape to its 'public' law role of constituting and regulating the free market sphere within which private contractual autonomy would reign supreme.[29] Instead, the core point of interest is provided by the fact that the ECJ does not and *cannot* engage at all with issues of its own legitimacy, or, indeed, the law-external legitimacy of its integrative-disintegrative jurisprudence. Fire insurance cartels are abolished with a grammatical wave of a judicial wand: no grounds are given for the decision.

In other words, formalism reaches its apogee within this judgment in a language of 'transcendental nonsense' (Cohen 1935).[30] Having once chosen the path of self-legitimating formalism, law not only loses all interconnection with its extra-legal environment, but also begins to run out of clear justificatory norms for its own operations. It is unable to engage openly with the facts of continuing national corporatist economic regulation; still less is it explicitly able to defend the application of competition law norms within, say, the legitimising normative idiom of economic constitutionalism. Instead, it returns to the dubious arts of 'reading the words on the page' and grammatically introspective self-legitimation, *but*, in view of the clear semantic *lacunae* within the scheme of European law, simultaneously imbues legal indeterminacy with its transcendental nonsensical content: the Treaty does not allow the ECJ to take note of schemes of national economic supervision, for the sole reason that the *selfsame* Court says that the Treaty does not allow it to do so.

Simply stated, and all potential regard for the legitimating law-internal function of formalism apart, von Jhering's 'heaven' of infinitesimally divisible legal norms is just that: a transcendental realm, veiled to the eyes of simple human reasoning. The application of its ethereal norms to the real-world sphere of human endeavour gives rise to miracles – the extension of a European competition law jurisdiction and the setting aside of long-standing national regulatory provision – for which no human rationale can be identified. For all that the ECJ's historical formalism might or might not have protected it from unwanted and legally unwarranted partisanship in clashes between national and neo-functionalist visions of the evolution of the European Community, it no longer furnished it with the adequate semantic or grammatical tools to address the rapidly advancing realities of European market integration. European law had bitten deep into politically legitimated complexes of national social-political regulation, unravelling century-old traditions, and had done so on the sole basis of a legal tautology.

This is the enduring weakness of formalism, and not simply within a European jurisdiction. Certainly, formalism is a powerful internal discourse of self-legitimation, jealously protective of law's political neutrality.[31] Nonetheless, it is also inherently flawed, unable, on its own terms, to make the necessary connection with its law-external environment, or to pursue the programme of *Rechtsverfassungsrecht*. Even Max Weber's formal legal rationality, trapped within classical models of legally secured economic exchange autonomy, lacks an enduring grammar of reality recognition. Its norms derive from and are judicially educed out of one, single, model of social reality – it cannot respond to other social models, let alone to a process of social evolution. Granted, in the case of German fire insurers, this happenstance might not have had all too great an impact: after all, notwithstanding the historical success of corporatist regulatory traditions, the dampening of inappropriate competition in insurance markets is possible through less economically distorting means.[32] Nonetheless, within the overall context of the evolution of the European market, and, above all, with regard to wholly legitimate national regulatory interests, such as consumer protection, some form of legal response that might capture the reality of social and political demands for positive market regulation was to prove to be indispensable.

It is in this sense, then, that the complex of market law cases, beginning with *Dassonville* [1974] and *Cassis de Dijon* [1977], and extending through to *Keck* [1993], might be argued to gain their constitution-building significance. Not only do such cases, delineating, as they do, the exact extent of the application of the vital market-building notion of free movement of goods [Articles 28 and 30 EC], govern the inter-relationship between European and national jurisdictions, they are also representative of European law's tentative efforts to move beyond formalism and to find a new basis for its judgments in 'facticity', or the legal observation of the facts of an extra-legal environment.

The jurisprudence on the exact jurisdiction of the deregulatory reach of the European free movement of goods provision [Article 28 EC Treaty] thus takes on the quasi-federalist function of identifying where the European legal jurisdiction ends and where its national counterparts begin. Equally, recognised Treaty exceptions to free movement, or their recognition as such by the ECJ (notions of health and safety, public policy, etc.), represent judicial approval of 'vital' national regulatory interests.[33] As was always the case in relation to the Interstate Commerce Clause of the US Constitution, the material treated by the Court was technical and economic in nature. Nevertheless, the impacts of technical adjudication were constitutional in character, exactly delineating the legitimate extents of national and European jurisdictions. However, within this constitutional jurisdiction, European formal legal rationality was now wearing exceptionally thin. As a consequence, the Court was required to look far beyond its formalist veil to identify new means for reality recognition and constitutional self-legitimation.

Beer is a particularly revealing substance in this regard.[34] Famously, the German *Reinheitsgebot* limited the material used in beer-making to wheat, malt and hops. Equally famously, such ancient regulation was to fall foul of European law, more particularly, its free movement of goods provisions. This was a potential tragedy for real ale enthusiasts, but was it a case of constitutional significance, exemplary of post-formalist judicial adjudication? Certainly: the decision that primary European law condoned the sale of other European beers, containing various additives, within German territory is representative of the judicial assertion of the dominance of the Rome Treaty above national legislative process. And, as such, it might also be taken in evidence of a neo-liberal judicial orientation: national cultural sensitivities were not to be allowed to distort the integration of a European market. Equally, however, the intense, if fumbling, efforts of the justices of the ECJ to understand the mechanics of beer making and the potential ill-effects of additives within beer, may also be argued to take their place, alongside, say, the *Brandeis Brief* of American constitutional history,[35] thus heralding a departure from ethereal formalist constructions and a return of law to the consideration of reality.

As former Advocate General Gordon Slynn was once drawn to remind an audience of common law judges:

> A further practical reason for the existence of differences between the techniques of statutory construction known to English Courts and the practice of the Court of Justice of the European Communities in interpreting disputed legal instruments lies perhaps in the extraordinary range of the measures presented for the European Court's scrutiny. (Slynn 1984: 420)

Granted, Lord Slynn's remarks might have been limited to the notion that the full range of civil law's interpretative methods dwarfs the restrictive methodologies of common law statutory interpretation.[36] However, it is also an appropriate descriptor of the fact that the ECJ has been remarkably forward in hearing economic and scientific evidence, and founding its judgments upon it.[37] Equally, with the notion of 'proportionality', it also established a doctrinal counterpart to scientific enquiry, or the presentation of scientific evidence within the courtroom. Rationalising its scientific approach within legal doctrine, the Court placed the onus upon national governments to *prove* that their 'restrictive' regulation had its basis in fact: governments were, from then on, to be required to demonstrate the real existence of the conditions which they claimed justified national regulation. In a threefold test, national regulation was required to be related to its aims, to be suited to achieving those goals, and to be the least (competition) distorting form of regulation available. Scientific inquiry would underpin the proportionality test. Accordingly, the German government's argument that the *Reinheitsgebot* was necessary in order to serve the purposes of consumer protection failed; science said otherwise – additives were not harmful to beer drinkers.

Clearly, at a meta-normative level of description of the legitimate European polity, such a judicial conclusion might be argued to be fully in accordance with a technocratic conception that views the European Communities as a 'rational' fourth branch of government, and argues that its law need only patrol and police the borders of rationality, deploying scientific evidence to ensure that the rationally construed European market is not subverted by illegitimate (irrational) national regulation.[38] Seen in this light, the ECJ was not a functionalist court pursuing simple integrationist goals; nor was it a mere agent court ever wary of its member state principals. Instead, the ECJ was engaged – in tandem with its technocratic Commission counterparts – in the rational unravelling of corporatism, the separating out of distributive policies from simple market regulatory goals with long overdue recourse to the theories and empirical studies of economic regulation.

Furthermore, such an analysis has much to recommend it. First, from a material perspective, since the Court's additional dictum that 'information' or labelling of the ingredients within beer should be an adequate measure of consumer protection has had, as its practical result, the exportation of 'pure' German beer to other jurisdictions, and not *vice versa*. And second, from a normative perspective, since the clear distinction drawn between socially re-distributive and simple regulatory goals acts to legitimate the Court's actions by placing them in a politically neutral arena of market economics, without prejudice to redistributive policies, which are, of necessity always subordinated to democratic political process.[39]

Yet, convincing as this technically rational tale is, it is not necessarily *our* story of the efforts of the ECJ to adapt its jurisprudence to the realities of European integration. Like many a court before it, the ECJ had also discovered that the unravelling of legitimate social interests, which its formalist jurisprudence had occasioned, had now created conflicts that could no longer be mediated within formalist grammar. Instead, beyond formally rational or politically legitimated law, the Court was again drawn into a legal materialisation debate – or the effort to give legal expression to the *Wirksamkeit* of the integration *telos*[40] – and was left to re-establish its interconnections with its extra-legal environment, desperately seeking a mediating form of legal norm (proportionality), in order to identify legitimate national regulatory concerns with recourse to 'science'. In other words, the court was seeking to reconstruct social reality within a academic scientific language, suitable for reception within the courtroom.

In this, of course, the ECJ was far from unique. Granted, the spectacular nature of European legal process – the subsuming of national regulatory processes within a supranational body of law, or, in more pejorative terms, the seizure of national competence by rampant primary European law – gave European legal processes of the materialisation of jurisprudence a profile that was apt to draw the attentions of theorists, less concerned with law-internal narratives of legal legitimation, and dedicated instead to the design of grand schemes to legitimise the overall process of European integration. Nonetheless, from the pragmatic legal rather than European theorist's point of view, the *problematique* of the construction of extra-political legal interconnection with the 'social' was a very old and mundane one, indeed, visible in the early nineteenth century jurisprudence of the US Supreme Court, warned against by Max Weber, and tackled theoretically head on by the 'free law movement' or *Freirechtsschule* of the Weimar Republic.

The realities of a process of European integration suddenly demanded courtroom appreciation of fact above norm: just as US justices had once been required to consider the material health rather than transcendental contractual status of female workers within American bakeries, the ECJ was now called upon to consider the material health of European beer drinkers. A materialisation impulse was observed in European law; the self-same materialisation impulse that had so greatly disturbed a Max Weber, who feared that doctrinally unfettered judges, seeking to marry law with social reality, would ultimately undermine the rule of law. Certainly, efforts to assess and address the health of European beer drinkers might not have had the same striking degree of constitutional significance as the endeavour to protect female workers from injurious industrial working conditions. Nonetheless, the descent into legal indeterminacy, which even this limited legal consideration of reality entailed, also bore with it a danger that social irrationality might begin to infect rational European law: how were the justices of the ECJ to judge the legitimacy or otherwise of culturally conditioned consumer cultures within the Federal Republic of Germany?

By the same token, however, processes of the materialisation of European law could also be cast in a more positive light. To a free law movement, indeterminacy was a positive force: determinate or formal law was the enemy of legal legitimacy within the broader social context of 'legitimate' social and political interests. Within the European setting, the real-world discovery that various national regulatory concerns could not simply be swept aside by formal European law, and the consequent materialisation of European law, was to be applauded rather than decried. Yet, even within this theoretical purview, European law was denied regulatory recourse to the materialising mechanisms that were, for example, developed by free law practitioners, and, in particular by Hugo Sinzheimer: within a negative integration process, the ECJ could not merely delegate appreciation of an extra-legal environment to the socialising and materialising lenses of 'special legislation'.[41]

Instead, the ECJ was left in the highly uncomfortable position of becoming a potentially socially liberating, but equally irrational, 'judge-king'. In other words, and in line with the writings of Eugen Ehrlich, the grandfather of the free law movement, they were *directly* confronted with the vital task of adapting law to reality: legislative mediation of justice demands remained an impossibility. Equally, scrabbling after the mechanisms that might structure and legitimate its interaction with social reality, at the same time avoiding the danger of simple romantic judicial re-creation of reality,[42] the ECJ made brave recourse to supposedly neutral reality-reconstructing discourses of science, or social science.[43] Science would furnish the vital observation mechanism between law and its extra-legal environment.

In a final analysis, however, and notwithstanding all its praiseworthy efforts to identify the material interconnection with social reality and extra-legal 'justice' demands, the Court had likewise plunged itself into the enduring legal controversy of formal versus material justice. Weber, of course, had warned against legal materialisation for very good reason. Materialisation impulses, notoriously difficult to construct in any convincing concrete manner, inevitably expose law to political controversy: even the neutrality of 'science' can be doubted (Chapter 4 (III.3), Chapter 6 (IV.1) and Chapter 7 (II.2)). The court that meddles in political and social realities courts the danger of political partisanship and places the rule of law in doubt. Formalism, and more particularly, Max Weber's formal rationality, is disconnected from social reality, or, at least, is disconnected to the extent that its founding paradigm of personal autonomy is an imputed constitution of society, rather than an adequate reflection of it;[44] nonetheless, at the same time, this imputed construction of society (pre-determined axiom of social organisation) also safeguards legal independence.

The eternal formal-material legal paradox accordingly returns with a vengeance: certainly, formalism may have imbued European law with authority, and, more particularly, may have established authoritative discourse between national and European legal orders. At the same time, however, and at the level of transcendental nonsense within judicial discourse, 'meaningless' formalism also threatened to bring about a collapse in legal authority. By the same token, material correction of formalist flaws, especially in the absence of legislative direction, was itself an inherent threat to the rationality and self-legitimating capacity of a European rule of law.

Seen in this light, eternal oscillation between formal and material aims must surely be a permanent feature of any legal order, let alone a European legal order. And indeed, the constant oscillation between formal and material jurisprudence is a characteristic feature of ECJ market jurisprudence in the late 1980s and early 1990s. More particularly, formal-material oscillation is to be found in the tendency of European law to retreat back into formalist jurisprudence and the transcendental nonsense of unfounded judicial pronouncement where science, or even social science, could no longer furnish law with a sufficiently protective legitimating veil for its extra-formalistic excursions. Thus, the bald and doctrinally incoherent observation in Sunday trading cases where the market met issues of religious observance that 'Article 28 EC does not apply to issues of Sunday trading'.[45] Further, formalistic nonsense is also identifiable within the curious effort to delineate more strictly the jurisdictional reach of Article 28 EC in the face of strategic efforts by European business to break down national anti-economic dumping regulation which was unpalatable to it, with the simple, if economically unfounded, distinction made between 'selling' and 'production' arrangements.[46]

## IV. The limits to market integration: constituting society beyond the market

None of this can be taken as *critique* of the ECJ: the constant oscillation between material and formal law-giving under conditions of legal indeterminacy has simply been a feature of all post-war jurisprudence, quite apart from the challenges posed by European integration. And indeed, in the constant battle to maintain internal (formalist) legitimacy, but not to lose an eye for external (material) justice demands, various instances of the ECJ's jurisprudential excursions have been far more subtle than initially seemed to be the case,[47] and, especially so, in the light of the disintegrative nature of processes of European integration. To reiterate: the ECJ is a court which is *explicitly* denied recourse to the luxury of closed politically constituted settlement; it is a court excluded from the axiomatic political-legal legitimation circle. Certainly, it is the constant theme of this volume that the *problematique* is one shared by all jurisprudential systems. Nonetheless, the continuing lack of an explicit sovereignty clause within European law,[48] and, more importantly, the continuing lack of a political constitution within Europe, makes it all the more visible within the jurisprudence of the Luxembourg Court.

The true significance of the challenge posed by *Rechtsverfassungsrecht* to the ECJ – or by the demand that it must somehow respond to the (non-traditionally, or non-democratically mediated) justice demands made by an extra-legal environment, all the while maintaining its self-legitimating, internal (but equally externally constitutive) legal discourse; arises most clearly where the market meets its explicit limits; more particularly, where the extra-legal environment possesses its own (self-generating) normative contours, which are not so easily captured within mediating scientific methodologies.[49]

Here, the analysis accordingly moves on to examine the Court's jurisprudential struggles at the interface between market integration and social redistribution, in order to consider putative organic inter-relationships amongst Europe's many legal orders or 'laws', as well as insoluble conflicts between equally legitimated legal jurisdictions, and to assess the challenges posed to law by the contested nature of European political process. As noted above, the defining feature of the integration story is the inevitable but unforeseen (self-) immersion of European law within redistributive battles, jurisdictional conflicts and political stand-offs. To this limited degree, perhaps, Jean Monnet and functionalists everywhere are undoubtedly correct: once commenced upon, the market integration process, whether it be given impetus by political agreement or by law, would seem to possess its own dynamic, reaching far beyond the economic realm to encompass all spheres of social and political life within Europe.

The following, then, (once again) represents a necessarily selective overview of significant happenings within European constitutionalism, charting the specific challenges posed to European law by the evolving social and political reality of European integration. The analysis is one that is sensitive to European political, social and economic realities, once again highlighting the historical relationships established between law and its extra-legal environment; but, is, likewise, one that rejects any simple form of interdisciplinarity and, instead, highlights law's *proprium* – its struggle to maintain its own and its social legitimacy. Equally, the analysis cannot, at this stage, hope definitively to identify the mechanics of a possible European *Rechtsverfassungsrecht*, or the instruments and mechanisms applied or not applied by European Law in the effort to find internal legitimation for its patterns of observation of, or discourse with, its external environment. Instead, it is simply an initial effort to analyse the actions of European courts in a realm of self-generating European polity-building that lies noticeably far beyond the reaches of any current theory of the legitimate nature of the European polity.

### IV.1. The limits to corporatist dissolution: constraining the self-defining European polity within the European market

Even if the underlying *ordo-liberal* precepts of Economic constitutionalism, or the methodological precepts of an economic analysis of law, can be argued to represent 'reality' – or to furnish law-giving under conditions of legal indeterminacy with a reality-adequate mediating discourse within which to identify and transform the facts of social organisation into legal norms[50] – neither, surely, would claim application to market spheres that interface or interconnect with the normative goals of social or welfare states.[51] In other words, at the interface between private and public economies, private exchange logic is of necessity – or at least beyond simple acts of protective national corporatism – legitimately distorted by redistributive aims that have been countenanced by (national) democratic processes.

In the 'normal' national setting, primary law would thus, at the very least, seek to steer clear of regulatory complexes, which entail a mixture of 'neutral' (apolitical) market regulation and redistributive provisions imposed by legislative process. Alternatively, national courts, despite often being given greater interpretational leeway by the existence of national constitutional catalogues of social rights, would not seek to embroil themselves in cases entailing direct confrontation between distinct and conflicting functional logics of pure market regulation and social welfare provision. As we have seen above, however, the sphere of European law possesses its own dynamic, which inevitably unveils underlying tensions between market and welfare logics, confronting national social regulation with the rationalising norms of European market law. In particular, with its technical-legal dedication to provisions of individual economic empowerment and the imposition of competition law, European law impacts directly upon the interface between private market economics (private exchange logic) and redistributive policy.

More specifically, and for the exemplary purposes of this analysis, European law impacts upon a national 'insurance interface', at which intricately constructed quasi-private commercial vehicles furnish social provision for public gain.[52] Corporatist (national) regulatory provision remains the enemy of rational (European) market exchange logic: the provision of social and welfare services through commercial vehicles, which are given various regulatory advantages within a private market is, therefore, constantly threatened by European law. Granted, the problem is partially one of European law's own making, in large part precipitated by earlier processes of judicial fact–norm translation, or the socially constitutive impact of a rights discourse within European law, which has seen the individual national citizen elevated to the status of European economic citizen (Everson 1995): a European *homo economicus*, endowed with a series of market rights that might be asserted not only against the national solidarity-securing collectivity (national regulation), but also against lesser quasi-private solidarity-securing collectivities, such as collective bargaining agreements or professional welfare provision associations.

However, although the problem is most readily apparent within primary European jurisprudence, it also reveals a clear and deeper deficit within the European polity, more particularly, a political failure to set clear limits to the market driven logic of European law. Accordingly, the 'social insurance' cases recently heard by the ECJ take on a particular (constitutional) significance as the lack of clear political limits to primary market regulation, and, more particularly, primary competition law, leave European law and judges in the uncomfortable position of being required to ascertain for themselves the exact limits of the European polity's normative desire to reconfigure market operations and market logic in the light of socially redistributive goals.

Engaging in explanation: in their status of *homo economicus*, a variety of individual Europeans have brought actions before the ECJ, arguing that national governments should no longer be able to exert a coercive force to enforce their membership within, and financial contributions to, quasi-private associations (insurance schemes) for the provision of pensions and welfare services. The provisions of European competition law, as well as free movement provisions, form the rhetorical basis for such arguments: quasi-private welfare provision associations, safeguarded from pure market competition by national regulatory laws that enforce membership within such schemes, are deemed both to engage in cartel-like behaviour, and to prevent individual Europeans from seeking provision from other (cross-border) welfare (insurance) providers. As a consequence, European competition law and free movement provisions might be re-cast in the guise of the major (de-)regulator of collective social redistribution within Europe, plunging European law into the very core of the formalist-materialist *problematique*.

Simple formal application of the European competition law paradigm would, naturally, be an inversely political act, destructive of social welfare throughout the continent. By the same token, however, any attempt on the part of the ECJ to ascertain the exact nature of material justice demands, or the legitimate extent of welfare provision within a private market, would be one fraught with difficulty. Science or social science offers very little mediating aid in this context: the stubborn application of economic analyses of law might or might not lead to the conclusion that quasi-private provision of public welfare is an inefficient mode of social organisation; such a conclusion, however, is but a poor mirror to an operational social reality that heartily approves of distortions within private market exchange logic, or at least does so at the private–public insurance interface.

It is thus here, by somewhat perverse accident, that Richard Posner's *critique* of 'ethereal' constitutional theory reaches its apogee:[53] no abstract theory of justice and no single theory of normative constitutional derivation can furnish the ECJ with the facts of a 'normative reality' found in its extra-legal environment. Equally, no method of legal interpretation, formal or material, is, of itself, a reality-adequate portal of observation unto a world beyond law. Instead, the only adequate assertion of social reality is, surely, the process of political contestation that draws the exact line in the sand of the insurance interface – the social reality of welfare provision is also a normative construction, and thus can only be 'legitimately' achieved and established following political debate.

Given this constellation, it is, perhaps, wholly unsurprising that the ECJ has, by and large, run like the Red Queen from its adjudicational responsibilities within social insurance cases; sidestepping the issue, and, more importantly, the application of EU competition law and free movement provisions, with reference to technical-legal cut-off criteria, such as a 'lack of cross-border effect', or the 'sub-competition threshold impact'.[54] Nonetheless, within the terms of this analysis, and with a specific eye to the evolution of a European

*Rechtsverfassungsrecht*, the Court's *dicta* in the case of *Albany* [1999] are illuminating.

Concluding that a collective insurance agreement, given coercive force by Dutch law, could continue to demand financial contributions from its membership, the ECJ declared, first, that the existence of a European, treaty-based, commitment to the processes of collective bargaining provided a substantive legal bulwark against the phenomenon of 'cherry-picking', the nemesis of all public insurance schemes.[55] With this statement, and its consequent refusal to allow quasi-private public welfare provision to be undermined by a wholly private European insurance market, the Court thus seemed to be beginning to sketch out, however tentatively, the contours of a substantive European constitutional commitment to universal welfare provision. Although not couched in the language of primary (constitutional) social rights, the higher legal recognition afforded processes of collective bargaining within the Treaty on European Union, proved to be sufficient technical legal basis for the judicial evolution of concrete limits to private market exchange logic within European law. The European legal order would appear to have come of age: simple functional logics of market integration would now cede to the normative desire of the European polity to ensure universal welfare provision.

Interestingly, however, although this cautious, but positive, judicial commitment to the evolution of a social Europe is undoubtedly significant, the judgment arguably contains a second, far clearer, commitment to the evolution of a European *Rechtsverfassungsrecht*. Simply stated, the Court was also furnished with clear evidence of the existence of economically abusive behaviour on the part of the collective insurance association (towards its contributors): the rates charged by the fund were far in excess of those charged by comparable schemes. Rather than tackle this behaviour head on, however, the ECJ referred the issue back to the national court for specific consideration under procedural considerations of 'administrative fairness'.[56]

It is this pronouncement, which proves most illuminating. Certainly, the imputation of a degree of social constitutionalism within European law is interesting in substantive terms, and presumably justified by explicit intergovernmentalist agreement on the continuing validity of collective bargaining within European labour relations.[57] Nonetheless, a very real *Rechtsverfassungsrecht* impetus is also present within the second element of the Court's reasoning: the Court was beginning to focus its constitutionalisation efforts not simply upon the evolution of substantive constitutional guarantees (for public–private welfare provision), but also upon the proceduralist reconfiguration of national political debate and decision-making.

The referral back to the national court retains its own *proviso*: various interests would seem to have been disregarded within the configuration of the insurance interface. An *invitatio ad offerendum* is accordingly made to national law. The ECJ cannot directly tackle abusive behaviour within member states: to do so would be to ensure the comprehensive application of a European economic rationality, which would destroy quasi-private provision at national level. Nonetheless, national law might yet play a constitutionalising role within European law, ensuring that all interests are properly represented within national collective bargaining processes, and safeguarding public social provision schemes from abusive private behaviour. By this token, rationalising European legal logics are extended to a public–private insurance interface (efficient provision), but pose no threat to normative political commitments to universal welfare provision. National political debate and exchange, restructured by European law, continues to draw the determining line in the sand between private and public economic logics.

### *IV.2. The limits to organic interconnection: adjudicating at the interface between Europe's laws*

If the social insurance cases are a measure of the adjudicative challenges posed to European law at the boundaries to 'pure' market integration, a startling indicator of the further legal challenges created by the death of axiom or pre-determined schemes of social organisation – in this case, the death of the axiom of jurisdictional definition – is furnished by a different court altogether, the German Constitutional Court (*Bundesverfassungsgericht*). The case of *Brunner* [1994], heard by the German Constitutional Court in the torrid political aftermath of the conclusion of the Maastricht Treaty on European Union is an instance of judicial decision-making that has attracted almost as much attention as the entire integration process taken together (MacCormick 1995; Weiler 1995; Joerges 1996a; Elftheriadis 1998; Everson 1998a). But, correctly so: the controversial issues raised by the judgment touch upon the central paradox within the integration process; a paradox that is, as yet, resistant to the rationalising impulses of Europe's eager constitution-makers – the absence of European legal sovereignty and the troubled co-existence of equally legitimate legal orders or jurisdictions with overlapping competences.[58]

The German Court's response to a private action denouncing the Maastricht Treaty as incompatible with the provisions of the German Constitution is not simply remarkable – in constitutional terms – for its culmination of the long-running judicial conflict whereby the economically oriented ECJ was slowly forced to develop its own catalogue of fundamental rights since national courts had threatened revolt, or had refused to allow European law to prevail above national catalogues of fundamental rights.[59] Equally, the judgment is not simply striking in the light of the Court's central (intergovernmentalist) finding that, in the service of provision of a constitutive *Grundnorm* to the EU, member states must – per normative force – remain the 'Masters of the Treaty'.

Certainly, the Court's consequential and circularly constructed assertion that, in order to be able to endow competence to the EU, member states must retain their own integral sovereignty, such that core legislative functions might never be alienated from socially homogeneous, and consequently democratic, national polities is highly significant:

> If the peoples of the individual states provide democratic legitimation through the agency of their national parliaments (as at present) limits are then set by virtue of the democratic principle to the extension of the European Communities function and powers. Each of the peoples of the individual states is the starting point for a state power relating to that people. The states need sufficiently important spheres of activity of their own in which the people of each can develop and articulate itself in a process of political will-formation which it legitimates and controls, in order thus to give legal expression to what binds the people together (to a greater or lesser degree of homogeneity) spiritually, socially and politically. (paragraph 44)

Equally, this apparent headlong return to communitarian visions of political organisation was the cause of much 'outraged' academic comment on the judgment. Nonetheless, whilst the analytical accuracy of much of such debate can yet be doubted,[60] the most notable feature within the judgment is surely the fact that this was the first judicial endeavour to give explicit attention to and to tackle the underlying constitutional disturbance within the European jurisdiction: the lack of European legal sovereignty – or the incommensurate nature of the competing claims for legal supremacy made by national and European legal orders – and the inability of European law to give coherent logical meaning to the 'organic' relationship that had been established between national and European legal orders.

In brief, the core issue tackled by the judgment was one of which court, or which legal system, might identify the exact limits to European law. At one level, as a creation of the ECJ, European law belongs within its jurisdictional ambit, so that its limits can only be legitimately determined by that Court upon the application of the rationality criteria of European law. At yet another level, however, and given that each exercise of the European jurisdiction encroaches upon the national jurisdiction, the limits to European law can also, or *must* also, be determined by national law in the light of its own jurisdictional criteria, or internal axiom of normative organisation.

As the following chapter demonstrates, this fact has the unusual consequence of transforming each and every instance of judicial adjudication (national and European) upon European law into a constitutional decision that delineates the exact breadth of national and European jurisdictions. Equally, however, it further underlines the inability of axiomatic, or predetermined, schemes of law within Europe to react appropriately to the facts of European integration. As the citation given demonstrates, the German Constitutional Court's location of the legitimate genesis of the European Union within the constitutive power of national normative systems of social organisation (national constitutions) might well be correct within the closed logic of the German Constitution; nevertheless, it is also a very poor reflection of a reality of European integration that has witnessed the authoritative assertion of European law above its supposedly constituent parts. The axiomatic normative battle has yet to be fought to its necessarily impossible conclusion: just as European law cannot take precedence over the integral, but sovereignty-bestowing, German Constitution, the rationality pursued by a German Constitutional Court similarly cannot be accepted within the integrationist logic of a ECJ.

In short, from being a matter of high constitutional theory, the existence of authoritative adjudication (or effective supremacy) can no longer be neutrally deduced from a single axiomatic *Grundnorm*, and has now become an explicit matter of the adjustment of norms to facts, and *vice versa*. The determinative issue is one of the *corporeal* elaboration of the organic relationship established and maintained between Europe's many (equally legitimate) laws. Axioms of legal organisation have foundered, with the result that the normative character of European legal evolution (its constitutional nature) can only be identified with regard to the concrete manner in which the various national and European legal orders present within the overall European jurisdiction observe, and respond to, the changing realities of European integration processes.

Once again, whilst the analysis cannot, at this stage, hope to identify the exact modes of reality observation practised by Europe's laws, one particular observation made by the German Constitutional Court is nonetheless of particular interest in this regard. Arguably, with its bold assertion that a(n) (integral) German constitutional jurisdiction would (impossibly) cede its sovereignty in line with the real-world evolution of a(n) (evolving) European polity, the constitutional court would not only seem to be offering up a discursive *invitatio ad offerendum* to its European counterpart, but would also appear (extraordinarily) to be admitting that the (normatively oriented) constitutional court is itself wholly dependent upon reality-proximate processes of legal observation of the extra-legal environment.

Where *evidence* might be presented to law demonstrating that the peoples of Europe have established an operational political reality – or a 'political Europe' of their own – law will respond, giving normative shape to factual political community in its turn:

> At the same time ... it becomes increasingly necessary to allow the democratic legitimation and influence provided by way of national parliaments to be accompanied by a representation of the peoples of the member states through a European Parliament ... [W]ith the establishment of union citizenship ... a legal bond is formed between the nationals of individual member states, which ... [although] it does not have

> a tightness comparable to the common nationality of a single state, provides a legally binding expression of the degree of *de facto* community already in existence flowing from the citizens of the Union [and which can] eventually become a part of the democratic legitimation of the European institutions, *to the extent that the conditions necessary for this purpose are fulfilled on the part of the peoples of Europe.* (emphasis added; paragraph 40)

Certainly, given the notion that various 'conditions' must be fulfilled prior to (German) legal recognition for political community in Europe, various authors might be drawn to seize upon this paragraph and to declare it to be proof of the unpalatable communitarian provenance of the judgment (Weiler 1995); in other words, the Court, or so it may be argued, is once again imposing (impossible) pre-conditions of spiritual and social concordance upon European democratisation processes. Nonetheless, and within the terms of an analysis that focuses specifically upon the incommensurate nature of equally legitimate legal orders, and, in particular, on the *Brunner* Court's efforts to overcome normative incommensurability through reality observation, the offer to treat made by the Court to the ECJ and to the peoples of Europe appears less in the guise of an exhortation to establish European cultural homogeneity, and more in the role of a further instrument of *Rechtsverfassungsrecht.*

If no logically coherent notion of legal authority (sovereignty of European law) can be established in order to govern relations between national and supranational law, this legal relationship, or organic web of European legal evolution, must instead be mediated by *Wirksamkeit*, or the ability of law to step beyond axiom to give normative force to operational reality.

### *IV.3. Law's limits in the evolving political community*

Positioned between axiom and reality, and equally trapped on the horns of the formalist-material legal dilemma, European law, or European legal reasoning, faces one final challenge that is posed by processes of European integration: the contingent, unexpected and uncertain European polity is evolving a political character that is far in advance of its own institutional structures. In other words, beyond intergovernmentalist agreement, and fully in line with RCHI analyses (McCowan 2003), supranationalist power constellations determine that, in addition, say, to adjudicating between the relative merits of national legislative provision and supranational primary law, European law has also been drawn into mediating directly between the competing claims for political primacy that are pursued by individual European institutions. As a consequence, European law also plays its part in determining the nature of the European polity, as well as the forms of political exchange (democracy) that govern that polity.

Distanced from its roots within 'pure' market regulation, and still without recourse to a definitive constitutional statement on the legitimate nature of the European polity, European law has also been called upon to contend with the myriad polity-constituting consequences of judging upon such overtly political areas within European law as the maintenance of the principle of institutional balance. Whilst this topic is dealt with in detail elsewhere (Chapter 6), it is important to remind ourselves briefly here that judicial decision-making upon, for example, the right of the European Parliament to challenge Council law-making or Commission regulation, necessarily immerses the Court within a process of polity pre-emption. Where intergovernmentalist failure to agree upon a normative framework for the emerging polity, or to countenance an increase in the competences of the European Parliament, is overtaken by factual development – or the courtroom agitation of a European Parliament for the endowment of competences commensurate with its growing democratically representative confidence[61] – legal indeterminacy translates into a politically constitutive role for the Court, with each decision that affirms or negates parliamentary powers having a broader impact upon the legitimate shape and character of a European polity. Thus, for example, to what degree are individual Europeans to be directly represented by their own 'European' Parliament rather than by their national governments? To what extent should Europe be governed by majoritarian political process within the Parliament, rather than by the technical decision-making of the European Commission? Should a Court be making these decisions at all?

Adjudicating within a realm of constitutive politics – and indeed inveigled into this position of polity pre-emption by the failure of a European political community to constitute itself properly – the ECJ is confronted with the task set out by the German Constitutional Court. It must directly assess the operational realities of an evolving European polity and its ability to form a political community. The question of how the ECJ has responded to this challenge forms the focus of Chapter 6. In the meantime, however, it is interesting to note that some form of response has been found. Nonetheless, as Koen Laenerts comments in relation to the case of *Les Vertes* [1992], formalism within this realm of explicit constitutional adjudication is also characterised by judicial retreat into transcendental nonsense:

> It is particularly interesting that the judges believed they could still appeal to the 'general scheme of the Treaty' immediately after a failure of the political process to solve the problem by specific provision in that same Treaty. *The truth of the matter is, of course, that it would have been unimaginable for the ECJ to deny legal protection to this political party.* (emphasis added; Laenerts 1992)

Adjudicating upon the right of the Green Party to assert its position within the European Parliament, the Court lays claim to a formal rationality for the decision. The 'general scheme of the Treaty', or so it is argued, provided the ECJ with adequate justification for a decision that countenanced institutional support for the Green Party. Nonetheless, formal rationality is little more than a chimera. The decision came hard on the heels of a political process that had failed to give clear expression to that right. Instead, as Laenerts makes clear, the judgment is founded in the reality-proximate reconfiguration of law.

Casting an eye on the operational realities present within, as well as the justice demands made by, a European polity, it is simply 'unconceivable' that any Court would decide otherwise. In Hermann Heller's terms, adequate protection for European parties thus forms a part of the justice demands of a European *Wirksamkeit*, to which a European law must and does respond. Clearly, the judgment is founded in legal patterns of reality observation and of translation of reality into law. However, beyond the simple fact that processes of European integration have advanced to the degree that European society now demands that all European political parties be given appropriate institutional support as a simple matter of course, the case of *Les Vertes* also leaves this analysis with one remaining question: which are the particular mechanics of fact–norm translation deployed by the ECJ? More presciently: behind a formalist veil of nonsensical adjudication, how does, or how can, the ECJ safeguard European law from potential infection by forces of social irrationality, and how does it maintain the internal legal coherence and integrity of European law?

## V. Between norm and fact: reflexive law and constitutional morphogenesis

'Between facts and norms', this final question brings us full circle to the starting point of the chapter: what particular contribution can interdisciplinarity make to the study of European law and, in particular, to the study of legal adjudication within Europe? Certainly, the guiding theme of this book, which argues that law within our modern societies must dispense with axiom, to relocate itself instead within a reality proximate process of fact–norm translation, demands an interdisciplinarity all of its own. Real-world structures of evolution of the European polity cannot simply be grasped with reference to legal norms alone. However, the banal act of putting the law 'in context' or, indeed, any grand theories or designs of study of the European legal system that seek to legitimise the actions of an ECJ with reference to pre-conceived visions of the legitimate shape and nature of the European polity, are of little aid in addressing the vital question of how European law responds to its evolving extra-legal environment, both translating happenings within that environment into sustaining legal norms, and maintaining its own authority and legitimacy.

Above all, however, putative interdisciplinaries, which not only fail 'to take the law seriously', but which also satisfy themselves with a fatally flawed methodology of normative pre-emption, seem curiously to disregard the underlying messages of established bodies of social and legal theory; bodies of theory that have long struggled with all the underlying paradoxes of real-world legal evolution. Certainly, theories of integration, such as neo-functionalism and intergovernmentalism, may have an explanatory or analytical force of their own – at least to the degree that they capture the motivations of various political actors within the European integration process. However, any attempt to analyse the evolution of European law in simple concert with these theories is unsatisfactory, disregarding of an 'internal' legal voice and legal narrative, as well as the challenges which such a narrative faces when seeking to adapt European law to a European reality.

The simple political will that Europe should be legitimised through intergovernmental action and agreement, or, alternatively, that supranational institutions should pursue a neo-functionalist agenda, is not *per se* commensurate with the real-world processes of European polity evolution to which European law must respond. As preliminary analysis demonstrates, an internal narrative of European legal evolution is not simply concerned with (veiled) pursuit of one or other grand vision of a legitimate *finalité* of European integration. Instead, it is caught on the horns of a material-formal legal dilemma, searching urgently for legal mechanisms, which both bridge the gap between law and a real-world, and which serve to legitimate Europe's law, or legal intervention within the evolving European polity. Certainly, preliminary analysis also reveals the gradual evolution of various legal modes to overcome this paralysing paradox – from the proportional application of 'scientific' modes of enquiry within the courtroom, to the procedural construction of a European polity (including its subordination to norms of administrative 'fairness'), and to the establishment of judicial dialogue between legal orders. Nonetheless, the exact mechanics of judicial translation of fact into binding (socially constitutive) law remain obscure, and, accordingly, a methodology of study must now be developed in the effort to furnish insights into the nature of European legal evolution.

'Bringing the eighties back in': perhaps one of the greatest ironies that bedevils current study of European law is the fact that the strongest impetus for European economic integration – crisis within the national welfare state and a national preparedness to withdraw from corporatist economic regulation (Chapter 1 (IV)) – was mirrored, and to a certain degree, given support by bodies of social and legal theory, whose re-addressing of the formal-material paradox within law was also derived from the recognition that materialist regulation and intervention at nation state level had failed to fulfil its own normative promise. At the same time, however, study of European law failed to make a connection with this body of scholarship (and, *vice versa*), such that it denied itself clear recourse to the theories and methodologies that were being evolved in the effort to overcome the abiding formalist-materialist paradox and to imbue modern law with a firm basis for legal evolution beyond axiomatic and pre-determined models of the welfare and social state settlement.

Between facts and norms, and as a part of the dual effort to establish an interconnection between law-internal narratives of legal legitimacy and extra-legal realities (social and political justice demands), a notion of 'reflexive' law was established in the endeavour to identify and legitimise patterns of observation between law and its environment. Two of the most famous social theories[62] that were evolved in the wake of the post-war failures within the interventionist state – systems theory (Luhmann) and the discursive theory of law (Habermas) – and which sought to furnish descriptors of a modern social reality, may have been wholly diverse in their world perspectives and methodologies, but nonetheless shared this much in common: the urging of their legal theoretical counterparts to move beyond simple formalist or interventionist (material) accounts of law in order to develop more subtle appreciations of the interactive nature of legal orders, which would forever be torn between their own coherent grammars and methodologies and the demands made by an extra-legal environment. Whether derived from notions of functional differentiation within society, or instead owing to a Habermasian belief in the normative primacy of political process, the critical issue was not, and is not, the simple mechanical act of 'placing the law in context'. Instead, the core *problematique* is a reflexive one of the identification of self-contained legal legitimacies[63] that are nonetheless immanent to social, economic and political realities, whether those realities are the systemic discourses of other social systems, or the vital integrative role of politics within society.

Between fact and norm, this current endeavour to identify a socially constitutive and self-constitutionalising *Rechtsverfassungsrecht* within European law is, therefore, similarly a pursuit of reflexive law within Europe and an effort to identify the mechanisms and mechanics that mediate between European law's internal legitimacy and its ability to respond to its extra-legal environment. However, it is also more than this: between facts and norms, the study also details the explicit death of constitutional axiom in Europe and the necessary admission that paradigms of formal, material and reflexive law must also be taken seriously at the meta-legal level. The story of the troubled evolution of Europe's law is thus also very much a story of disintegration of the axiom of national constitutional settlement, of failings within pre-ordained and pre-emptive normative visions of the legitimate shape of the European polity, and of law's struggle to retain and regain self-legitimation structures; structures that pay due regard to extra-legal realities, as well as the justice demands established within such realities, and to the further challenge of reconstituting these demands within legal norms. Denied recourse to constitutional axiom, Europe's constitutionalising law is forced to consider more closely the paradoxical demands made by its internal and external environments. It is forced to take social and legal theory seriously.

At the constitutional level, the story is one of legal reaction to the failures in paradigms (axioms) of social organisation. Better stated, the legal task is one of adaptation to a social reality that is far too complex to be captured within pre-emptive paradigms of social organisation. The legal task is not a revolutionary one of replacing paradigm with paradigm, but is instead one of responding to enduring extra-legal revolution with a constantly self-legitimating law. The task is onerous, and, to borrow from a Marxist idiom that has already been plundered by reflexive legal theorists, entails a process of 'constitutional morphogenesis', or radical re-orientation of law, away from paralysing pre-determined paradigms and axioms of societal organisation to the self-legitimating observation of complex social reality:

> If there is no means of escaping a paradoxical situation, for example, in the manner achieved by Whitehead and Russel in their theory of logical types, paradoxes paralyse the observer and either lead to a collapse of his or her construction of the world or to increased complexity in his or her representation of the world. The latter case can be characterised as morphogenesis (Krippendorff 1984: 45).[64]

'Morphogenesis', at a constitutional level, entails response to ever changing and ever complex social reality. *Rechtsverfassungsrecht* gives constancy to morphogenesis, supplying law with its own enduring methodology of fact observation and norm translation.

This study isolates two potential focal points for constitutional morphogenesis within the realm of European law (including national and European legal orders): the interface between national and European jurisdictions (Article 234), at which adjustments are made to the competing claims of individual legal orders to normative primacy; and the political interface between European institutions (the principle of the balance of powers), at which European law must directly address and adjudicate between deferent political visions of the legitimate nature of an evolving European polity. The methodology of study is drawn from legal sociology, relying on structured interview techniques and textual/contextual analysis in order to unveil hidden narratives of legal self-legitimation. The underlying theoretical direction, however, remains open, drawing on all potential analyses that might aid in the establishment of reflexive law within Europe.

By this token, the self-legitimating mechanisms of *Rechtsverfassungsrecht* remain obscure, to be educed from legal narrative rather than deduced from one legal theory. Nonetheless, and if the insights gained during this preliminary retelling of the story of European legal integration might be accepted, the analysis can be pre-empted to a certain degree. Where constitutional morphogenesis within Europe is founded within the politically rationalising powers of procedural notions, such as 'proportionality' and 'administrative fairness', as well as a process of dialogue between still autonomous national and European legal jurisdictions, the socially constitutive and self-constitutionalising powers of Europe's law would seem to lie, not in any substantive vision of the nature of the legitimate European polity (a rights discourse), but rather within the procedural ability of European law (national and European) to structure extra-legal political discourse.

## Notes

1 Relative late-comers to the European academic extravaganza; though, solid analysis, possibly far in advance of other disciplines, has been provided, by, amongst others, Lepsius (1990, 1991).
2 Respectively attributable to or represented by, Haas (1964), Keohane (1986), Burley and Mattli (1993), Moravscik (1993), Marks, Hooghe and Blank (1996), Weiler (1981), Garrett (1992), Mestmäcker (1969, 2003), Ipsen (1972), Majone (1994, 2005).
3 Taking the theory of technocratic governance, or the appellation of the European Communities as a Fourth Branch of Government, as an example: 'technocratic governance' is not simply an analytical tool to describe the role played by Commission agencies and committees within European governance (i.e., they are neither executive nor legislative in character), it is also a normative prescription: neither the Commission nor its agencies should ever stray into policy-making areas requiring direct political oversight (i.e., redistributive issues). 'Functionalism' is perhaps somewhat more difficult to categorise as a dual descriptive-normative academic tool. Thus, with its hidden agenda of forcing political integration within Europe by means of economic integration (Majone 2005), it is more easily identified as an operational rather than analytical tool. Nonetheless, it still possesses its own normative agenda and embodies the concomitant assumption that the only legitimate European polity is a polity that is fully integrated in all of its economic, social and political facets.
4 In other words, it can no longer simply be analysed in terms of closed processes of constitutional reasoning which pay little or no attention to the economic and political contexts in which it occurs.
5 The sobriquet 'law in context' is thus, perhaps, the worst example of current European legal thinking to pay due regard to distinguished intellectual traditions of legal and social theory – certainly, many diverse schools of legal thought and talented legal academics gather under the 'law in context' label as a form of flag of convenience (not least Jo Shaw herself). However, as a concept, it is wholly empty: what is the context, and why is it relevant to law?
6 In other words, the act of formalist interpretation down from first principles is generally dependent upon the existence of those first principles. Note, however, that formalist interpretation can also exist within a pre- or post-constitutional setting; see below, Section III.1.
7 In other words, the actions of the ECJ may be compared with those of the Supreme Court of the 1930s, which reshaped the US Constitution in order to allow for wholesale legislative intervention into spheres of private (economic) autonomy (Ackerman 1993).
8 Now much modified (Slaughter and Mattli 1998: 206).
9 The notion of the European communities as an 'association of functional integration' was introduced into debate by Hans-Peter Ibsen. It is perhaps best regarded as a partner notion, not to simple functionalism, with its long-term agenda of political integration, but to neo-functionalism, at least to the degree

that supranational institutions of European integration (Commission, ECJ, etc.) ensure that integration is a controlled and therefore legitimate process, constrained by the pursuit of stated integration aims (stated in the treaties).

10 From Kennedy's point of view of course, an activist lawyer is not a threat to established orders of social solidarity, etc., but a progressive force that might save law from regressive conservative forces – if only he or she could. By the same token, however, formalist reasoning can also prove a bulwark and protection against abusive regimes; see, with specific reference to apartheid in South Africa, Klare (1998).

11 With specific reference to the notable success of the European Parliament in increasing its rights of standing under Article 230 EC (ex 173).

12 And indeed, it is unlikely that its proponents would claim that it could do.

13 A disregard perhaps shared by systems theorists; or perhaps not, given that a recent article in the genre characaterises internal legal disciplinary discourses as a form of 'theology', see Teubner (2004).

14 For commentaries on a very complex author, Kennedy (1988), Teubner (2005).

15 Predating Kelsen, and his theory of scientific derivation of legal norms, the application of the Napoleonic *Code Civil* within continental Europe had thrown up its own 'democratising' legal heroes. Primary amongst these were Friedrich Carl von Savigny (1779–1861) and Rudolf von Jhering (1818–1892), whose refined schemes of legal interpretation (grammatical, semantic, schematic, teleological and analogous – the latter notion contributed by von Jhering) promised that hermeneutically sealed legal interpretation and application would ensure that the intentions of the authors of legal codes would not be subverted by a political judiciary. Savigny, in particular, is the progenitor of Weber's notion of formal legal rationality. Both authors continue to contribute to the education of lawyers to this day.

16 And this, perhaps, is the clearest indication of current limits to interdisciplinarity. Triadic dispute resolution rests upon the independence of the judiciary. The temptation to the political scientist, however, is to measure independence in terms of institutional power structures, class backgrounds, etc. With this effort, worthy as it might be in its own terms, the argument nonetheless fails to pay due account to law-internal efforts to maintain political neutrality – von Jhering's heaven of infinitesimally divisible legal norms may not be attainable (see below, note 50), but is designed to lock law into a democratic mandate – and thus has little applicability to law-internal efforts to establish its own *normative* independence.

17 *van Gend & Loos* [1963], *Costa* v *ENEL* [1964].

18 For full details of the corporatist barrier to the integration of European market regulation, see the theoretical chapters and individual empirical studies in: Majone (1996). Once again, Majone's recent insights are also illuminating. Command and control economics demanded segregation of national economies: this then constituted the most significant barrier to economic integration within Europe (2005: 197).

19 In essence, functionalism, in its most purposive form, aimed to bring about political integration 'by stealth', or by the prior integration of national economies (Majone 2005, Chapter 2), See the insightful *critique* of the motivations of Jean Monnet and Robert Schuman by Milward (1996).

20 Whilst legal materialisation efforts may have been a part of the legal theory discourse in pre-war years, conscious practice of socialised law-making by lawyers rather than their political overlords, gradually developed throughout the course of the 1960s, perhaps reaching its apogee in consumer protection law. For a fine example of the conscious art, with specific reference to consumer law, see Micklitz and Reich (1980).

21 Arguing that the wording of various provisions of the Treaty did not suggest that the member states had intended to afford it direct effect. For full detailed analysis of the various objections raised, see Stein (1981: 5–9), Slynn, (1984), Lenaerts (1992).

22 Corresponding to the role ascribed to it by neo-functionalist theory.

23 And here, perhaps, the joke might at last be said to be on the English constitutional theorist, Dicey. No lover of constitutionally secured individual rights (1930), Dicey habitually restated his commitment to 'the law of the land' as the primary means of protecting individuals (in a negative liberal construction), arguing that not one constitutional right had spared the opponents of the French Revolution, or saved one African American from the full exegesis of systems of slavery and oppression (1926). And yet, a law, if not of the land, but of the European market, explicitly committed to the language of individual right, has been the primary guarantor in our time of exactly those notions of liberal private autonomy of which Dicey so heartily approved – Europe's legal language is one of rights, but its effect is one of the negative carving out of spheres of private autonomy, as member states are required to desist from legislative action that would harm the market, or legislative encroachment upon the secured economic spheres of individual Europeans (citizens of European law).

24 See, for full details, including explicit application of the term in case law, Slynn (1984: 415–417). Generally though, the significance of the Court's melding of civil law traditions of interpretation is largely overlooked: conflict between common and civil law tradition grabs the imagination, but likewise obscures the fact that the application of the Napoleonic *Code Civil* tradition throughout civil law Europe was greeted in differentiated ways. Looking at the doctrinal *problematique* through exclusively German lenses, the leap from teleological reasoning to an *effet nécessaire* may be striking. If a francophone judge is sitting alongside, however, the gap is not all too great (again, rather perversely, not since a French tradition places any great worth on individual rights-based empowerment – famously it does not; but rather, since a French civil tradition is committed to its counterpart – the realisation of the *common* project of the code).

25 Formulations deployed respectively by the Court and its Advocate General in *van Gend & Loos* [1963] and, *Costa* v *ENEL* [1964]. The notion of 'organicism' is, of course, an early alarm call within European law: here pre-political efforts to create interconnection between national and supranational jurisdictions of European Law also clearly stray into the dangerous 'romanticism', or (in Weber's terms), value irrationalism, which haunted the free law movement or *Freirechtsschule* , and, especially their precursor, Eugen Ehrlich (1987). Thus, Ehrlich himself was a great pains to avoid romanticism or irrationality within free law: lawyers should, by contrast be trained in (social) scientific methodologies, in order to enable them to recognise social demands in a methodological manner (Chapter 7 (II.2)). Nonetheless, he also recognised that releasing law from restraints of formal reasoning might also give rise to the danger of the rebirth of the judiciary as 'judge-kings', guided only by their own irrational and partial personalities. At this level, then, Ehrlich's well-meaning efforts to create extra-legal interconnections with society can also be seen as a precursor to the sickening contra-factual romanticism of Nazism (see, in particular, the worst excesses of a Carl Schmidt – for detail of his most unpalatable, post-1933 and pre-1945, formulations, McCormick (1997)). In the notable efforts of Weiler to give character to the integral relationship between national and European law of course, 'organicism' is shorn of darker meaning and distilled down into the professional process of the mutual socialisation of national and European lawyers (1993, 1994). However, and, indeed, once again, whilst these analyses cannot

be disputed on their own terms – also echoing Max Weber's writings on legal professionalisation (a professionalisation that is dangerous in Weber's analysis since it opens up a door to unwarranted 'legal materialisation', (1969)) – they are of limited relevance within this study, failing ultimately to make the connection to the deep-seated normative efforts of law to connect with its social environment – and the magnitude of the challenge that this poses to law (see below, Section IV).

26 See above, note 23.

27 Note, Giandomenico Majone is probably correct in his assertion that the unexpected evolution of the European market during the 1980s is likewise attributable to a change in political attitude to the economics of wealth creation and welfare provision throughout the continent: the mixture of social and market regulatory goals within the post-war corporate state had stagnated European economies – rapid overhaul was necessary if welfare bills were to be met (1994). Note also, however, that the Single European Act also sounded the death-knell for theories that argued that the European polity was legitimised by processes of 'exit, voice and loyalty' – or the notion that member states always had their say in the construction of Europe (Weiler 1981).

28 In other words, the 'private' constitutionalism established by European law in the 1960s can be argued to have been rationalised by the Court in line with *ordo-liberal* theories of the Economic Constitution. European law had now taken on a 'public' constitutional role, not simply forcing member states to desist from application of potentially distorting corporatist regulation (creating the constitutive limits to the market), but also regulating the internal activities of the market (competition law). See above, for full details of *ordo-liberal* theory and economic constitutionalism, and in particular, their application to a European market setting, the works of Mestmäcker (1969, 1994, 2003).

29 Within a European setting, economic constitutionalism can be argued to share the normative-analytical flaws of, say, neo-functionalist and principal agency theories of European integration – just because the notion can be used to legitimise processes of European integration, it does not necessarily follow that it does so. However, within its national setting and in terms of its underlying *ordo-liberal* economic theory, it also shares much in common with economic analyses of law, and might thus claim a larger degree of *factual* underpinning, at least as regards quantifiable processes of cause and effect (see, for an exemplary exposition of the underlying genius of the art Kleinhenz (1978)). As a social science methodology that claims to reflect social reality, economic constitutionalism therefore also possesses considerable normative power. Article 28 and the four freedoms could easily be argued to represent the limits of the constituted European market, safeguarding it against undue encroachment of protective national legislation. Equally, Articles 81 and 82 EC can be identified as market-internal regulators of economic freedom. However, the European Economic Constitution has since undoubtedly been superseded by material and social European regulation, much to the disgust both of Anglo Saxon economic analysis and Germanic economic constitutionalism (Majone 2005; Mestmäcker 1994).

30 The term was coined by Felix Cohen, who, in his study of the legal recognition of corporations within individual US states, noted that law could no longer coherently justify its decisions within a purely formal legal analysis: von Jhering's heaven of infinitesimally divisible legal norms was unobtainable in practice. In the light of this finding, formal law, continuing to eschew examination of reality, began to look ridiculous – a corporation existed, and was subject to legal norms, simply because the law said it existed.

31 See, in stark response to a US critical legal scholarship that built on Cohen's insights, Schauer (1988). In this argument, the comprehensive rejection of formalism is commensurate to throwing away the baby with the bath water. Formalism ensures judicial impartiality; it protects legal authority against accusations that it is pursuing partisan political goals. See, also, above note 15, for formalism's vital role in locking law into a democratic mandate.

32 Within insurance markets, the notion of the solvency margin (realisable capital funds maintained by insurers) is argued to guard against insurance market failure without distorting competition.

33 And, at the same time, heralds the beginnings of the secondary legislative competences of the communities (more specifically, the Commission). See, for details of the deregulatory–reregulatory paradigm within European law, Joerges (1996b), Vos (1999).

34 *Commission* v *Germany* [1987] 1227.

35 See *Muller* v *Oregon* and the *Brandeis Brief* (1908): the *Brandeis Brief* is the first noted effort to persuade the US constitutional court to take empirical socio-economic evidence seriously. Famously, lawyers sought to persuade the US Supreme Court to consider the issue of working conditions for women with reference to potential physical injury rather than simple contractual status. The Court was asked to take note of 'science', or studies of the real impacts of work on women. Looking back at the *Brandeis Brief* a century later, however, the dangers of legal materialisation, or the wedding of law to factual reality, are, also readily apparent. What might have been progressive jurisprudence in 1900 is now, from the feminist perspective, little more than a paternalistic encroachment into the world of working women. Law had simply imposed a stylised romantic structure within which 'weak' women would be afforded protection to allow them to fulfil their roles as 'mothers' and 'wives' in 'service of the nation'.

36 Now largely defunct and partially so by virtue of European civil law influence.

37 For a recent example of European law's extraordinary degree of reliance upon science, and the dangers this entails, see, the hearings in *Pfizer* [2002], more particularly, the failed effort of the Court of First Instance to understand what 'science' is. See Chapter 4 for full details.

38 Giandomenico Majone's recent work has clarified his underlying understanding of European law within his overall analysis: European law should restrict itself to 'negative integration', protecting the rational sphere of the internal market (2005).

39 And this represents the often overlooked democratic and social solidarity-securing element within technocratic governance theory. Majone does not dismiss social interventionist regulation; he merely argues that it should be strictly distinguished from market regulation (and be reserved to national polities).

40 To reiterate: the rationality of negative legal integration necessarily met its limits as European law was confronted with the potentially 'legitimate' regulatory interests of politically legitimated national jurisdictions. If the 'operational reality' or *Wirksamkeit* of the European integration process was one that demanded due European regard for legitimate national interests, some form of mediating norm (proportionality) and legal mechanism (scientific evidence) had to be identified in order to allow for the establishment of equilibrium between national and supranational jurisdictions.

41 Summarising the material legal legitimation efforts of Hugo Sinzheimer (1875–1945), his vital contribution remains the recognition that law must serve the social demands that are created by evolving social reality. However, in a final analysis, his concern that law should reflect reality led him to argue in favour of

a legislative explosion. The legislature should furnish codes for areas of social organisation that no longer bore any relation to law's 'formalist' self-legitimating perceptions of a world 'justly' ruled by private legal autonomy. Specifically, with regard to a labour market, lawyers should be trained in and cognisant of the methodologies of social science and reality recognition. However, theirs should not be the final task of adapting law to reality. Instead, that competence continued to reside within the legislature – specialised codes (which would be subject to formal canons of interpretation) would be the engines of reality proximate legal evolution (Sinzheimer 1977)).

42 Ehlich, too, was concerned that lawyers need be constrained by scientific methodologies. However, failing to develop a legislative role in the combating of legal indeterminacy, Ehrlich also recognised the dangers that judges would simply become 'judge-kings', no longer controllable by society or, indeed, by the law.

43 Note, however, that Sinzheimer's approach and methodology, allowing for the recognition of social realities that had departed from the imputed legal social reality construct of private autonomy, though promoting of legal training in social science, still demanded direct political legitimation for material law.

44 In other words, Weber's promotion of individual liberal (economic) autonomy surely also owes to a normative 'world view', and is not simply a lesson learned from 'material' history.

45 *Torfaen Borough Council* v *B & Q plc* [1989], *Stoke-on-Trent and Norwich City Councils* v *B & Q plc* [1992] ECR.

46 The infamous *Keck* jurisprudence [1993]. Although the vagaries of *Keck* may have been corrected in subsequent cases, contemporary commentary was right to ascribe a certain helplessness and doctrinal hopelessness to the Court on this occasion (Chalmers 1994; Reich 1994). Naturally, this difficulty has also infected other areas of ECJ economic jurisprudence, with perhaps the greatest controversy caused by its formalist application of freedom of services provisions (Article 42 EC) to an Irish constitutional ban on abortion (*Society for the Protection of Unborn Children* v *Grogan* [1991]); see, for a powerful attack upon the Court for its 'disingenuous' jurisprudence, Coppel and Aiden O'Neill (1992).

47 Above all, with regard to the abortion issue, where Coppel and O'Neil's analysis might be argued to be a touch harsh – after all, the Court did furnish a political breathing space to the Irish Constitution, such that intergovernmentalist politics could exempt this provision from the exegeses of European economic law (in the 1992 Maastricht Treaty). Other, subtle, examples also abound (Joerges 2002b).

48 Note, however, that the proposed treaty on constitutional union did not establish the undisputed 'sovereignty' of European law.

49 Note, however, that these normative contours are sometimes created by law itself, more particularly, by rights discourses.

50 Clearly, a somewhat moot point: Richard A. Posner, for example, might argue that his studies of cause and effect are 'real', or at least far more real than any reality disregarding constitutional theory (1998: 1); his detractors, however, have always been many and multifarious. And, with all due regard and respect for the talents of legal economic theorists, an overall doubt must, at the very least, be considered – economic analysis inevitably contains its own integral normative precepts, to which its methodologies of reality construction are attached. The point is explicit within economic constitutionalism, it is founded within ordo-*'liberal'* (*ordoliberalismus*) precepts.

51 Hard-line economic theorists argue that their models should be applicable throughout the sphere of economic organisation. Nonetheless, the desire, here, is to avoid complex *critique* of economic legal analysis. Suffice it to say, economic

legal analysis is also a useful legal tool for the purposes of establishment of *Rechtsverfassungsrecht* – the authors of this volume, however, would reject its application to areas of social organisation specifically dedicated to redistribution.

52 The issue concerns the status of public–private social insurance providers throughout Europe (the provision of social insurance through 'private' organisations, such as professional associations, is an old European model) and a series of tricky 'social insurance cases', referred to the ECJ by a variety of European jurisdictions, see *Poucet and Pistre* (joined cases) [1993], *Albany*, *Drijvende*, *Bokken and Bretjens* (joined cases) [1999] and *Pavel Pavlov* (joined cases) [2000]. See, for full details of the intricacies of the cases, Everson (2003a).

53 Perversity provided by the fact that Posner's overall economic analysis would probably be wholly dismissive of the European practice of public–private welfare provision.

54 In particular, in *Poucet and Pistre* (joined cases) [1993] and *Pavel Pavlov* (joined cases) [2000]. In these cases, the professional associations offering welfare provision were held to be so small as not to qualify for consideration under European competition rules – the national jurisdiction was thus preserved.

55 Or the process of leaching out of 'good' risks from common funds by private insurers, so that poorly financed 'bad' risks form the basis of consequently under-funded public provision.

56 Importantly, the Dutch legal system did not allow for judicial review of the welfare fund established by the collective bargaining agreement. Accordingly, the ECJ was also requesting Dutch courts to adapt their own legal order: to alter it in order to allow for consideration of procedural fairness.

57 Equally, the argument can be made that the Court was thus acting as a principal of its intergovernmentalist masters.

58 In other words, a paradox still readily apparent within the draft constitutional treaty on European Union.

59 One of the causes of action being that the Treaty infringed upon the fundamental right to property; a notion rejected by the Court, albeit only on the basis that monetary stability was not deemed to be a property right. For details of the development of fundamental rights jurisprudence by the ECJ, Laenerts (1992: 128–130).

60 Joseph Weiler, (1995), has famously attributed the Court's mention of spiritual and social homogeneity to a backward looking, communitarian (or, indeed, to a Schmittian) view of nationhood, which, he argues, is an unnecessary and destructive barrier to the evolution of cosmopolitan democracy within Europe. Here, however, in addition to noting: (1) that this argument seems overstated, given that the 'spiritual' sobriquet only appears in one paragraph of the judgment (albeit one of the pivotal paragraphs); and (2) that the argumentative reasoning followed seems to owe more to rhetoric rather than philosophical accuracy (Hermann Heller is surely the source of the offending paragraph?) – Weiler's broadside on the Court might be argued to have wholly missed the point. Kantian democratic ideals are equally trapped within the flaws of the liberal paradigm that guides modern law – Kant also demands philosophical concordance with the republic and, thus, gives birth to his own slaves. The German Court was not creating an unwarranted and old-fashioned barrier to European democratic integration; on the contrary, it was struggling to circumnavigate – again in a judicial form of reality observation – the incommensurate consequences of application of the conventional legal axiom of closed constitutionalism. Certainly, this study cannot countenance any vision of democracy founded in invented or imputed notions of a pre-political polity (Chapters 1 and 7). Nonetheless, it is not the aim of this book to take issue with outdated pre-political conceptions of

the settled constitutional polity. Instead, the study is engaged in the far harder task of overcoming the undue closure impulses inherent to supposedly universal constitutional ideals. See, also, Everson (1998a).

61 A theme reproduced in all cases in which the European Parliament has sought to expand its rights of standing under Article 234 EC Treaty. See *'Les Vertes'* [1986], *Comitology* [1988], *Re Radioactive food* [1990].

62 Temporarily leaving aside the simple leap into the abyss, which deconstructivist jurisprudence was brave enough to take. See Teubner (2005) on the distinctions within continental social and legal theory (constructivist theory versus deconstruction – that is, Germany versus France), and, more particularly, on the nihilistic tendencies inherent to acts of legal deconstruction.

63 The normative elements within systems theory are often overlooked: systems theory does aspire to a social integrative legitimacy of sorts. Granted, the effort is highly controversial within systems theory itself. Nonetheless, consideration of, say, human rights discourses, within systems theory does hint at a socially constitutive role for patterns of legal observation (Luhmann 1965; Teubner 2004). See, also, for efforts to recast network theory in a socially-integrative light by means of the maintaining of the openness of legal systems to all future social operations, Laduer (1997).

64 For further commentary on morphogenesis, see Teubner (2004) and Luhmann (1991: 71).

Chapter 3

# Forgetting law

## I. Law and non-law in the convention process

This chapter addresses an age-old paradox in its heightened modern form: constitutions are the simultaneous source *and* product of 'law', but consideration of the nature and character of the 'law' is often strangely absent from political constitution-building processes. From a critical legal perspective, 'law' might be, and, indeed, often is, construed as playing a 'thick' role within the making of constitutions; first, by virtue of its innate normative ability to 'give force' to the emerging constitution; second, and in vital contrast, due to the inevitable existence of 'constitutional indeterminacy' and the role that adjudicative law plays in the 'filling in' of constitutional *lacunae*; and third, and highly significantly so, since law might also be perceived as entailing a duty to 'adapt' the rarefied – yet indeterminate – constitution to social reality (materialisation impulses).[1] In stark contrast, however, where constitution-building processes are viewed as being primarily political moments, law is assigned a concomitantly 'thin' constitutional role and deemed to be an object, rather than a catalyst, of constitutional debate and change. In this view, the 'active' role of politics is 'to make the constitution'; the 'passive' role of law, by comparison, is assumed simply to be one of 'adjudicating' upon the constitution.

At one level, politically constitutive forgetfulness, or lack of regard for law (or for the particular nature of legal process) within the act of the constituting of the polity, is easily comprehended in terms of the self-contained *Grundnorm*. The constitutive act is not merely the source of law; by the same token, it also predates law, and should, thus, be shielded from any potential, legally derived, assault upon its normative content. If the constitutive act is commensurate with the assertion of the dominance of a particular polity-creating programme, it would be curious, indeed, were the constitutive moment to be contaminated at birth by any admission of future contingency, both in relation to the practical business of constitutional application, and with regard to any normative spectre that might be cast upon the longevity of the constituted polity and its material programme of social renewal (or, in terms of the origin of the constitutive act, the polity 'of the revolution'). If the aim of a constitution is the perpetuation of the substantive goals of *the* constituted polity (or, the material aims of the revolution), the alternative vision presented here of an evolutionary polity founded in the constant adaptation of constitutional application to evolving social reality cannot but be anathema (Ackerman 1984; Holmes 1994; Preuß 1994b).

Powerful and simple as this explanation for disjunction between constitution and law is, it might nonetheless be questioned. As Chapter 2 demonstrated and the following chapters underline, legal indeterminacy is a daily fact of adjudicative life, whether law-giving is a simple matter of application of private legal norms, or whether it is related to a 'higher' judicial assertion of the 'meaning' of 'primary', or putatively constitutional, law. No matter how much a constitutional convention might seek to give enduring life to the particular contours of a constitutive moment and constituted polity, the constitutional text remains a series of empty shells around which a multitude of interests, values and ideas cluster and clamour for voice. Equally, however, the pragmatic recognition of law's indeterminate limits can also transmute into a normative *critique* of the entrenched (reactionary) polity, as legal 'materialisation', or legal efforts to give normative effect to evolving social reality, conjoin with a normative preference for the enduring primacy of political process, with the result that the constitutive moment is relocated within the perpetual evolution of the polity (or eternal spirit of revolution).[2] Constitutional settlement can, therefore, be argued to be a potential act of false political violence against the revolution, rather than a substantive expression of revolutionary justice. Legal and constitutional indeterminacy is accordingly assigned a positive force – indeterminacy is a constitutive channel for the legal appraisal of social reality, and for legal recognition for the social and political justice demands, which such social reality entails.

Such critical legal doubts about the 'passive' constitutional character of law, as well as concerns about the mooted ease with which political constitution-building is seemingly distinguished from constitutional adjudication, apply to all putative constitutive acts. However, these doubts are surely only intensified with regard to the European Union, within which law (national and European) has traditionally played an elemental role in the 'constitutionalisation' of an emergent and socially complex Europe. Adopting the critical stance, it is readily apparent that the recent European Constitutional Convention, made up of national and European parliamentarians, as well as the representatives of supranational and governmental governance organs, assigned only a subsidiary role to European law, allowing forces of non-law (politics) to play the major part in setting the constitutional agenda for the European Union. By the same token, it might thus be argued that the Convention's inattention to 'thick' law-led constitution-building could not but detract from its claim to be initiating an informed constitutive debate within Europe. Equally, the failure to consider law and legal process within existing processes of European constitution-building was one further undermining feature within the Convention's efforts to furnish Europe with its determinative constitutive moment:[3] the reality of European integration is clearly one of continuing re-adjustment between the contested poles of an evolving polity, and cannot be successfully obscured or veiled by the promotion of grand schemes of purported normative convergence and entrenchment. Furthermore, the issue is not simply the pragmatic one that continuing fundamental disagreement on the goals of European integration necessarily undermines the effort to instantiate a *final* European polity. Instead, given a positive aim to relocate the revolutionary moment outside of a constitutional settlement, and within evolving social reality, the Convention's endeavour to create a European constitutional settlement may also be discredited in normative terms.

In common with its famous Philadelphian counterpart, the European Convention missed a prescient opportunity to address and publicise the more complex role that law has played and will continue to play in a necessarily open-ended process of constitution-building in Europe. More specifically, it failed to investigate the creative forces that lie behind formalist narratives of constitutional 'adjudication'. It failed to understand or even to assess the forces that might potentially 'legitimate' Europe's 'hidden' constitution-building: namely, the vigorous efforts of national and European law to adapt incomplete, even misleading, normative constructions of reality to a complex and ever changing real-world of European integration, as well as to its very particular social and political justice demands. In particular, it failed to convince European publics of the inspirational and potentially socially-integrative force of the open-ended process of European legal integration: its underlying potential to at last correct the abiding flaw in liberal constitutional settlement, or its exclusionary tendencies; not by means of a comprehensive re-settlement throughout Europe, but, rather, by its adaptation of European constitutionalism to a post-settlement constitutional reality, where notions, such as (national) non-discrimination, together with mechanisms of legal adaptation to a real-world, would, at last, free the *res publica* of its dependency upon slaves. Failing to pay due attention to the stumbling efforts of European law to overcome the vital shortcomings within the settled paradigms of liberal constitutional settlement, the European Convention also failed to underline and draw due strength from the European Union's hesitant and tentative contribution to the experimental process of the creation of a fully 'universal' European polity.[4]

Accordingly, the following analysis takes a closer look at the paradoxes of the political constitutional act, in order to shed greater light on the more intricate relationship that is generally woven between constitution, law and politics. It likewise moves on to consider one of the primary legal mechanisms governing civilised constitutionalist advance within Europe: or, the preliminary reference procedure which governs relations between national and European judiciaries at the non-authoritative interface between Europe's sovereign (constitutional) orders [Article 234 EC] – a mechanism largely ignored by a 'reforming' European Convention. And finally, it seeks to establish a methodology within which an empirical study of this potential instrument of constitutional morphogenesis might help to establish the normative contours of Europe's existing constitutionalism, or its *Rechtsverfassungsrecht*.

## II. Law and non-law in the constitution-building process

For Alexander Hamilton, one thing was very clear: the constitution was necessarily antecedent, not only to daily politics, but also to law. The dual pre-political and pre-legal character of the constitution was manifest in the right of constitutional judges to overturn legislation, not because one might 'suppose a superiority of the judicial to the legislative power', but because 'the power of the people is superior to both' (*Federalist Papers* 1961: 468). In so far as the judges remained true to 'fundamental' laws and did not, 'on the pretence of repugnancy ..., substitute their own pleasure to the constitutional intention of the legislature', they were, in such cases, merely giving voice to the original constitutive voice of the people (*Federalist Papers* 1961: 468–469). Constitutive power was derived from, and the Constitution was the expression of, the substantive aims of the revolutionary polity. The fruits of the constitutional moment, in other words, were elevated beyond the realm of human bargaining and institutional operation, whilst the bundle of compromises, obscurities and equivocations that Madison, at least, had felt inevitably marked each and every (constitutional or otherwise) deliberative legislative process (*Federalist Papers* 1961: 229)[5] were lent a retroactive air of normative infallibility, as the constitutive will of the people was formed within the Philadelphia Convention and given force by the US Constitution.

The retrospective attribution of a normative circle-squaring function to the constitution-building process may readily be identified as a device to lend axiomatic 'theoretical propriety' (*Federalist Papers* 1961: 230) to a constructed and necessarily idealised scheme of human government that nonetheless claims primacy over daily human relations, independently of whether such relations are political or legal in character. Less apparent within this process, however, is the manner in which a desire for future normative perfection may also colour contemporary perceptions of the workings of 'real-world' institutions of human government, and, more particularly, of law. Alternatively, the reification of the constitutional convention process above the mundane reality of commonplace political compromise, perennial social re-alignment and conditional judicial pronouncement can lead to a paradox, whereby the act of the creation of the primary legal instrument and source of the force of law (the constitution) is largely divorced, not only from all consideration of the internal character of law and legal operation, but also from careful analysis of the exact relationship maintained between 'post-constitutional' law and the constituted society which it claims to regulate.

In the setting of the first US constitutional moment, such a paradox is manifest in a peculiarly 'thin' conception of the law that would draw force from and give force to the US Constitution. Madison's stated concerns about the inevitable indeterminacy of language within the Constitution[6] were thus to be countered by Hamilton's simple conviction that political conflict on the meaning of constitutional primacy could be settled with recourse to an original constituted will of the people as directly represented by the scientifically disposed (doctrinal) 'JUGDMENT' of 'independent' federal judges (*Federalist Papers* 1961: 469).[7] The impetus for constitutional adjudication was accordingly a formal one: norms of adjudication would be deduced out of the final constitutive text.

Seen in this light then, the first US constitutional moment, or, at least, the view taken of it by its distinguished commentators, was one that drew a sharp distinction between the constitution, political process and law.[8] The substantive ideals of the 1776 Revolution, concretised within the political hurly-burly of the Philadelphian Convention, were to be raised out of the sphere of political discourse and contestation. Both the 'self-evident truths' of the Revolution, and the polity to which they were to be ascribed, '[W]e the people',[9] were to be entrenched in higher law. Equally, the day-to-day political process would not only become subordinate to that higher law, but would also be forever overseen by a derived and necessarily constrained law of constitutional adjudication. At one level, then, the US Constitution gave birth to Ackerman's 'counter-majoritarian difficulty' (Ackerman 1984), and therefore preserved the famous philosophical trio's perception of the determining ideals of the Revolution against majoritarian assault by subsequent generations of Americans. At yet another level, however, it also furnished the impetus for the evolution of a range of refined mechanics and theories of constitutional adjudication; all dedicated to ensuring that whatever apparent indeterminacies were to arise within the text of the Constitution, its 'meaning' would remain constant – be that meaning determined within the framework of 'originalism' or within that of 'textually immanent' interpretation.[10]

Leaving aside the tricky question of whether counter-majoritarian tendencies may be justified at normative level – many a good argument can be and is made in favour of the constitutional binding of future generations[11] – the strict distinction drawn between constitution, politics and law that was established by the founding fathers of the US Constitution might thus be argued to have set in motion the process whereby, 'JUDGMENT', or constitutional adjudication, became an ever more rarefied art, increasingly distanced from the social reality to which a US Constitution applied. Certainly, theories and methodologies constraining constitutional adjudication do have much in common with the formalist notions of law, established and promoted by such theorists as Savigny and von Jhering. As such, they must, therefore, also be recognised and prized: not only since they form a part of the vital effort to furnish law with a degree of self-legitimation,[12] but also since they seek to ensure that the supposedly socially consolidating 'will' of a polity is not subverted by the political and social peccadilloes of its own constitutional justices. Nonetheless, evermore differentiated efforts to dissect constitutional norms in the endeavour to perfect Hamilton's art of 'JUDGMENT', or to attain von Jhering's heaven of infinitesimally derived legal norms, have necessarily also resulted in the disjunction of constitutional theory and constitutional adjudication from reality; retarding the recognition of extra-legal reality by law, and denying the potential of an indeterminate constitutional law to give voice and normative power to the justice demands made by a 'revolutionary' polity, which lives on far beyond the moment of constitutional instantiation. With this, a realm of American constitutional adjudication and theory is today subject not only to the increasing frustrations of Richard Posner, and above all, his angry plea that constitutional theory return to considerations of 'facts' (1998: 2), but also to the more measured considerations of Cass Sunstein, who seeks the reconnection of constitutional justices with 'social facts' (1993). All sides of the academic spectrum agree: the historical US Constitution is increasingly divorced from the American reality, which it claims to govern.

In brief, then, formally conceived constitutional adjudication may preserve legal integrity, as well as seek to serve the aims and goals of a fixed revolutionary polity. Seen in isolation, however, it fails to establish a vitally reflexive and legitimating relationship between the constitution and its constantly evolving social environment. Once again, the point is both pragmatic and normative. The existence of legal indeterminacy, as Madison noted, is a simple function of the imprecision of all human language. Equally, however, theories of constitutional adjudication, designed to overcome legal indeterminacy with reference to the original will of constitution makers or to refined notions of textual immanence, vitally fail to ascribe any normative power to the notion of constitutional indeterminacy, locking the polity into (potentially reactionary) adherence to instantiated revolution, rather than freeing the spirit of perpetual revolution far beyond constitutional settlement.

The touching, if naïve, recourse of the Philadelphia Convention to formalist perceptions of the law and constitutional adjudication, and concomitant lack of consideration for the realities of legal process and societal evolution has, however, also found its recent modern echo within the European convention process. In particular, within a self-nominating European 'Constitutional Convention', which, whilst seeking clearly to delineate the individual competences of both the Union and the member states, paid little or no attention to the primary judicial mechanism of real-world competence apportionment and adjudication between member states and the supranational community: the decisional functions exercised within the preliminary reference procedure (see Section III). Despite increasingly audible concerns about the sustainability of the Article 234 EC procedure,[13] the Convention, shadowing its Philadelphian counterpart, predictably concentrated its few efforts to reconstitute 'legal process' upon the securing of the efficiency and the 'independence' of the Justices of the European Courts (CONV 636/03).[14]

Torn between a need to ensure continued national representation in the matter of appointment of justices to the newly named 'Court of Justice of the European Union' (Article III-353 draft constitutional treaty) and a desire to establish a genuine European jurisdiction, debate within the Convention's discussion circle on the European Court of Justice (ECJ) dabbled briefly with issues of individual representation before the Court under Article 230 EC Treaty,[15] but likewise failed to connect with a wider debate taking place within the Convention upon subsidiarity, or the relationship between the interlocking national/supranational orders and sovereignties of the re-founded European Union. Subsidiarity would remain a matter for political re-adjustment between the national parliaments of the Union. Article 234, the institutional fulcrum governing vital judicial relations between national and European jurisdictions would not be amended, or even addressed. Instead, the integrity of a new constitutional order would be safeguarded and served by persons 'whose independence is beyond doubt and who possess the ability required for appointment to high office' (Article III-365 draft constitutional treaty).[16]

With the reference to 'independence', as well as to 'judicial competence', the constitutional faith of the European Convention would thus seem equally to have been placed in Hamilton's process of 'JUDGMENT', whereby the particular norms of European constitutional adjudication would be infinitesimally derived from the general norms of the European Constitution by a professimalised judiciory. As a result, the Convention can likewise be argued to be reproductive of existing reductionist perceptions of the nature and role of legal process within the evolution of the European Union. Granted, the oral submission made by the President of the ECJ to the Convention, that 'the Court's case law ... has (already) begun' to confer a 'constitutional character on the Community's legal system' (CONV 572/03:1), might, at first glance, be viewed to be a highly political assertion; reminding the Convention members, lest they ever forget, that their assumption of a constitutional mantel had come relatively late in a long established constitutionalisation game. Digging deeper, however, the President's comments can also, by contrast, be viewed as being indicative of the continuing dominance of a formalist legal account of the development of a European law which is distinguished by its simple equation of the ECJ's doctrinal pursuit of 'direct effect' and 'supremacy' with a *de facto* higher or constitutional legal legitimacy for the European legal order as a whole:

> Tucked away in the fairytale Duchy of Luxembourg and blessed, until recently, with benign neglect both by the powers that be and the mass

> media, the Court of Justice of the European Communities has fashioned a constitutional framework for a federal type of Europe. (Stein 1981: 1)

In other words, even prior to the coming of the European Convention, with its promise of a 'true' constitution, the higher law of the treaties had furnished sufficient and adequate primary norms out of which a European judiciary might fashion a law with a constitutional character through its own neutral process of 'JUDGMENT'. With or without a constitution, European law already approximates the heaven of infinite norms, in which constitutional legitimacy might be located within the independent judicial identification of the constituted will of the 'Masters of the Treaty', or of the 'peoples of Europe'.

Equally, the Convention's lack of attention to legal process, and, in particular, to the post-constitutive relationships maintained between constitution, politics and law, might also be argued to be reproductive of a further reductionist perception of European legal evolution. In other words, the Convention's unwillingness directly to address the substantive process of adjudication within the European Courts and their satellite national counterparts, may also be suggested to be reflective of the realist strand within political science (and politics), which has long argued that European judicial process is merely an obscuring adjunct to the political. To restate a common view

> [L]aw functions both as a mask and a shield. It hides and protects the promotion of one particular set of objectives against contending objectives in the purely political sphere. (Burley & Mattli 1993: 72)

Transposing to the minds of Convention members, then, 'JUDGMENT' within European law, with its air of constitutional adjudicative neutrality, would simply serve to mask the pursuit of whichever political programme lay behind the draft constitutional treaty.

Law as simply authoritative-given versus law as politicised chimera: this dual reductionism furnishes a further indicator of the inadequacy of the traditional perceptions of law-giving and legal adjudication within the European Union and European Convention. Prevailing, dichotomous, yet operationally congruent,[17] views of legal process within Europe, founded either in a notion of law and its courts as a force which is independent from, but which 'neutrally' governs, the social and the political, or within a vision of law as servitor and protector of an individual political agenda may dominate European constitutional debate,[18] but must also be identified as being wholly divorced from the reality of the European legal process.

Between facts and norms, each legal and political view of 'law and lawyers' in the evolution of the European Union has traditionally betrayed an inability to bridge the gap between idealised pre-political normative orders of government and the reality of governance in a rapidly changing world. The non-settlement of Europe notwithstanding, formalist legal commentary (inexorably pre-conditioned by sovereignty paradigms) has eschewed any meaningful investigation of the real-world conflicts inherent to governance in a sphere of on-going integration. Complacently, it has, instead, remained trapped within a paradigm of hierarchical legal norms that has facilitated its simple 'declaration' of the supremacy of the European legal order over those of the member states. By the same token, however, political science and politics have betrayed a concomitant realist inability to afford analytical value to 'the factual power of the normative', busying themselves, instead, with an exposure of the political substance within legal pronouncements, but not looking further to identify the normative constraints and constructive impulses that law itself embodies, moulds and perpetuates (Habermas 1994: 9–11).

Within 'real-world' historical integration processes, rude challenges to the formalist supremacy of European law (*Brunner* [1984]), together with clear indications of the power of legal constructions, such as the *acquis commuanitaire*,[19] to determine the governing *telos* of Europe,[20] hint at a far more complex relationship between constitution, law and politics. Equally, they clearly underline the inadequacy of the existing characterisations of legal operation within Europe. Within the Convention, however, the apparent reproduction of reductionist formalist and/or realist perceptions of European legal processes, likewise raise the spectre of renewed analytical ossification. With the European normative circle squared through a semantic claim to 'the constituting of Europe', and 'theoretical propriety' likewise established by means of an idealised constitutional antecedent to daily politics and law, the daily and constitutionally significant response of European legal processes to the yawning chasm which continues to exist between our state-derived pre-political constitutional orders, and a form of governance in Europe that is marked by the breakdown of traditional polities, may now be further masked by convenient assumptions that law's 'JUDGMENT' can be refashioned as a simple expression of Europe's constitutive will.

The notion of 'we, the peoples of Europe', however, is surely a chimera; a myth even more ethereal than Madison's 'we, the people of America', and a poor basis indeed for the legitimacy of a European law that has struggled to adapt itself to an evolving social reality within Europe. Even more critically, however, the myth that 'we, the peoples of Europe' might ever be properly served by determinate processes of European constitutionalism, is both simple wishful-thinking and anathema to a notion of post-settlement constitutionalism that is founded within the positive nature of constitutional indeterminacy – or the avenues that it opens up for a form of constitutionalism, which facilitates the on-going adaptation of law to social reality, and which gives constitutive voice to evolving social and political justice demands within an extra-legal environment.

## III. The reference procedure and the making of the European constitution

Given the Convention's overall mandate more clearly to specify the individual competences of the Union and the member states, its explicit efforts to identify the supremacy of European Law (Article I-10)[21] and to incorporate the ECHR within EU norms (CONV 354/02), its further endeavours to establish a single legal personality for the Union (CONV 691/03) and its discussion on enhanced justiciability for the concept of subsidiarity (CONV 286/02: 8), the claim that debate on the future constitution of Europe within this forum was largely characterised by its 'thin' conception of law may initially appear to be a strange one.

Nonetheless, if set against the evolutionary context of a process of European integration driven by the early declaration of European legal specificity and supremacy, the negative, but 'real-world' and market-building, judicial integration of the 1980s, as well as the consequent unforeseen unravelling of national complexes of social, economic and cultural regulation (Joerges 1996a), the Convention's discussions retain a fatal air of abstraction. The force of law within Europe is not derived simply from the declaratory content of treaties, but instead educes from a complex process of differentiated normative legal response to the 'real-world' requirements of a demanding integration *telos*.

Between facts and norms, Europe's law is divorced from the comforting axioms of constitutional settlement, and must instead engage in a process of normative adaptation to the facts of the evolving European polity. More particularly, however, such a legal process within Europe can be *explicitly* distinguished from conventional constitutional adjudication. Even at the purely normative level, Europe's law is readily exposed as an 'unsettled' law, without recourse to any one definitive norm of constitutional derivation (*Kompetenz-Kompeten*).[22] Accordingly, the preliminary reference mechanism of Article 234 EC becomes vital to this study for three reasons.

Establishing a functionally differentiated, rather than a hierarchical relationship between national and European courts, whereby the ECJ would judge upon the meaning of European law, whilst national courts would apply that meaning, the preliminary reference procedure proves significant: first, because it is the manifest legal institutional expression of the defining status of Europe's law as a paradoxically non-authoritative, authoritative law of adjudication; second, and in the absence of an undisputed norm of constitutional derivation (sovereignty), because it provides the focal point for the establishment of an alternative 'organic'[23] and non-authoritative relationship between Europe's authoritative legal orders; and third, because 'organicism' also extends to the substance of judicial decision-making within the reference procedure. Article 234 EC is thus the primary point of contact between the norms of European law and the facts of European integration, furnishing the vital institutional fulcrum for the confrontation between and balancing of rarefied European legal norms against their real-world impact within member state societies. It is the vital point at which the battle to overcome the formalist-materialisation paradox is fought, and at which Europe's law must both legitimate itself and legitimate its constitutive effects within a wider social, economic and political environment.

As famously noted (Weiler 1993, 1994), Article 234, the cornerstone of the European legal system, is embedded within a mutual relationship between the ECJ and national courts, which, at an initial operational level, equally famously furnishes uniformity of legal interpretation throughout Europe. At a deeper level, however, the relationship between national and European judges also builds the legitimating fulcrum for a European law, which notoriously derives its formal normative power from the member states and their constitutional settlements ('Masters of the Treaty'); and yet, with each and every competence unravelling adjudicative operation potentially undermines both those selfsame national frameworks and its own normatively coherent existence. At the practical level, each and every decision to expand, say, an individual European right within national jurisdictions, becomes a decision that is undermining of national settlement and national sovereignty, as individual Europeans break free of the sphere of personal autonomy pre-ordained by the national political collective in order to pursue their rights as European citizens. The axiomatic paradox is startlingly apparent: if European law derives its normative force from the sovereign legal orders of the member states (*Herren der Verträge*), but at the same time, in asserting its jurisdiction, undermines national sovereignty, the potential issue is not only one of the evisceration of national legal orders, but, by circular consequence, is also one of the invalidation of the legitimacy of the European legal order.

Seen in this light, European legal process must thus necessarily embody intra-constitutional dialogue and adjudication, whereby the claims and demands of competing normative legal orders are measured and weighed up against one another in an endeavour to identify the overall equilibrium. Each legal order (national or European) may be authoritative within its own decisional logic. Nonetheless, at the limits to the reach of its own jurisdiction, or the interface created between national and European law by virtue of Article 234 EC, it finds itself in a non-authoritative realm of discourse between legal orders. On isolated occasions, such legal processes are explicit and their constitutional consequences readily apparent as both national constitutions and the breadth of the jurisdiction of European law are amended in their interpretation, or expanded or restricted in their scope by means of high profile jurisprudence.[24] More usually, however, constitutional significance must be distilled out of the daily cases and the daily business of a treadmill of national referral to the ECJ under Article 234 (Everson 2003a).[25]

Identified by the ECJ as a vital guarantor of the 'rule of law' within the Union (ECJ 1999), the reference procedure and process of dialogue thus initiated between the European Court and its national counterparts, might, therefore, be identified as a complex matrix of (1) material response to the real-world demands made of the European legal system[26] together with (2) normative re-adjustment between distinct legal orders as the simple facts of integration not only strain the norms of European treaties, but also undermine national constitutional settlements, and ultimately challenge the 'organic unity' (Shaw 1996) of normative legal governance within Europe as a whole.

Within this complex matrix, concerns necessarily arise as to the appropriateness of a 'thin' perception of the law or constitutional legal process that maintains the European order. Quite apart from commonplace modern doubts about the ancient ability of judges, or the 'living oracles of law' (Katz and Blackstone 1979), to embody the original constitutive will of the people by means of doctrinal 'JUDGMENT',[27] the dual challenges of multiple competing claims to normative loyalty and necessary normative adjustment to the factual circumstances of integration, immediately indicate that, although the independence of judges might yet play its part, the source of the force of Europe's 'organically whole law' must surely derived from a more complex well-spring than a simple legal formalism educed from a single pre-legal constitutive will.

In a very real sense, then, Article 234 EC is a primary mechanism of constitutional morphogenesis within Europe (Krippendorff 1984). The paradigm of a sovereign legal order with a clear limit to its authoritative jurisdiction is one that cannot capture the realities of the non-authoritative confrontation, discourse and re-adjustment between authoritative legal orders. Equally, it cannot explain the re-adjustment of non-authoritative authoritative law to the facts of European integration: the materialisation efforts undertaken by Europe's law, and its concomitant endeavour to retain integral legal legitimacy. Article 234 EC would thus seem to represent the primary institutional mechanism, within which the patterns of observation maintained between self-contained authoritative legal orders and an evolving European polity are extended far beyond simple axioms of sovereignty, in order to take note of and respond to the complex normative constellation of adjudication at the non-authoritative interface between authoritative legal orders.

Refined notions of constitutional adjudication may or may not have relevance within single legal orders. They are, however, highly imperfect aids to interpretation *between* authoritative legal orders. By the same token, however, the established paradigms of the closed constitution or settled constitutional polity, cannot respond to the contested facts of European integration and the incremental establishment of a European polity. Nonetheless, given these contingencies, Europe has not witnessed a breakdown in the paradigm and/or the recasting, say, of Article 234 EC as a hierarchical institution of adjudicative appeal within a sovereign and authoritative European legal order. Instead, the legal process that has focused on Article 234 EC appears to have widened the horizons of constitutional adjudication, and to have enabled the establishment of a reflexive relationship between European law's internal imperative for self-legitimation and an extra-legal environment of evolving economic, social and political reality.

## IV. Judges, lawyers and the source of the force of law

The identification of the preliminary reference procedure as an institution of constitutional morphogenesis cannot, in itself, furnish a legitimating narrative of Europe's law, and, in particular, of its constitutional impact. It does not give a clear account of the exact contours that are reflexively established between law and society. Instead, the term 'organicism' at once gives us an initial vocabulary within which to conceive of the new post-paradigmatic relationships between national and European law, as well as new interconnections between Europe's law and evolving social and operational reality, but likewise alerts us to the dangers of withdrawal from the axiomatic paradigms of adjudication, whether they be drawn from a general body of traditional legal formalism, or from the theory and practice of constitutional adjudication.

Formal adjudication, it is noted, preserves law from the dangers of partisanship. The grammar and semantics of formalism both provide a bulwark against the perversion of the (legislative or constitutional) will of the polity and also preserve the internal integrity of law.[28] Such a statement, however, extends far beyond an identification of the social hazards posed by the personal vices of a potentially malfeasant judiciary. Instead, the act of breaking away from axiomatic adjudicative models necessarily confronts the law anew with the formalist-materialist paradox, with the extreme difficulties and dangers attendant upon efforts to socialise law without direct recourse to the authoritative will of a constituted polity or, indeed, a single authoritative legislature. The efforts to identify the mechanisms of a socially reflexive law, such as the holding up of science or social science as a legally accessible mirror to society, are not merely potentially flawed in themselves (Chapter 2 (III.2) and Chapter 7 (III.2)). Instead, and by exact virtue of their potential flaws, they also cast doubt on the legitimacy of legal fact–norm translation, and raise the spectre of the self-appointed 'judge-king' who, lost in his own partiality, does not possess the requisite authority either to maintain the integrity of law or to promote social cohesion.[29]

In other words, notions of organicism must be rescued from their potentially destructive romanticism and refashioned to furnish a transparent, coherent and compelling narrative of socially reflexive law. This, however, is far from being an easy task,[30] especially when the analysis is not committed to any one 'theory' of socially reflexive law.[31] Instead, this book commits itself, without theoretical prejudice, to a marriage of social and legal theory with the mechanics of socio-legal research. The endeavour is one of the identification of the real-world contours of *Rechtsverfassungsrecht*.

The following effort to build a 'thick' conception of the law that better reflects its role in European constitution-building processes is thus founded in the empirical study of the existing Article 234 EC Treaty reference procedure and the internal-legal perceptions of 'political' constitution-building; more particularly, on the narratives of UK judges and barristers in relation to their individual experience within the courtroom and to legal participation, or the lack thereof, within the convention process. Equally, in concentrating upon the internal legal narrative of lawyers and judges engaged within the institutional mechanisms of constitutional morphogenesis, the study seeks to identify which, of all of the possible mechanisms of socially reflexive interconnection between law and its extra-legal environment, is privileged by Europe's law. Furthermore, it also seeks to analyse the strengths and weaknesses of European legal discourse from the practical viewpoint of whether law can translate norm into fact and fact into norm, and thus establish (within a real-world of European integration) a self-legitimating and socially sensitive European constitutionalism, or *Rechtsverfassungsrecht*.

### *IV.1. Data-set and methodology*

The data-set upon which a following chapter is based comprises 44 replies to questionnaires, initially sent out to lawyers and judges (166 within the original sample) and five semi-structured interviews. The data-set targeted the London chambers of barristers and the Judges of the English (and Welsh) High Court and Courts of Appeal, as well as the House of Lords (the final Court of Appeal for the United Kingdom as a whole).

In differentiating and analysing 'constitutional adjudication' and the 'thick' role played by law within European constitution-building, empirical instruments were designed in line with the underlying assumption that lawyers would themselves adopt a formalist legal idiom when narrating their experiences both within European law and with reference to the convention process. Accordingly, whilst direct questions were asked on the constitutional character of European law and adjudication, as well as its impact upon national legal systems, various 'indicators' were also developed, both to identify fundamental and potentially constitutionally significant shifts within legal process, and to assess the quality or provenance of 'non-formalist' legal debate.

The indicators comprised:

(a) Potential changes in the language and instruments of legal argument: marked courtroom shifts to rights-based and principle-based legal argument being presumed to be indicative of distinct constitutional argument, and to provide a yardstick against which determining constitutional ideologies (rights-based individualism versus procedural governance) might be measured.

(b) Potential changes in the forms and geographical provenance of evidence presented to the court: greater use of non-legal and non-national material within legal processes being presumed to be indicative of 'the limits to formalist argument'; more particularly, the search of law for sources of legitimation beyond traditional normative legal frameworks (such as the national constitution) and beyond the traditional nation state.
(c) Potential changes in the style of legal argumentation: varying degrees of informality between courts and marked shifts in legal argumentation – from confrontation to investigation – being presumed to be indicative of a move beyond formal reasoning within coherent normative orders to non-formalist adjustment between normative orders.

The limited extent of the data-set nonetheless also raises a presumption of a degree of distortion within the results:

(a) The English legal system is distinguished from its continental counterparts. Seen in this light, marked shifts in the language and instruments of legal argumentation within English courts may also be indicative of the adoption of continental legal tools (principles, rights) that have proven to improve the efficiency and working of the UK legal system.
(b) Likewise, common law has historically been marked by a confrontational courtroom style. Shifts to investigative styles may also be indicative of a simple joint legal learning process rather than a deeper constitutional re-adjustment.
(c) Responses to surveys and requests for structured interviews also suggest that the data-set is distorted by a process of self-selection, whereby only those lawyers who already have a strong interest in the evolution of the European legal order have joined the study.

Notwithstanding all such potential distortions, however, the following chapter, in beginning to sketch out the potential contours of a European *Rechtsverfassungsrecht* demonstrates the wealth and potential of a European legal discourse that is daily confronted with the onerous task of categorising and giving voice to an emergent European polity.

## Notes

1 Again, to argue in Hermann Heller's terms, constitutional indeterminacy is a positive force for normative good: it is the indeterminacy within constitutional provisions, which allows for the adaptation of law to operational social reality and the justice demands which such reality entails.
2 In other words, an alternative view of the revolutionary polity is pursued here. Rather than consider the 'revolutionary polity' to be commensurate with the polity that is entrenched within the constitutive act, the analysis focuses upon an

unsettled and unconstrained revolutionary polity in which politics has primacy. Note, however, for the purposes of this analysis, that 'unconstrained perpetual revolution' is not to be considered commensurate with its Marxist counterpart. The defining feature of constitutional morphogenesis, as well as *Rechtsverfassungsrecht*, remains its liberal impetus, albeit a liberal impetus that always courts illiberality.

3 Note, however, that the European Convention was not, in fact, given a mandate to create Europe's 'constitution'. Instead, its intergovernmentalist masters had urged the Convention to engage with the altogether more modest tasks of the investigation of possible improvements to the mode of governance within Europe. Following Laeken and Nice, reform was required to ease the management of the Union, largely in response to its increased membership. The transformation of the Convention into a Constitutional Convention and, in particular, its efforts to furnish Europe with one (take it or leave it) draft constitutional treaty, was an 'assumed mandate'. For the vital role played by Valerie Giscard d'Estang in re-directing the Convention's efforts (plus, importantly, on the failure of the Convention to establish a republican moment of constitutional transition in the Habermasian tradition) see Magnette (2003)). Although this book is not particularly concerned with any misguided efforts to force a politically constitutive moment within Europe, a strong *critique* must nonetheless be made of the 'masters of the Convention' – by what right did they assume the constitutive powers of the European polity? Was the whole constitutional process within Europe simply hijacked by the personal ambition of a few 'elder European statesmen' to furnish history with a new body of 'European saints' to complement Monnet and Schuman?

4 In other words, both the pursuit of 'non-discrimination' (in relation to nationality) that opens up the closed polity to the concerns of individuals external to the republic (Joerges 2002a) and the preparedness to step beyond socially atrophying axiom to found normative governance schemes within social reality.

5 Particularly in relation to the division of powers between state and federal level: the contradictions within the Constitution indicating that the 'convention must have been compelled to sacrifice theoretical propriety to the force of extraneous consideration' (1961: 230).

6 An indeterminacy in part deriving from the fact that 'no language is so copious as to supply words and phrases for every complex idea, or so correct as not to include many equivocally denoting different ideas' (1961: 229). Madison as proto-type post-modernist? Perhaps not. But the inherent existence of indeterminacy within language and law is clearly pinpointed.

7 The formalist yet 'antiquarian' link to William Blackstone's scheme, whereby judges represented the original constitutive will of the people above the executive power of the Crown, is clear. Judges are to be seen as 'the depository of the laws; the living oracles, who must decide in all cases of doubt, and who are bound by an oath to decide according to the law of the land. Their knowledge of that law is derived from experience and study ... and from being long personally accustomed to the judicial decisions of their predecessors' (Katz and Blackstone 1979: I.69).

8 Famously, there are great distinctions between the authors of the Federalist Papers generally, and between Madison and Hamilton in particular. In brief, the far more intricate considerations of the workings of democracy and the law evinced by Madison's support for decentralised government (functional separation of powers between President, House of Representatives, Congress and states), mark the beginnings of the pluralist tradition of constitutional thought, which lays a lesser emphasis upon the primacy of the political collective and greater emphasis upon the recognition of the necessity of the dispersal of power amongst

different groups and institutions – although, note, by confusing counterpoint, that Madison was also responsible for the totalising 'myth' of the notion of 'we the (American) people'; a myth designed to give the constitution a normative force above and beyond the individual claims to sovereignty of individual US states.

9 Note, even though the notion of 'we the people' was a myth created by Madison to ensure the constitutive primacy of the US Constitution, the Philadelphia Convention shared the same inclusive universal liberal aspirations as its revolutionary French counterpart; the reach of the polity was not to be de-limited by any exclusionary or 'pre-political' notion of an 'ethnic' American nation, bound by lines of blood, language or culture. Instead, philosophical concordance with the ideals of the Revolution would form the basis for inclusion within the American Republic. Nonetheless, leaving all universalist aspirations aside, the concretisation of the revolutionary ideal within the US Constitution set in motion a dual process of exclusion, as formalist schemes of constitutional interpretation retarded the recognition of the justice demands of groups within the US nation (the *res publica* had its slaves in a very real sense), and likewise determined that an American polity would be justified in disregarding the justice claims of other nations in consideration of its own national self-interest.

10 Again, though presented in somewhat reductionist terms, the two major governing strands within theories of constitutional adjudication might be distinguished as follows: first, theories founded in originalism seek to reproduce the aims and goals of the framers of the constitution; second, theories founded within textual-immanence seek to combat the potential perversion of the constitution through a demand that constitutional justices restrict themselves to applying the literal meaning of the constitution.

11 And certainly so within the proceduralist Habermasian conception of binding of future generations to the circular process of definition and re-definition of the constitution through political process (Habermas 1994; Alexy 1994). Likewise, it may be doubted whether the US Constitution did, in fact, bind future generations to the destructive degree of preventing the adaptation of the constitution to social justice demands – see, only, Ackerman's famous investigation of the second constitutive moment within the New Deal (1991), or his assertion that we should never under-estimate the creativity of the 'closed' liberal revolution (1992: 3). See, however, Chapter 7 below.

12 In other words, furnishing constitutional justices with a mechanism whereby they might claim that their constitutional adjudication is due to a law-internal methodology, so that it is not prone to accusations of political partiality.

13 General concerns about the ability of the European legal system to process the volume of cases placed before it are increasing (Rasmussen 2000). By the same token, however, each unexpected, but inevitable, encroachment of European law into technical legal areas, such as company law, not originally foreseen as being within the ambit of EC law, must surely raise doubts about the technical ability of a small number of generalist EU justices to meet the technical legal demands of EU legal evolution.

14 See, for European Convention submissions, http://european-convention.eu.int/. The 'Final report of the discussion circle of the Court of Justice' contains a limited discussion that strangely excludes the major concern of the judges of the European courts (as expressed in their submission to the Nice IGC): namely, the necessity of maintaining the unity of the Community law system by means of the preliminary reference procedure (ECJ 1999). See, only, Chalmers (2004) for detailed description of the Court's concerns about any proposed amendments to the preliminary reference procedure. In the Court's own words: 'Any reorganization

of the preliminary ruling procedure on a national or regional basis ... involves a serious risk of shattering the unity of Community law, which constitutes one of the cornerstones of the Union. ... Jurisdiction to determine the final and binding interpretation of a Community rule, as well as the validity of that rule, should therefore be vested in a single court covering the whole of the Union' (at p.28). Note, also, the Court's continuing 'formalist' efforts to establish its own hierarchical dominance over national courts; a dominance that might nonetheless be doubted: see Chapter 4 below.

15 Suggesting an amendment to that Article (Article III-356(4) draft constitutional treaty), which would ensure individual standing before the Court to challenge any regulatory act of direct concern to individual Europeans (see Chapter 6).

16 Interestingly, debate within the discussion circle on independence was heated, if sparse. The current EU treaty, with its guarantee for the 'independence' of the Court of Auditors and lack of similar guarantee for the Court of Justice drew excoriating comment from Convention members (see, only, 'Contribution de Mme Elena Paciotti sur l'independence des juges de la Cour de Justice (CERCLE I – WD 12)). Similarly, the compromise struck between national and European interests in the matter of the appointment of justices to the Court – a compromise founded upon the establishment of an EU level panel to advise on the suitability of candidates proposed by the member states – was also subject to the criticisms of those who felt that the presence of a (European) parliamentary representative on that panel (Article III-357 proposed constitutional treaty) would compromise the 'political' independence of the Court (see, 'UK comments, as sent by Baroness Scotland of Asthal (CIRCLE I – WD 19) and 'Remarks by Reinhard Rack on the Draft final report of the Discussion Circle on the Court of Justice (CIRCLE I – WD13)).

17 After all, as Chapter 2 (III.1) demonstrates, the functionalist integration agenda has been well served by legal formalism in practice.

18 A general conflict, which has an effect far beyond the realm of European law, noted and bemoaned by Habermas as presenting a fatal weakness within many attempts to fashion governance orders that are both effective and moral (1994). Within the Habermasian analysis, however, the notion of 'legalism' replaces the more pejorative term 'formalism', echoing Savigny and von Jhering, and paying due homage to the underlying commitment of 'structured' lawyers, such as Stein, to dedicate careful legal analysis to the service of the democratic norms of the constitutional legal state (*Rechtsstaat*).

19 Now applying as a pre-condition for membership within the Union.

20 A power perhaps best reflected within the convention process by the efforts of Justice Iglesias to remind the discussion circle on the ECJ of the vital constitutional role played by the Court in elevating economic rights to the status of personal rights within a supposed European Economic Constitution (CONV 572/03:6).

21 Potentially a redundant measure; however, it is tempting to conclude that the European Convention was concerned to see an end to the efforts of Courts, such as the *Bundesverfassungsgericht*, to adjudicate on the limits of EU jurisdiction.

22 Importantly, this was a problem not solved by the European Constitutional Convention. European law was afforded explicit supremacy rather than sovereignty – *plus ça change* in the world of European normative incoherence.

23 The formulation adopted by the justices of the ECJ to describe the relationship between European and national legal orders (*van Gend & Loos* [1963]; *Costa v ENEL* [1964]). In the meantime, the term has also become a common feature within academic descriptions of the nature of that relationship (Shaw 1996).

24 Exemplary, the German Constitutional Court's demand that creeping judicial Europeanisation be curbed (*Brunner* [1994]), together with the ECJ's (responsive?) restriction in the jurisdictional reach of Article 28 Consolidated Treaty (*Keck* [1993]). See above, Chapter 2 (IV.2).

25 With reference to the unforeseen unravelling of national social policy, the constitutionally significant redistributive consequence of the social insurance cases and the dialogue between national and European legal orders.

26 And, after all, all treaty content notwithstanding, the market must function, whilst, and increasingly so, joint national and European police powers must be exercised in areas such as asylum policy.

27 And here reference is simply made to the problem of 'legal indeterminacy' in its semantic/grammatical constellation (Kennedy 1986).

28 For a modern reiteration of the vital services performed by formalism, see, again, and only, Schauer (1988).

29 See Chapter 2. The stakes are high, indeed. To reiterate, the *Freirechtsschule* , in its inspirational character, inspires the major part of this volume. Nonetheless, the dangers inherent within this movement must also be recognised. Although such authors were anathema to the Third Reich, their insistence on a direct connection between law and society (in particular, Ehrlich's degree of romanticism) may likewise, and very perversely so, have also set the scene for the romantic veil that National Socialist Law drew over its authoritative and inhuman jurisprudence – romantic concepts such as '*das Volk*' are surely a constant threat. See, for the marginalised personal position of the School within the Weimar Republic, Rotthleuthner (1988).

30 And indeed, we should remember that Max Weber ultimately withdraws from the effort, warning against inherent materialisation tendencies, no matter how attractive they might be. Note, however, that much Anglo-Saxon comment upon Max Weber fails to penetrate the normative sadness which permeates his writings (Trubek 1972). The dismissal of Marxist historicism as an irrational natural law may at first glance hint at Weberian disapproval for all materialisation tendencies. Nonetheless, the point is ultimately not that Weber disdained all efforts to socialise law. Merely, that he felt that the dangers inherent within socialisation were too great to engage with.

31 Either within a proceduralist normative format (the leading example, of course, being Habermas), or within more functionalist efforts to dissect and describe ever more accurately the mechanics of interaction between functionally differentiated societies and their functionally differentiated law; see, for example, Teubner (1989, 1993).

Chapter 4

# Adjudicating non-authoritative law

## I. Lawyers, (self-) illusion and the making of the constitution

The notion of *Rechtsverfassungsrecht* is the product of an academic mind (Wiethölter 2003). Furthermore, it is the specific product of the age-old social and legal theory effort to capture and address the formalist-materialist paradox within law. As such, it would be surprising, indeed, were its dual elements of self-justification and reconnection of law with society to be current within the discourses or 'consciousness' of practising lawyers: constant and detailed consideration of how processes of 'law-giving' are 'justified' at the limits to authoritative legal orders would, perhaps, detract too greatly from the daily business of legal evolution within courtrooms and chambers.[1] After all, which lawyer or judge involved in the prosaic application of common market fisheries regulation would give a thought to the role that he or she might or might not be playing in the dual constitution of society and of a law whose legitimacy likewise resides within its social responsiveness?

Nonetheless, within this study, it is not so much the absence of direct legal consideration of the socially constitutive and self-legitimating nature of Europe's law that is of particular interest. Instead, it is the form which this absence takes. In short: the immediate impression left by empirical investigation is one of a law which is highly practised in addressing the formalist-materialist paradox at a practical, if not a theoretical, level through an illusionary language of legal application that privileges the formalist semantic, but likewise veils deeper efforts to adapt seemingly monolithic law to constantly evolving social reality.

Thus, perhaps the most striking of all interview responses gathered within the data-set was that of a Court of Appeal judge on the question of whether the reference procedure entailed constitutional consequences within the legal order. Even in relation to *Factortame*,[2] a case with unparalleled constitutional impact both within English and EU normative orders, legal self-narrative is wholly abrogating of law-driven constitutional consequence (Interview 109):[3]

IE: Even when I was deciding the *Factortame* litigation, I didn't feel there was a tension other than the fact that the government of the day wanted one result and that didn't seem to the court to [be] the result, which was provided for in European law.

IR: Did you not have any kind of greater constitutional sense of your role at that moment?

IE: No, I don't think I did in the sense that I saw what it involved, but my approach was, well, that's what you've signed up to. And it's rather like getting married. It is, of course, a huge commitment, but once you've done it, well, then, you say, well, is this or is this not part of the deal? (laughs).[4]

The humour is indicative; the legislative process may lead us where we would not wish to go, but what can the poor lawyer do? In the legal world, norms are self-fulfilling. The constitutive will expressed by European treaties remains pre-legal and self-fulfilling by simple virtue of impartial and independent 'JUDGMENT' in the courts. The possibility that laughter might also mask a judicial *choice* not to draw the domestic constitutional line in the sand, in the manner of the *Bundesverfassungsgericht*, is seemingly not an assertion that immediately appeals to the legal mind.

Nonetheless, the following data drawn from legal perceptions of the reference procedure matrix, as well as of the convention process, reinforces the immediate suspicion of a layered process of legal (self-) illusion, in which a professional formalist narrative does, on occasion, give way to constitutional re-alignment processes that owe a far lesser debt to formalism, and a far greater one to the need to re-adjust formalist normative constructs to the more prosaic demands posed by the real-world. The reality that lurks beneath formalist discourse is one of practical adjustment between equally authoritative legal orders, as well as one of legal 'materialisation', or the adaptation of law to its extra-legal environment. Finally, however, and highly significantly so, a formalist narrative of constitutional adjudication is, once again, reinforced by personal narratives of 'service' to law, rather than 'agency' in legal or constitutional change.

## II. The formalist narrative of European constitution-building

At the heart of a dominant formalist narrative of European law lies a strange paradox. When asked whether the European legal system *already*, and without reference to the work of the European Convention, comprised a 'constitutional order', the vast majority of questionnaire respondents, answered 'yes', overwhelmingly justifying this appellation in formalist legal terms:

> 'As the supreme law within the sphere of its application overriding legislation' (Barrister 75); 'It contains a hierarchy of legal norms which

> result in the disapplication of other rules where the latter are inconsistent' (Barrister 20); 'It is concerned with the allocation of power to different sources of law' (Appeal Court Judge 109); '[It] provides a written document giving individuals enforceable rights and freedoms and overrides other inconsistent law' (Barrister 43).

Consistent with a formalist analysis, the mechanisms of 'constitutional recognition' are wholly legal-internal in character, determining that where the boxes of 'supremacy', 'norm-hierarchy', 'division of powers'[5] and 'enforceable rights' can be ticked, the European legal system might be elevated to constitutional status without reference to social, cultural or political influences, or, indeed, even to the European Convention. And yet, a vital inconsistency nonetheless arises in this narrative with regard to the exact extent that formalist paradigms of law remain, in their purest Kelsen-led manifestation, dependent upon the identification of the 'pre-legal' and 'pre-political' constitutive moment and 'source of law' (*Grundnorm*).

Within a European legal order educed from international treaties rather than from founding moments, the establishment of a hierarchical legal order replete with individual rights and a division of powers can thus be argued to be more a matter of factual re-adjustment to the integration *telos* than one of normative deduction. And, indeed, two questionnaire responses at least hint at a wholly political origin for constitutionality as national and European sovereignties are re-aligned in an on-going waltz of legislative contestation. Europe thus builds a constitutional order '[I]n the sense that it can override parliamentary sovereignty' (Barrister 83), and to the degree that '[T]he abeyance of UK parliamentary sovereignty plainly has constitutional significance (but I may have misunderstood the question)' (Law Lord 149). Furthermore, one response explicitly emphasises the vital importance of a 'practical' post-constitutive process of acceptance of the constitutionality of the European order, not within national societies, but within the legal systems of the member states:

> The seminal case law of the ECJ, *which has been accepted by the member states courts including the UK Courts*, established the EC Treaty as a fundamental (and supreme) part of national law. The TEU is a prototype for further integration. (Barrister 76; emphasis added)

With this inchoate notion of 'acceptance', threat is thus posed to a formalist narrative, as 'organicism' within the European legal order begins to undermine the wholly self-referential character of formalist discourse, contaminating it with vague sociological concepts that cannot simply be captured within a 'pure' legal semantic. The linguistic hint of a potential higher judicial embarrassment with regard to the limits to formalist narrative ('but I may have misunderstood the question') is nonetheless spared, as unwillingness to admit that a formalist claim to constitutionality rests solely upon the simple legal acceptance of the practical political and legal processes of the erosion of national sovereignty is seemingly given a more constructive form in the formalist narrative's re-assertion of the 'conditional' nature of European legal supremacy. Thus, in an English legal formulation, constitutionality remains wholly dependent upon the continued vigour of the enabling 1972 European Communities Act:

> It constrains the UK legislative and judicial bodies' freedom of action *so long as* the 1972 Act subsists. (Barrister 46; emphasis added)

Meanwhile, in an interesting case of borrowing between legal orders, the formula adopted by the *Bundesverfassungsgericht*, when seeking to give a name to the EU beast in a normatively consistent manner, is reproduced within the assertion that European constitutionality is to be found within national *Grundnorms*:

> It attributes powers to Community institutions and controls the basis for their exercise. It is not an autonomous order because from the national perspective at least the member states remain 'Masters of the Treaty'. (Barrister 49)[6]

In short, then, all uncertainty as to the provenance of the existing European 'constitutional' order notwithstanding, a formalist narrative of European law is nonetheless constructed. Certainly, the formalist dish is served with a very strong pinch of transcendental nonsense: how can any formalist order exist in the absence of one, undisputed, constitutive norm? Nonetheless, with nonsensical elevation of the notion of 'contingency' to the transcendental status of self-evident legal norm, the advocacy and adjudicative actions of lawyers and judges are legitimated within formal discourse, as a presumption of constitutionality and 'theoretical propriety' within European law raises courtroom pronouncement to the status of socially and politically neutral 'JUDGMENT'.

For those, who are not wholly convinced by this contingent narrative, however, the vital neutrality of the law – its self-contained status as servitor of the constitutional moment – is further reinforced by legal perceptions or non-perceptions of the constitutional convention process underway within Europe at that time.[7] With the vast majority of respondents professing no interest in the European Convention whatsoever (38),[8] the cocooning attributes of a formalist narrative of the status of European law are supplemented by an account of the profession of law, which adds force to the assertion that the constitutive act is a pre-legal moment, which deals with issues of non-law, such as the '[P]*olitical* process of rationalisation of fundamental principles of EC law' (Barrister 76; emphasis added), in which lawyers, mere handmaidens to the constitutive will, have and, indeed, should have, no interest whatsoever. Judicial opinion is adamant (Interview 109):

IR: Have you been following the debate around the European Convention?
IE: I don't regard that as part of my job and I don't regard myself as having sufficient spare time to want to devote that time to that particular thing. As it's in the course of development.

'That particular thing', or, in the words of another lawyer, '[T]he nature of the emerging constitution, concepts of democratic legitimacy' (Judge 154), might hold an interest for practising lawyers in their capacity as private citizens. And indeed, as private citizens, lawyers might even express regret about the distance of the Convention from the ordinary European, similar to those expressed by a general public (Interview 4):

IR: But do you feel part of it?
IE: I don't feel that actually I am participating in something which seems to me to be very important. I feel much further away from what's going on even, if this is possible, than I do in a general election in this country where I know that casting my vote is going have remarkably little effect on the outcome anyway (laughs). But I mind more about this (laughs).[9]

Laughing regret is permitted within the private, non-legal, discourse of European lawyers. Nonetheless, logics of formalism and professionalism further dictate that, even where lawyers do become a part of convention processes, furnishing 'expert legal advice' to national politicians or European Convention members, the driving impression remains one of a constitutive process, which is not only to be seen as 'non-law', but which is also to be forcefully shielded from contamination by the legal issues of 'daily practice' (Interview 20):

IR: Have you been following the debate around the European Convention?
IE: I've been following it a bit, not as much as I would like. A member of the Euro team in these chambers, Professor Takis Tridimas, is, in fact, the chairman of the group of 15 legal experts who is working on part of the constitution. And I know that Takis is . . . tremendously proud and pleased that he is doing that work. And I think that we are all sort of deliberately standing a little bit away because, you know, we wouldn't wish to put him in a position as we discuss other things with him; *cases we're working*. We don't want to make it difficult for him (emphasis added).

In brief conclusion, then, a dominant formalist account of European legal process reinforces traditional impressions of a stark distinction between constitution-making and the process of constitutional or legal adjudication. The European Convention lies in a realm of 'non-law', which should never be contaminated by legal practice, or by concrete legal cases concerned with the 'reality' of European integration. Legal process, in contrast, is neutral in character: educed from a circle squaring, if nonsensically contingent, constitutional settlement, law regulates its social environment with sole reference to its *own* socially and politically neutral values.

## III. Argumentation, evidence, problem-solving and strains in the formalist narrative

Obvious weaknesses within a formalist account of European legal processes can, nonetheless, be distilled from the accounts of daily practice within national courts at the interface between national and European normative orders. In particular, barristers, the convincing engines of legal argumentation within English courts, when asked whether they feel themselves to be an active part of a process of European constitution-building (as opposed to constitutional adjudication) are clear in their immediate response: '[U]nquestionably' (Interview 4).

Certainly, such responses may be cast in formalist terms (Interview 20):

IR: Do you feel you are part of the process of European constitution building?

IE: Yes, I do ... I accept that, for example, EU law is supreme over national law and so on. But you find that that concept is not as familiar to some lawyers, to some judges. Or, at least, it's not as acceptable ... you feel part of it when you're making arguments to prove in court that, well, ok, domestic law might say this but it can't stand. The statute has to be struck down because it's contrary to this provision in the EC Treaty. And then you feel that when you succeed in that kind of argument that you are sort of part of applying the system.

In other words, the act of building the European constitution lies in educating the domestic legal system upon the concrete mechanisms of an existing European constitution rather than in a 'consensual' act of re-adjustment of the sovereign reach of the domestic legal order.

The essential self-contradiction within this account of lawyerly persuasion, however, becomes more apparent as the legal narrative admits non-legal elements within its educational crusade (Interview 4):

IR: Well, do you feel, when you are working, that your job is part of a European legal order that is itself the foundation of a European constitution?

IE: And the foundation of having a Europe that doesn't tear itself to pieces yet again as it's done three times over. Unquestionably.

The contradiction similarly becomes ever more evident in a judicial disclaiming of a constitutional role (Interview 109):

IR: Do you feel that you are part of a process of European constitution-building?
IE: No, I don't feel it, at least not in my judicial capacity ...
IR: So you don't see your role in the courtroom, dealing with an EU case, using various European principles as part of the debate, the discussion going on, you don't feel that is part of the constitution.
IE: Well, it clearly is to some extent. It depends; I don't [know] whether [we're] talking about a *European* Constitution or a national constitution. Insofar as it's a European Constitution, the quarrels which have existed between the powers of the Commission and the powers of the Council, for instance, or either of those two and the Parliament, I haven't actually – there have been cases doing this – but I think they've all been in the ECJ. I certainly haven't been involved in any such cases in this country (emphasis added).

The 'Europeanness' of the supposed Constitution is telling: a formalist disclaimer of any constitutional function. Nonetheless, the *explicit* omission of consideration of constitutional consequence within national law is also, once again, implicitly indicative of a subsequent stated awareness that the two systems are inextricably linked within in a 'marriage' of entwined constitutional consequence (Interview 109):

IR: I want to move on somewhere else now. I want to talk more generally about the EU Constitution, or potential EU Constitution. Do you feel the same loyalty to European law that you feel to national law?
IE: In so far as European law – you're there referring to the law of the European Community or European Union – the answer is yes, totally. *But I don't accept the premise that they are distinct* (emphasis added).

What, then, is the glue that holds the marriage of legal orders together? Once again, the presence of ill-defined 'organicism' is tangible. In short, and notwithstanding all formalist efforts to compensate for inherent axiomatic inconsistency, or for the lack of a European *Grundnorm*, through notions of 'contingent supremacy', the matrix of normative and factual re-adjustment within the reference procedure necessarily remains the focus of a constitution-building process which must search much further in its pursuit of rationally constructed legitimating norms than the simple 'theoretical propriety' of a pre-legal, pre-political constitutive will.

### *III.1. Judicial dialogue: the basis for normative re-alignment?*

The measure of an alternative non-formalist source of constitution-building is not, however, to be found within the specific intensity of the judicial dialogue maintained between ECJ and national courts: marriage between Europe's legal orders is not marked by fervent exchange of conjugal rights. Instead, legal narrative reveals various factors that militate against constant interchange between the distinct normative orders that form the European legal system.

At a political level, the underlying reluctance of national governments to submit their actions to European judicial oversight, taken together with the general observation that the parties to a case (or rather their advocates) play the central role in determining whether an ECJ reference will be requested,[10] determines that much potential national–European judicial dialogue is rudely cut off at domestic source (Interview 4):

IR: How willing are UK judges to make an ECJ reference?
IE: I didn't realise how easy it was to oppose a reference ... when I came back to the UK ... I started doing a lot of Government cases. Usually, the Government doesn't want a reference. Usually, the Government says it's perfectly clear.

Similarly, internal legal values, such as the need to provide speedy judgment, may discourage individual judges from engaging directly with the ECJ. Equally, political issues, such as the desire of a lower court to reach its own judgment, may also stand in the way of a reference to the ECJ.[11]

Instead, a yardstick for the presence of non-formalist constitution-building within the reference procedure may be found in the 'quality' of discourse. Such quality is manifest not simply in the fact that '[t]here's no spiritual reluctance to refer at all' (Interview 109). Nor is it to be wholly deduced from a surprising, if occasional, lack of formality in this 'obviously very new and a one off' relationship between national and European Courts (Interview 109):

> I don't ring up an ECJ judge saying I've got this problem. The nearest I've got to that, which I have done two or three times, is when I've had a case to which the answer seems to me to be [so] obvious, that I have rung acquaintances there who are in the Court and said we are currently minded to say that this is *Acte Claire* and there is no problem here. Can you see a problem in us doing that? And, on each occasion so far, they have said no, save on one occasion when they said we do have one such reference coming before us from another court which covers the same material and for my part I think the answer that you propose is the one that will probably be come to, but you might do better to wait and see what happens to that.

Instead, it can be found in the general preparedness of national judges to consider and incorporate the norms, mores and principles (legal grammar) of Community law within their own legal systems (Interview 49):

> I think English judges, on the whole, are appropriately willing to make references. It would be quite wrong, I think, to equate the making of frequent references with being a good European. It's not like that at all. Judges have a number of considerations to balance, one of which is giving judgments within a reasonable time ... I think what one sees in England is that judges are becoming much more confident in applying Community law for themselves. I don't mean that they tend to apply it in a *little Englander or xenophobic* sort of way. I think, on the whole, they bend over backwards to be fair. The cases that are referred on the whole are cases that should be referred because the answer is going to be important for other member states as well (emphasis added).

Interestingly, the marriage of Europe's law at the non-authoritative interface between authoritative legal orders would also seem to be characterised by legal internalisation of the European principle of (national) non-discrimination, or by the notion that an issue confronting one polity may also be of direct concern to others. In the absence of a definitive sovereignty and hierarchy-defining norm, and forced, instead, into necessary substituting dialogue, Europe's law loses its many referential landmarks within the self-interest of individual national polities, or indeed, the self-interest of a supranational polity, to approach a form of universality which is founded, not within philosophical concordance with the *res publica*, but, rather, in its exact opposite – the recognition that the self-interest of the republic has lost its legal primacy.

### *III.2. Legal language and constitution-building*

The integration of Community law, and more importantly, the Community legal method, within national legal systems might thus, of itself, be argued to reflect a process of constitution-building; a form of constitution-building, moreover, with its own inspirational aspiration to legal universality. Furthermore, however, marked shifts in the modes and tools of legal argumentation across the member states of the Union also tell a clear tale of re-alignment within once-isolated national legal perceptions of the meaning and importance of normative government.

Equally, on some occasions, marked shifts can clearly illustrate a new understanding of the nature of the national polity or 'European polity in waiting'. Within the UK context, for example, the introduction of European 'rights' to a polity more accustomed to a negative liberal regime of freedoms[12] has contributed to a judicial evolution of a new understanding of the 'rule of law', which is measured in terms of the equality of rights (Interview 49 (Barrister) commenting on *Factortame*):

> But I think one of the principal factors at work was the feeling of the English judges that if citizens from other community states could obtain these injunctions by relying on Community law, then surely British people should be allowed to obtain them as well. *Incidentally, the case wasn't followed in Scotland. So there's a difference now between England and Scotland* (emphasis added).

The fact that the process of integration of Community law into national legal systems has not been one of the simple joint adoption of a single constitutional (rights-based or otherwise) understanding is, however, immediately confirmed by the continuing differentiation between the judicial patterns of observation of the extra-legal environment within which they operate. Thus, Scottish and English judges have a very different view of the justice demands, or deeper philosophical precepts of self-constitution, pertaining within particular segments of the UK polity: in this judicial analysis, Scotland remained, at least at the time that the interviews were conducted, wholly committed to the negative construction of spheres of personal autonomy.[13] Instead, the complexities of a constitution-building process rooted, not in the pursuit of a single constitutive will, but in the process of re-alignment between multiple self-contained normative orders is readily apparent in the choice of different courts within the Community legal order to place a different emphasis upon particular instruments of European law as befits the individual 'extra-legal' conditions pertaining within the forum (Interview 49):

> I think there are ways of presenting EU law in Luxembourg which differ from the ways in which you might present it in the United Kingdom. You raised earlier the example of subsidiarity which is a very good one. Mention the word to an English judge and most of them will nod briskly and say they understand what that means and they understand its importance. You mention it in Luxembourg and you get a tired smile as if to say well we know that had to go into the treaty ... but!

Once beyond the formalist veil, the peculiarities of the European legal constitution-building discourse become more apparent as lawyers themselves note that the major shifts within the grammar and semantics of the European legal system have centred not, as might have been expected, around the increased incidence of substantive legal concepts, such as rights, but within a marked shift to European principles of interpretation, such as purposive reasoning,[14] as well as the concept most often cited by our respondents, that of 'proportionality'.

A long-standing and powerful instrument of Community law, which supplies the yardstick of constitutionality within the ECJ's efforts to distinguish between national and European competences (Maduro 1997), proportionality is also confirmed within the current data-set as a vital instrument of judicial self-justification, which furnishes the courts with a precision proceduralist tool with which to assess the competing political claims of different sources of authority. Interviewee 109 concedes that European legal language has entered the UK courtroom. More importantly, however, it has also begun to contribute to the re-structuring of UK law:

> Because concepts of which the European Court of Justice and also quite often the European Court of Human Rights have made use, such as the German concept of proportionality [have proved useful]. *Those, as one can easily see, have gradually been discovered by the judges as being useful intellectual tools for tackling problems which are common to any political system [in] which judges and politicians [operate]* (emphasis added).

The notion of judicial 'discovery' is pivotal. The formalist paradigm of neutral 'JUDGMENT' is swept away as the courts struggle to adjust their judicial role to a reality of uncertain normative authority and competing claims to political authority. Proportionality, a practical procedural test of whether political means are suited to social ends (Chapter 2, Section III.2), furnishes courts with a neutrally flavoured instrument of adjudication that no longer directly relies on the expression of constitutive will, but, at the same time, affords the courts a measure of protection from the realist political claim that they are substituting 'their own pleasure to the constitutional intention of the legislature'.

With this, the contours of alternate constitutive authorities within the European legal system begin to emerge. Within the legal system itself, theoretical propriety is, perhaps, redirected away from the people's constitutive voice to a 'legal constitutionalism', or *Rechtsverfassungsrecht*, whereby law seeks, in each and every adjudicative act, a renewed normative force in its ability to ground 'JUDGMENT', not in ancient precedent, but in the proceduralised weighing up of immediate fact.

Equally, however, law's complementary constitutive force, or the normative ability of *Rechtsverfassungsrecht* to structure fact through procedural adjudication, is also hinted at, as counsel considers the effects of proportionality upon their own clients (Interview 4):

> If you are, again coming back to proportionality, if you are on the government side of the case and therefore you are trying to explain that a particular response was proportionate, you're usually involved in quite a difficult exercise because you are trying to look at what seemed to be a reasonable thing to do at the time and then to explain, expose why it was proportional. Now, it may indeed be proportional. This is not … necessarily … an exercise in falsification. That's not what I'm suggesting.

> But the problem is likely to be that intellectually it wasn't initially approached as, 'is the [decision] proportionate?' It was approached as, 'given various policy constraints, and different political objectives, is this the right thing to do?' Now, that probably gets you out to something that more or less was proportionate, but you have to rethink it almost in order to present it as proportional.

If the modern measure of deliberative legitimacy is to be found in the process of self-reflection whereby political debate is shielded from irrational self-interest,[15] then, a necessary discovery process of legal self-legitimation, becomes, by the same token, a socially-constitutive norm, as policy-making, policy constraints and governing interests are subject to re-formulation and review within a paradigm of factual appraisal, which does not deny political decision-making, but does require that it be shorn of any hidden self-interest and that it be justified in relation to prevailing conditions within a real-world of political contestation.

### *III.3. Evidence and constitution-building*

The particular difficulties which law faces when it moves beyond its own normative narrative, however, are similarly manifest in relation to further noted changes within (UK) courtrooms of the European legal system – in particular, with regard to a greater noted reliance upon 'scientific' representations of real-world conditions.

As a necessary factual compliment to the 'discovered' principles of normative re-adjustment, such as proportionality (Chapter 2 (III.2)), renewed European recourse to economic or cultural studies of the conditions pertaining within 'real' markets might thus be argued to mirror historical constitutional moments, such as early twentieth-century social constitutional re-alignment within the United States, when law departed from precedent and 'JUDGMENT' to ground its decisions in scientific studies of prevailing social conditions, instead (Chapter 2 (III.2)).

Although it is perhaps lacking in the immediate upheaval of necessary constitutional response to potentially revolutionary social inequality under conditions of rapid industrialisation, recourse to science and social science is a feature of legal discourse within Europe (Interview 109):

IR: Have you noticed any more sorts of socio-economic studies brought in as evidence?

IE: Yes, ah, well certainly economic studies. I don't know about socio; there have been a whole series of cases on the beer trade … and whether it's easy to persuade a bitter drinker to move to lager.

Certainly, a degree of judicial vagueness about the distinction between science proper and social science might be noted. Nonetheless, the appearance of 'non-legal' material in courtrooms throughout the European legal system is a further indication of the limits to formalist reasoning and the necessarily constitutive role which law has been required to play in bringing the multiple and competing norms of a European legal system closer to the realities of an emerging European society.

However, the effort to 'socialise' law, releasing it from the pre-conceived formalist paradigms that can be and are founded within the society whose constitutive will it claims to represent, continues to suffer from the selfsame inconstancies that plagued early twentieth-century efforts to re-found law as a sociological discipline. A claim might thus be made that law can re-invent both itself and its authority within a 'scientific' paradigm that is no longer marked by 'imagined' normativism, but is instead underpinned by the truth-claims of analytical methodologies rooted within social reality rather than social reconstruction. Nonetheless, the endeavour to shatter axiom and unveil reality likewise appears to be illusory, as 'scientific discipline' not only reveals that it is itself, and in common with law, a 'constructed reality', but also proves to be difficult to translate into the existing structures of normative law. Indeed, an impression is often left that the use of scientific material only serves to further instrumentalist aims (Interview 4):

> You could certainly find yourself presenting [economic material]. You would quite often find that you were trying to commission economic material. And then you have the usual fun interface between law and economics where you have the lawyers trying to explain to the economists what they want. And the economists saying but I don't understand at all. I build my model like this. That's fine, it's not going to help you because I [still] won't be able to present material that actually explains to the court what I need to show. Again, it's a matter of either looking for material which is already there and finding a way of packaging it so that it fits within the framework of what you need to run the argument as; or, if you don't have the material, seeing whether there is any way that it could be commissioned that could be any good. That is, of course, usually then subject to the objection that you went out looking for material.[16]

### *III.4. 'Workability' and constitution-building*

Even if the image of lawyers as 'socially legitimated law-givers for Europe' has failed immediately to convince, the increased incidence of the use of material evidence within the courtrooms of the European legal system does, however, still contain its own constitution-building and constitutionally legitimating potential. More particularly, it does so when seen in conjunction with a marked degree of what can provisionally be termed 'workability'[17] within the self-perception of European lawyers.

Ostensibly a description of purposive reasoning within European law, one barrister's statement that '[I]t's trying to make it work rather than interpret exactly what it is' (Interview 20) thus furnishes a final key to an understanding of the constitutive impulses that guide and legitimate legal constitution-building processes within Europe.

In other words, the need to *find solutions* within a complex interlocking series of normative orders that must also adapt themselves to an evolving European reality entails a rationality pressure which forces the legal system to rise above any easily accepted normative or implicit political self-interest in its search for mechanisms to guide the development of European law. Within this framework, although scientific evidence may be flawed, it is nonetheless an aid in the effort to circumnavigate political interest, social need and normative constraints in order to furnish judgments that ease rather than hinder the integration *telos*.

Often simply an accidental rationalising force, which is reproduced across European institutions for a variety of reasons,[18] 'workability' must be starkly distinguished from functionalism. 'Workability' has nothing to do with any grand ideological scheme to force the pace of integration within differentiated, yet interconnected, spheres of European society, in the eternal hope that economic integration will induce comparable evolution in its social and political counterparts (Chapter 2 (I)). Instead, the simple rationalising pressure to 'make Europe and its legal system work' is not only to be identified as a non-formalist constitutional building task, but can also be argued to be a self-legitimating legal mechanism: the challenge of meeting *telos* through facilitative problem-solving replaces illusionary axiom in order to provide the vital link between law and the society by which it is constituted and which it, in turn, constitutes.

In this sense, then, workability is related to Heller's conception of *Wirksamkeit* (Chapter 1 (II)). Certainly, the exact patterns of legal appreciation of operational social realities, as well as the justice demands that such realities entail, remains obscure: science cannot be the sole adjudicative measure of achieved patterns of social operation, together with their inherent normative commitments. Nonetheless, in seeking to give effective force to integration processes, law is undoubtedly engaged in a form of bridging fact and norm and of reality translation – and, more importantly, a form of legal reality translation that no longer brooks any peace with supposed immutable axioms of national legal organisation.

## IV. Servants to or agents of the constitution-building process?

A final twist in the (self-) illusionary presentation of law is, however, apparent within descriptions furnished by lawyers of their role in the courtroom, and, more particularly, their relationship with their clients. At one level, the narratives of lawyers (rather than judges) about their professional roles confirm the existence of an obscured non-formalist account of constitution-building within the European legal system. Legal counsels are the convinced European engines of a legal evolution which seeks to meet the demands of the integration process. Judges, on the other hand, remain true to their national normative orders and must be inveigled into acceptance of the European order (Interview 4):

> They come with a different amount of acquired knowledge. They come with different preconceptions as to what the law is about ... it requires you to look at the case you are doing differently and also to try to see how, if you're running an English law argument and a Euro argument, how you can get the two to mesh so that the judge is not going to be terribly upset by all this funny foreign law and have the natural reflex which is to push it as far to one side as he can conveniently manage.

Similarly, 'funny foreign law' can also be forcefully deployed to pursue client-led visions of the polity (in this case, a rights-based vision) which are foreign to the domestic order (Interview 20):

> I felt the client did feel that she was part [of a European polity], that she was relying on EU law to get her rights, which she was, on an objective view, entitled to, but which the domestic law didn't give her. [We went to the Court in] Luxembourg and, in the end, as I say, we lost, but then I did feel that we were all part of this bigger system.

And yet, such clear intimations of polity-building lawyerly agency in a European constitution-building process are also immediately suppressed. The prevailing logic is of service to the law; a self-contained professionalism which (1) derives from the duty to serve the client (Interview 20):

> Clearly, as barristers, we're essentially sort of mouthpieces for our clients and so it may be that, in particular cases, I would be arguing that EU law doesn't apply here, because that's in my client's interest, so you will take different attitudes towards it depending on your client's interest in a particular case.

And (2), as a consequence, dismisses any special status for European law and its norms, '[T]here's no magic about EU law. It's another weapon in the armoury' (Interview 49); and, instead, (3) locates its explicit efforts to persuade national judges to accept the norms, principles and the *telos* of a European legal system firmly in the neutral and didactic sphere of professional legal education (Interview 4):

> You will be trying to explain, if it is a judge who has never really looked at the case law of the European Court before, you'll be trying to explain that it won't read the same way as an English case reads ... And you'll be saying, of course, you know, I'm showing you a case where the facts are slightly different from the present case, but the statement of principle is to be found here. I'm going to show you another three cases where you will find the same statement of principle. I'm therefore going to invite you to be prepared to accept that the statement of principle probably is a general statement of principle. Now, let's see what it does if you apply it to the case that is actually in front of you.

With this, the circle of (self-) illusion is complete. Even where the logic of the formalist paradigm appears strained, the new paths of courtroom legal evolution followed retain their 'neutral' character – a neutrality prompted and necessitated by the lawyer's professional duty to the client.

## V. Thick law: from adjudication to constitution-building

Politics is politics, law is law and never the twain shall meet; but neither shall they pollute the constitutive moment. For us, the most pressing paradox is, perhaps, the fact that our traditional understanding of constitution-building processes has long weaved a close and (for the constitution) determinative relationship between 'law' and 'politics';[19] and yet, it has founded this relationship upon a strangely disembodied view of both 'law' and 'politics'. Constitutional conventions, of course, cannot but be marked by political disputation. Nonetheless, the constitutive moment is emptied of all contestation as the constitution is created, and the gulf between facts and norms established, as an equally neutered law adopts the mantle of the living oracle of the constitutive will, shielded only from its own potentially socially disruptive influence by formalism and the veil of judicial 'independence'.

Facts are facts and norms are norms and the never the twain shall meet: the most surprising conclusion of this survey is the continued narrative power of formalist accounts of the origins and the force of law, not only in the light of a century of critical legal scepticism, but in the face of a political-legal entity, the European Union, which has, time and again, demonstrated the redundancy of axiomatic constructions of society. Eschewing even the Habermasian effort to re-found norms in fact by means of the constituting and re-constituting effects of political discourse, legal narrative withdraws beneath its formalist cloak and refuses to play any but the most technical of roles in a realm of 'non-law'. By the same token, the European convention process, with a realist belief in the power of politics to direct law, dabbles briefly within a sphere of judicial politics, restating the primacy of the European Union for the benefit of recalcitrant national judiciaries

(Chapter 3 (III)), but likewise places renewed faith in the age-old mechanism of judicial independence to effect 'its' constitution, or its political programme for the entrenchment of a particular European polity (consolidation of the revolution).[20]

And yet, the survey also re-confirms various underlying reasons for a 'noble' legal endeavour to retain a formalist character. Formalist fiction or doctrinal purity retains its power to convince: to depart from the axiom of once-constituted governance is to place the origins of law in doubt and to risk the relativist dead-ends of critical jurisprudence,[21] or to court, as did the *Freirechtsschule* or 'free' law movement (Chapter 2, Chapter 7 (III.2)), the implication of the legal system in transient societal trends or imperfect scientific appreciation of reality. By this token, the pejoratively flavoured appellation of legal narrative as a (self-) illusion is wholly unfair: a profession of law works with imperfect formalist means; at the same time, however, law thus shields itself from the more obvious follies of academic endeavours to found legal origin in ever more elusive realities.

Such potential unfairness is likewise heightened by the simple fact that narratives of (self-) illusion, once unravelled, reveal the extraordinary creativity of a legal system which has, in the daily courtroom round, responded sensitively both to normative *lacunae* and to factual demands, not only adapting to the integration *telos*, but also compensating, through problem-solving ('workability') and the structuring of an extra-legal political environment, for lacking political settlement. More revealingly, however, an experimental process of European *Rechtsverfassungsrecht*, and, in particular, its imposition of deliberation-inducing rationality standards (proportionality) upon external political debate, would also seem to represent an experimental, yet highly creative, response to the formalist-materialist legal paradox, which a settlement unravelling and unsettled integration process has made explicit. The eternal problem posed by the necessary process of legal materialisation remains the inherent danger that, in seeking to identify and satisfy the 'justice demands' of an extra-legal environment, law will itself be implicated within material demands (value irrationalism), losing both its internal normative coherence, and its external socially consolidating authority, as it cedes its vital social neutrality.

Nevertheless, within the novel and re-invigorated proceduralism of the European legal order, its proactively constitutive, yet non-directive, relationship with a form of politics that acts as the courtroom mirror to social reality, Europe's law offers us an experimental potential for a more differentiated understanding of constitution-building processes within and beyond constitutional conventions. More specifically, the relationship of *Rechtsverfassungsrecht* with (experimental) notions of deliberative democracy (underpinned by legal notions of proportionality) appears to establish the vital link between on-going political processes, or 'politics', which retains its primacy in the matter of identifying social reality, and a legal order with its self-legitimating procedural rationality. In short: *Rechtsverfassungsrecht* appears to represent a process of legal self-constitution and concomitant societal constitution, which forcefully explodes the constitution-building/constitutional adjudication paradigm, and yet, in its proceduralist character, retains a degree of legitimacy.

Finally, however, it must also be noted that the mechanics of *Rechtsverfassungsrecht* are limited and may also be subject to a certain degree of disturbing analysis. Above all, English legal history, forever faced with its own problem of shifting centres of normative and factual power,[22] often argues that the only *locus* for legal and constitutional legitimacy within the United Kingdom lies in a legal professionalism by means of which a very small group of lawyers ensure constitutional stability and civility through the imposition of their own 'professionally' constrained mores upon the political and social attitudes of a restricted group of professional entrants (Simpson 1987). And indeed, certain indications do exist in support of the argument that such a professional securing of a European legal future is likewise developing within the United Kingdom and beyond (Schepel and Wesseling 1997).[23] Nonetheless, such sources for constitutional legitimacy, accompanied as they often are by visions of wood-panelled walls and port wine, are as disquieting as they are comforting: should the evolution of a European constitutionalism ever be entrusted to the hands of so few, and, above all, such a self-selecting few?

Accordingly, it is, at the very least, perhaps time to draw aside isolationist legal veils, in order to reveal the full extent of evolutionary legal constitutionalism in all its flawed glory. Likewise, the existing contours of legal constitutionalism should be investigated as closely as possible for all their possible failings. As a consequence, the analysis now moves on to tackle one of the trickiest challenges posed to *Rechtsverfassungsrecht*: direct political conflict between contesting and contrasting visions of the legitimate shape of the European polity and the evolution of explicit 'principles' of constitutional adjudication between them; 'principles' which might play their own part in ensuring that legal indeterminacy within Europe is a positive force, expressive of a desire to socialise Europe in line with the real-world nature of a European polity and its justice demands.

## Notes

1 Within the German, this dual concept of law-giving and justification for (legitimation of) law-giving can also be rendered within one punning word: *Rechtsverfassungsrecht*. The best English translation possible – justif(y)ication, however, does not quite capture the literary elegance of the original. *Rechtsverfassungsrecht* is deployed by Wiethölter (2003) to capture the dual self-justificatory and juridification tendencies of all law within society, including the prosaic norms of private law. Conflation of the two terms *Rechtsverfassungsrecht* and *Rechtsverfassungsrecht* is, perhaps, not quite faithful to the intricacies of

the originating theory. Nonetheless, within this study at least, the far more expansive term of '*Rechtsverfassungsrecht*' is preferred and used to denote both terms, although its semantics do not immediately capture the vital notion of self-justification, specifically since it does capture the dual constitutive nature of law: the particular defining feature of European law remains its duality; a duality that is constituting of society, even as, in response to society, Law constitutes itself.

2 *Factortame Ltd* [1996] (House of Lords and ECJ) reversing the age-old rule that the Crown might not be held liable for its acts and establishing the principle of state liability at European legal level.

3 Note, in the following, that IR denotes interviewer, whilst IE denotes interviewee.

4 Note, responses have been edited for ease of comprehension. As the inclusion of laughter indicates, a full-scale discourse analysis might have been conducted upon the data-set, and indeed would have given very salient results. Nonetheless, for the purposes of this analysis, simple textual analysis does suffice to provide insight into a legal consciousness.

5 Note, however, that the notion of a 'division of powers' also has an undeniably European and 'unsettled' air. Rather than the more common formula of an allocation of power to different institutions within a unitary sovereign order, the talk is of the allocation of power to 'different sources of law'. In other words, the plurality of a traditional division of powers is radicalised and extended to encompass the division of powers between plural polities (sovereign legal orders).

6 The notion that EU law derives its force from national legal orders is reinforced by questionnaire responses to the question of how lawyers viewed the EU legal order. We offered contributors 4 choices: (1) self-contained part of UK law; (2) an irritant within UK law; (3) an integral part of UK law; and (4) other. Thirty-four replies said it was an integral part of UK law: of those 24 were Barristers, 2 were High Court Judges, 7 were Appeal Court Judges and one was a Law Lord.

7 The data-set was created whilst the European Convention was conferring.

8 Many, indeed, confusing it with the European Convention of Human Rights. This is a further rather disturbing confirmation of the European Convention's utter failure to fulfil its very basic mandate of the promotion of informed debate on European governance, or its self-appointed task of including the peoples of Europe within a constitutive act. Respondents to questionnaires were largely self-nominating. Generally speaking, only those lawyers with a specific interest in European law were drawn to reply. Surely the most informed of all groups within society on European law, the respondents nevertheless evinced a startling degree of ignorance about the Convention that was then actively underway.

9 Humour here also giving a clear indication of the potentially distorting self-selecting nature of the data-set sample; lawyers who responded to the survey overwhelmingly evinced strong pro-European views.

10 All lawyers interviewed in the survey indicated that opposition to a reference by one of the parties to a case will often lead to a refusal to refer.

11 'Some of them are feeling they ought have a crack at it. And if they're wrong then a higher court can say they're wrong and that court can make a reference. So, for example, a high court judge might decide that he should decide the point and that if he's wrong it should be the Court of Appeal that makes the reference ...' (Interview 4).

12 See, for detailed investigation of the United Kingdom's alternative vision of liberality, where the measure of personal autonomy is to be found in the negative notion of non-discrimination (do as you will, as long as you do no harm to others), rather than the positive ascription of rights, Grey (1989).

13 See, above, note 12. Note, however, that the Human Right Act (2001), applying to the whole of the United Kingdom, has altered the politically constituted nature of the UK polity, at least to the limited degree that Parliament must now explicitly voice its desires to overturn rights. Whilst Courts have yet to digest the implications of the Act fully, changes within judicial perceptions of the UK polity are becoming apparent.

14 A concept that has extended beyond the European legal system to 'pollute' purely domestic reasoning: 'Well yes. I think there are so many examples now of courts reading statutes in a [purposive] way. Not only statutes I might add, but contracts' (Interview 49).

15 A general Habermasian perception given particular force in relation to the creation of a constituted Europe, when Habermas exhorts a European populace to engage in the 'painful' task of severing subjective ties to engage in a European political community (2001).

16 Note, judicial appreciation of scientific evidence is marked by courtroom incomprehension throughout the realm of European law, and, in particular in relation to the notion of risk, or the application of the precautionary principle. See, only, the following tortuous exchange in oral pleadings before the Court of First Instance in the case of *Pfizer* [2002]: *Professor Phillips*: You get the organisms in chickens; the organisms are transmitted to man and the rest of it flows. If you cannot demonstrate the rest of it, the whole thing comes to a stop. I do insist that no harm has been done. You have the potential and the hazard but it is not translated into a risk. That is my understanding of all the scientific evidence I have read. *Judge Laenerts:* Is that not to some extent playing on the words? You say it is a hazard and we had this morning the distinction between hazard and risk. If you have a hazard, it may become a risk. Is that not playing on the words? *Professor Phillips:* No. I do not believe it is. If you are defining your risk as the use of growth promoter in animals leading to resistance in animals, the hazard is translated into a risk ... What happens to those organisms once they contaminate food ... once they are ingested by man all has to be assessed before you say that you can turn the hazard into what is the risk, to me, which is the infection in man. I thought that was what we were talking about.

17 The term 'workability' is chosen for a variety of normative reasons (see below). Importantly, however, it is also chosen in preference to the grammatically more appealing notion of 'functionality'; a term, which is revealed to encompass a variety of potentially distorting processes of political accommodation within European law-making. See Chapter 6 (I).

18 Within our survey, for example, the rationalising effects of multi-lingualism were also confirmed: 'You are addressing a multi-lingual court in one of the languages of the Community. You have to plead in the way that expressly recognises that facts of [different] legislation. That recognises the fact that for many people the language of the court is not their language ... My test for pleading in Luxembourg, what I say must be so clear, so easy to follow and so attractive that I seduce the court away from listening to others' (Interview 4).

19 Either a thin perception, in that law constrains politics; or a thick perception, whereby law and politics influence and shape each other (Habermas 1994).

20 Note, again, however, that whilst this analysis has very little room for detailed consideration of the nature and shape of the (largely defunct) draft European constitutional treaty, that treaty, too, is marked by extraordinarily pluralistic understandings of the European polity. With the potential to mean many different things to many different people, the treaty is not merely indeterminate in the

sense that all legal language is necessarily indeterminate, instead, it is explicitly indeterminate, presenting, for example, wholly contrasting and incompatible visions of the forms of democracy that should be maintained within the European polity (Chapter 5 (I)).

21 In other words, to deconstruct beyond all meaning and jump into the normative abyss of wholly non-authoritative law.

22 In other words, common already is a law absent a clear *Grundnorm* (lack of clear UK constitutional settlement).

23 For strong *critique* of the very small number of academic authors who form the core of the European legal movement, and thus determine its mores.

Chapter 5

# Constitutionalising the institutional balance of powers

> The classical efficiency criterion of Pareto-superiority is incapable of distinguishing among the political frameworks I consider in this paper – because each framework would predictably make some people worse off than each of its rivals, none is preferable on Paretian grounds. More fundamental principles of legitimacy are necessary to assess the competing claims of alternative frameworks
>
> Bruce Ackerman (2000: 646).

## I. Institutional balance within the European polity

In Jean-Paul Jacqué's seminal analysis (1990),[1] the Community principle of the 'institutional balance of powers' is identified as the vital constitutional fulcrum that has smoothed the path of increasingly intense integration between the nation states of Europe. Not only is it sensitive to the residual, yet integral national imperative for sovereignty, it is also facilitative of supranational integrative impulses. It is the 'static' (Jacqué 2004: 384) higher legal principle that has vouchsafed the strictly delineated exercise of integral competences both to the member states and to the Communities, and which has guaranteed an ordered and orderly process of integration in which law has disciplined and dissipated political conflict on the existing and the proposed nature of a 'dynamic' European polity (Jacqué 2004: 384). *De facto* increases in and accrual of powers by individual institutions would never be tolerated. Instead, re-apportionment of power would always be subject to explicit agreement (preferably treaty-based). The formal application of an entrenched and intransigent legal map of apportioned powers, it is thus argued, has proven to be the grease that has oiled the wheels of an uncertain and innovative integration process.

Given these formidable constitutional antecedents, the current debate on the state and nature of the balance of powers within the European Union might be considered to be normatively parsimonious, indeed. In a post-Convention environment, the effort to avoid the potential 'Nirvana fallacy' that the governance of the contingent Union might ever be founded in coherent and comprehensive principles of governmental organisation (Cram 2002) now seems to have dissolved into a game of political catchpenny in which the complex institutional arrangements of the current and proposed European Union are minutely analysed in order to ascertain which bodies amongst the institutional *mêlée* of the European Parliament, Council, Commission, national governments and national parliaments might or might not have been the winners and the losers in a tortuous re-apportionment of real (if not readily grasped at the formal level) powers of initiative within the European Union.[2]

Nonetheless, this low-level politicisation of the principle of the institutional balance of powers (the undignified scramble for powers of influence between, say, the Council and the Commission) should not be dismissed too readily – at a normative level of analysis – as an aberrant 'real-world' intrusion into a world of perfectionist constitutional formalism; a temporary assault on an axiomatic sphere of principled institutional organisation that will more or less slowly re-establish itself once the political fires over the meanings of the proposed constitutional treaty have been (judicially) dampened down; or, alternatively, once the draft constitution has been consigned to the historical dustbin.

Instead, such pragmatic political debates are, at once, both an affirmation of Ackerman's generalisable dictum, uttered with regard to the separation of powers principle (Ackerman 2000), that simple institutional shifts in power entail far more than simple efficiency gains between distinct bodies of governance and government, *and* a confirmation of the specifically explicit problems attendant upon a *sui generis* 'process' of European integration. On the one hand, the current political conflict within and on the nature of the institutional balance is merely the tip of the iceberg of an immanent crisis of normative legitimation within the European Union, which asks the question of 'for the benefit of whom' should power be balanced, or, in the light of more recent developments, 'separated'. On the other hand, contemporary bickering is also a continuation of the deep-seated political and social rumblings that have always underlain judicial pronouncement on and the application of the principle of the institutional balance – a vivid reminder and affirmation that formalist application of higher principles is often a veil for dynamic, rather than static, judicial re-adjustment to an ever changing *praxis* of social and political organisation.

Seen in this light, the current controversy over the meaning of institutional balance is thus, above all, a specific expression of the general tension created by the supranational impetus, which has increasingly seen competences traditionally reserved to the national polity transferred to international governmental organisations such as the European Union, with all the consequent concern about the democracy deficit to which such transfers give rise. As one influential commentator has noted, the coupling of international integration and democracy does not entail a case of 'love at first sight' (Stein 2001).

Instead, complex institutional machinations on whether the Council or the Commission should have primacy over an increasingly integrated EU foreign policy[3] (or, indeed, whether national parliaments should have a greater say in restricting the scope of EU policy-making) are a surface expression of far more deep-seated democratic concerns and doubts about who might best, as well as when and where and how, give voice to the 'common' (supranational) or, alternatively, 'divisible' (national) interests of a dynamic European polity.

More particularly, and vitally so in the context of this analysis, the explicit appearance of specifically 'majoritarian' democratic principles within the proposed constitutional treaty (Article I-46),[4] as well as the strengthening of the position of the European Parliament within the legislative process, has also further increased tensions within the effort to lessen the EU democratic deficit between two distinct and contrasting positions: first, between efforts which retain (albeit somewhat diffusely) the underlying ethos of the institutional balance (Articles I-11(2), I-12(6) and I-45 of the proposed constitutional treaty), and which seek to maintain the institutional distinctions drawn between national and supranational polities, as well as between the institutions which represent each common or divisible interest; and second, between concepts that posit their democratising hopes within a contrasting principle of the 'separation of powers' that (albeit currently somewhat faintly) echoes the traditional triadic distinctions between executive, legislative and judicial government, and which is beginning to re-fashion the European legislative process as a majoritarian expression of an indivisible European will.

Following Ackerman's argument, it must be recognised that each proposed or argued for adjustment within the political constellation or institutional framework of the European Union will not only give birth to winners and losers at institutional level, but will also entail fundamental, if highly indistinct, alterations in the social and political *praxis* of the underlying legitimation of the Union. Equally, if Ackerman's assertion that the winners and losers in the changing political frameworks game cannot be equalised through the mere application of *pareto* efficiency criteria, then an initial imperative might seem to be one of the translation of such social and political *praxis* into universal normative legitimacy through the identification of a higher (and undisputed) substantive governing ideal within the principle of the balance of powers, or alternatively, within its emergent competitor, the principle of the separation of powers.

In short, if Europe is an indivisible polity possessed of one common will, then its Constitution and the judicial application of that Constitution should clearly reflect this fact. However, and it is a big 'however', it is *precisely* this possibility, the potential for the emergence of *one* 'substantive' governing principle of European Union, that the uncertain process of European integration and current vigorous debate on the mechanics of the balance have thrown into doubt. Underlying Jacqué's seminal analysis of the nature of the institutional balance is the fundamental recognition that the European polity has always been and remains *sui generis*, at least (or *only*) to the degree that both its *telos* and its destination are openly contested. In this area of competing national, supranational, private and public interests, the greatest legal virtue identified for the principle of the institutional balance by commentators remains (Jacqué 1990), therefore, precisely 'this', its essentialist, formalist and proceduralist nature.

In a tautology *par excellence*, while the ebbs and flows of political and social conflict might come and go, the constitutional principle of the balance of powers has remained and, indeed, will continue to remain untroubled, regulating the advancement of the Union through its formal and inviolate demand that each institution might only act within the limits of its competences. The politics of Europe and the European polity are dynamic; its governing law, however, is static (Jacqué 1990).

Or is it? Whilst the following analysis cannot but conclude that, under *sui generis* conditions of explicit polity contestation, a higher law would be ill-advised to focus its constitutional efforts upon the identification of 'thick' substantive governing principles, the simple acceptance of the once and forever formalist nature of a procedurally flavoured (or essentialist) legal principle of institutional balance must, perforce, be cast into doubt. Not least, since the notion of 'balance' might, by itself, imply some sort of substantive view of a lasting equilibrium between national and supranational forces (Joerges and Neyer 1997), but also, and more vividly so, since the concrete legal application of the institutional balance has indeed changed, both over time and outside concrete treaty re-negotiations, giving us a glimpse of European law as an active, as well as a latent, actor in the process of European polity formation and transformation.[5]

Moving away from formalist conceptions of proceduralism and moving to a legal theoretical analysis of the process of European integration, the core issue and question would, accordingly, seem to be one of the 'principled' mechanics of the judicial adjustment of the constitutional stricture to social and political *praxis*. As Ackerman again reminds us, fundamental conflict on the meaning of underlying constitutional principles, such as the separation of powers or the rule of law, has always been present within institutional arrangements and constitutional adjudication on these arrangements. Within a *sui generis* process of European integration, however, such fundamental conflict is not only a corollary of polity formation and development, but is, rather, a defining characteristic of the necessarily uncertain *telos* of the European polity.

Seen in this light, normative legitimation is thus, perhaps, less a matter of the formalist application of the institutional fulcrums of higher law, and even less a matter of the identification of eternally contingent substantive governance principles. Instead, to echo the themes of *Rechtsverfassungsrecht* and constitutional morphogenesis reproduced throughout this book, normative legitimation must surely be found in the principled judicial practice of fact–norm translation. More particularly, within an explicitly constitutional jurisdiction, confronted constantly with contrasting visions of the legitimate shape of the future European polity, it is to be found within law-internal principles, which facilitate *praxis* recognition and approbation without succumbing to the particularising stain of judicial/legal embroilment within social and political contestation.

## II. Dynamic politics and static law: the high stakes of judicial interventionism

> The most important aim of the Constitution is to avoid a repetition of the developments, which, in the Weimar Republic, led to the abolition of the separation of powers, and thus to the collapse of the rule of law. The path to the complete surrender of the doctrine of separation of powers through the *Ermächtigungsgesetz* of 1933 took its first open form in the excessively wide interpretation of Article 48(2) of the Weimar Constitution in favour of the executive (*Re Tax on Malt Barley* [1964] paragraph 20).

With this startling admission of judicial fallibility, the *Rheinland-Pfalz* Finance Court reminded us, in its challenging 1964 judgment rejecting the executive transfer of 'legislative' competence to the European Economic Community under the, then, Article 24 of the German Constitution,[6] of just how high the stakes of judicial interventionism can be in the area of constitutional adjudication on institutional powers. Repeating a common theme of this book, the well-intentioned but ill-formed and inchoate 'free law' (Ehrlich 1987; Rotthleuthner 1988; Grosswald-Curran 2003) of the Weimar Republic, the first explicit effort to adapt the norms of law to the realities of social and political evolution, appeared, to this Court at least, to have ended in tragic judicial adventurism and the betrayal of the 'primary' jurisprudential function, that of the maintenance of the 'rule of law'. Certainly, Hermann Heller might have preached in favour of legal indeterminacy in pursuit of a reflexive social constitutionalism. However, as a simple matter of historical record, indeterminate judicial adjudication had not effected the cause of adaptation of law to 'just' social demands, but had, instead, ended in the lawless abyss of the Third Reich.

### *II.1. Static adjudication*

This vital statement thus provides the key to a first understanding of Jean-Paul Jacqué's laudation in favour of the 'constitutionally static' interpretation of the European Union's principle of institutional balance. *Meroni* [1958], the first judicial statement of the principle of institutional balance (at that time consolidated within Article 4 of the EEC Treaty) was decided, a bare 13 years from the end of the Second World War, and still within the context of the 'moral' rescue of the western European nation state from its pre-war political and legal turpitude. Seen in this light, the ban on institutional delegations of power and the injunction that each and every institution of the Community (more precisely in the case of *Meroni*, of the High Authority[7]) might only act within the limits of its competences, appears less within its modern guise as a troublesome barrier to the establishment of efficient government throughout the European Union (Majone 1988, 2005), and more as an appeal for the powerful reiteration (and application to the 'new' Europe) of Montesquieu's underlying justification for his scheme of a separation of powers.

Jacqué spells it out explicitly: the 'conservatory' element within the balance of powers at this time had little if anything to do with maintaining a political balance between the dynamic supranational interest in integration and a necessary residual member state interest in the maintenance of national normative and political integrity (Dashwood 1998), and everything to do with a 'protective function' in its most general terms:

> [F]or the Court, the principle is a substitute for the principle of the separation of powers, which in Montesquieu's original exposition of his philosophy, aimed to protect individuals against the abuse of power. In the absence of a separation of powers, the principle of institutional balance made it possible to guarantee to undertakings that a modification of the institutional balance would not call into question the decision-making process envisaged by the treaties and the accompanying guarantees provided by the treaties (Jacqué 2004: 384).

In other words, 'constitutional staticism', grounded within the notion of a 'protective function' within the institutional balance, relates initially to a wholly autonomous legal logic and legal function of constraining political expansionism in the service of an individual liberty which is secured in the European setting, not by 'rights',[8] but by the law-internal principles of the rule of law and legal certainty. The social danger to be guarded against is the tyranny of the arbitrary exercise of power. The concomitant legal danger is one of judicial embroilment within arbitrary politics by means of an expansive constitutional jurisdiction; the counter-legal solution, one of strict adherence to a formalistic process of adjudication that maintains the rule of law, or, in other words, maintains the limits to institutional competence, as encapsulated within the positivised legal order. Seen in this light, the strangely disappointing formulation of the principle of institutional balance by the *Meroni* Court, a formulation importantly and recently confirmed by Advocate General Geelhoed in the latest of a tortuous line of 'Comitology cases',[9] gains in significance.

Thus, the bald statement that 'the balance of powers which is characteristic of the institutional structure of the Community must be regarded as a fundamental guarantee' (*Meroni*), is not merely a formalistic *non sequitur*, a superfluous statement that the Court will apply the law of the treaties (more specifically, the apportionment of institutional competences) as it literally stands, but is, instead, a radical judicial commitment to self-restrained exercise of judicial competence in order to maintain the settled architecture of European political governance, and so to safeguard the liberty of the European citizen. The primary judicial function is one of adherence to a legal internal regulative norm, the securing of individual liberty.[10] The fundamental mode of judicial operation is one of rejection of extra-legal considerations and the maintenance of a law-internal legal formalism through the literal application of positive law.

The 'protective function' within the institutional balance remains a guiding feature of the ECJ's, and, more particularly, its Attorney Generals', rhetorical mode of its 'principled' application. Advocate General Tesauro's pronouncement, found within his opinion on *Re Generalised Tariff Preferences* [1995], is exemplary:

> The central feature of this case law, which is quite unambiguous is the Court's constant attention to the rigorous preservation of the institutional balance, *as it has gradually evolved following amendments to the original text of the treaties* [a]. It is precisely in order to ensure that balance, *by means of an adequate and consistent system of legal protection* [b], taking particular account of the progressive strengthening of the Parliament's role, especially in the legislative process, *that the Court has repeatedly affirmed the latter's right to bring legal proceedings* [c] (emphasis added). (paragraph 19)

As emphasis [b] demonstrates, the aim of the Court seemingly remains its commitment to a specifically legal system of 'protection': the ECJ acts *precisely* to ensure internal consistency within the logic of the legal application of the principle of institutional balance. And yet, even within this clear restatement of the Court's dedication to its own internal logic of 'legal protection', there are also very clear indications of a further troublesome element within the ECJ's institutional balance jurisprudence. As emphasis [a] readily reveals and emphasis [c] impliedly confirms, the ECJ's adjudicational purview is once again distinguished from other constitutional jurisdictions: rather than simply being charged with the preservation of a constitutionally settled apportionment of powers, the Court is called upon to play a critical role within an evolutionary constitutional process, whereby a rapid series of Treaty amendments,[11] together with various fundamental instances of secondary Community legislation,[12] result in large-scale upheavals within the political constellation of the EU institutional balance; a balance which the Court is then called upon to explicate.[13]

This, then, forms the second element within Jacqué's plea for the maintenance of constitutional staticism. Ensuring static, stable, adequate and logically coherent jurisprudence on the institutional balance is no longer just a matter of rescuing Europe from the moral *malaise* of the early twentieth century. Instead, it is also a crucial element within the awkward and always troublesome mechanics of judicial response to an underlying alteration in the politics of constitutional evolution.

Constitutional staticism must be maintained in the face of unprecedented political and constitutive dynamism. The series of Intergovernmental Conferences that have dominated the European integration *telos* over the last 20 years, taken cumulatively together with the spillover institutional effects of a series of more or less *ad hoc* legislative and administrative efforts to ensure the efficient governance of the European Union,[14] have fundamentally remoulded the European polity; not just once in one striking 'constitutional event', but over and over again in a rapidly unfolding series of often contested measures of polity evolution. Equally, the meaning of this contested polity evolution is fought out daily in concrete battles on substantive policy-making and policy initiatives as treaty amendments are constantly tested before the Court.

Taking Ackerman's dictum to heart, the augmenting of parliamentary powers, be it by means of increased prerogatives or increased standing before the Court,[15] matters: it recasts the European polity as a representative (majoritarian) supranational entity and creates its own losers, especially amongst institutions dedicated to the maintenance of the integrity of national interest or to the efficiency-oriented technocratic character of the European Union. By the same and reverse token, however, the *ad hoc* daily efforts to overcome the efficiency iniquities of non-delegation principles through contingent legislative mechanisms, such as the Comitology Decision of 1986 – giving greater powers to 'expert' decision-makers within European institutional structures (Vos 1999) – trail their own deprived institutions and polities in their wake as majoritarian supranational and organic national interests potentially cede to an overriding technocratic rationale. Incremental, yet meaningful and politically contested constitutional evolution impacts constantly upon a sphere of fundamental legal protection and does so in the course of normal political decision-making. In this scenario, then, the interpretative hurdles of judicial operation are magnified as the ancient constitutional task of ensuring general protection from abusive tyranny is supplemented by the demand for novel judicial mechanics of disciplined constitutional evolution, or for 'principled constitutional morphogenesis' under normal political conditions.

The task of maintaining constitutional staticism under conditions of political dynamism is thus, at its core, one of facilitating political change whilst retaining legal integrity. Advocate General van Gerven, in his efforts to distinguish earlier ECJ case law on institutional comitology structures (see '*Comitology*' [1988])[16] in the case of *Re Radioactive food* [1990], explicitly details both the political realities of an incremental process of constitutionalism within the Union, and the difficulties that law faces in responding to it (St. Clair Bradley 1991). The natural temptation within the political process is for institutions and the interests that gather around them to seek to utilise the law to further their own positions of power; to encourage the ECJ to fill in the 'empty' shell of an evolutive European constitutionalism with judgments on substantive policy matters that cast an empowering judicial eye this way and that way amongst the winners and losers in the daily political battle for institutional dominance. As van Gerven notes, Council negotiations, prior to the Single European Act, may have approved of an increased role for the European Parliament in the governance of European states.[17] Nonetheless, they were still hostile to an expansion in the Parliament's standing under Article 230 EC (ex 173 EC). At the same time, however, they were also marked by the cold but realistic recognition amongst various national representatives that the mixture of parliamentary activism and the existence of a legal channel for its expression could not but result in the evolution of increased parliamentary powers, especially in the vital area of their practical legal assertion under Article 230 EC: [l]es institutions communautaires étaient sous l'emprise d'une constitution évolutive et qu'un jour la jurisprudence dommerait *de facto* ce droit au Parlement.[18]

By the same token, however, Advocate General van Gerven responds to political perceptions that law is an actor rather than neutral arbiter in the evolutionary constitutional process, emphasising, even as he overturns the jurisprudence, the vital effort of the ECJ within '*Comitology*' [1998] to maintain a rigid distinction between daily decision-making and politically instigated constitutional change and the commitment of European law to a static legal constitutionalism founded in the 'protective function' of European law. Though ostensibly an issue touching upon the efficiency of administrative governance within the European Union, '*Comitology*' it seems, revolved, at its core, around the matter of a parliamentary request to the Court for an 'alteration in the institutional balance in its favour':

> Had the Court accepted that proposal, it might have been interpreted as interference by the Court in the very delicate question of institutional balance as between the Community institutions endowed with legislative powers or prerogatives and thus as interference in the political decision-making process, even though the Court had previously stated (although it impliedly contradicted that in the *Comitology* case) that the judicial settlement of conflicts must be considered separately from the political means of settling them. (paragraph 5)

This, then, is the specific key to judicial difficulty. The Court is not simply called upon to adjudicate upon the constitutional meaning of explicit treaty-based alterations within the institutional balance, but is also called upon to do so within the whirl of daily political decision-making. Both '*Comitology*' and *Re Radioactive food* concerned substantive political conflict constellations: either contestation about the efficiency-based demand for administrative delegation under the Comitology Decision, or conflict on the degree of immediacy necessary within quasi-executive responses to potentially contaminated food. In the light of constant amendments to the institutional prerogatives within the treaties, however, and, in particular, the political demand for their constant judicial explication, such cases also necessarily confront the ECJ with an evolutionary constitutional role – 'who' might challenge 'what', 'when' and 'on what basis' – inherent within which there is an immediate danger that the Court will not only be intervening directly into daily politics, but will also be usurping a typically polity-driven constitutive role in the apportioning of institutional competences and political powers.

In short then, van Gerven's unusually unequivocal enunciation of the problems facing a modern ECJ confirm that Jacqué's particular, though academic, preoccupation with the maintenance of constitutional staticism is also a necessary and vital consideration within the real-world doctrine of the ECJ: the interpretative difficulties facing courts are seemingly very much multiplied within evolutionary constitutional process. Further, however, and vitally so, Advocate General van Gerven, the ECJ and the Court of First Instance's unfolding interpretation and application of the principle of institutional balance reveal that, although the incremental and evolutionary nature of European constitutionalism might be considered *sui generis*, at least to the degree that the *telos* of European integration remains 'explicitly' uncertain, certain parallels can still be drawn to seemingly traditional processes of constitutional adjudication, and, in particular, to the historical difficulties inherent to the process of adjudication between plural political forces that so haunted the judiciary of the Weimar Republic.

### *II.2. Transcendental nonsense and constitutional adjudication*

So begins van Gerven's final effort in *Re Radioactive food* to ground his finding that Parliament's prerogative had been infringed, since it had not been given sufficient practical political opportunity to offer up an opinion on the Council and Commission measures limiting the dangers of the entry of foodstuffs contaminated by radiation into the European Union:

> The distinction I have just outlined between the interpretation of the Treaty with a view to ensuring that there is an adequate and coherent system of legal protection and its interpretation in a manner, which might not interfere with the delicate political balance between the institutions, is in my view an essential one. (paragraph 6)

Once again, van Gerven is at great pains to distinguish a legal role in furnishing fundamental 'legal protection' from a political or constitutive role in determining the shape of Europe's governing institutions and its underlying polity. More explicitly:

> That distinction has important practical consequences. Whereas establishing (or re-establishing) an institutional balance between the Council, the Commission and the Parliament – *a matter which I consider is not the province of the courts* – entails giving the Parliament as full a right of action as the Council and the Commission enjoy, that is not the case if the aim is to ensure that the Parliament enjoys effective legal protection. (paragraph 6; emphasis added)

Slowly but surely, van Gerven assures his audience that it is not the provenance of the ECJ to usurp what would be an overtly constitutive role, or, indeed, a practical political function, in furnishing the European Parliament with the same status within the institutional balance as that enjoyed by the Commission or the Council. The aim of the Court is not to shape the European polity, nor is it to dictate the shape of day-to-day policy-making. Instead, allowing the Parliament to challenge activities of the Council and the Commission is merely a matter of facilitating the Parliament's assertion of its 'rights' and 'prerogatives' within European law. In legal doctrinal terms, the adjudicational operation is one carried out wholly within the legal internal logic of *effet utile*:

> [I]t is because the Parliament must be permitted to bring actions in order to defend its rights, powers and prerogatives adequately itself, in the same way as other persons or institutions. (paragraph 9)

'To every right, a remedy': with this fundamental tenet of juridical dogma, this particular representative of the European legal system at once gives material form to a potentially wholly inchoate notion of legal protection, and signals to a political polity that its constitutive powers will never be alienated by virtue of judicial embroilment within the day-to-day political posturing of institutional interests.

The subordination of the scope of the notion of 'fundamental legal protection' to the logic of *effet utile* is one subsequently approved of by the European judiciary. Logically speaking, however, the vital goal underlying the notion of a separation of powers – that of protection for the individual from abusive power – might be used to extend the doctrine *ad nauseam*, emptying it of its meaning and leaving *all* exercises of power subject to constant challenge from individuals who fear that their rights might have been infringed. If the purpose of a separation or a balance of powers is to protect the individual (or the individual institution), then surely all individuals (and all individual institutions) should be free to challenge all acts of governance that have arguably been undertaken to the prejudice of the balance of powers?

'No', intone both the ECJ and the Court of First Instance: the balance of powers principle does not embody a '*Rechtsgut*', or a legal value 'in its own right', the possible infringement of which would give any party the right to challenge the exercise of power in the 'general interest', or in the 'common good':

> It follows from the Court's case law that the seriousness of the alleged infringement [of the institutional balance] by the institution concerned or the extent of its adverse impact on the observance of fundamental rights cannot justify an exception to the absolute bars to proceedings laid down by the Treaty. Thus, an alleged infringement of the institutional balance cannot give rise to an exception to the admissibility rules governing actions for annulment laid down by the Treaty.[19]

A judicial viewpoint that is again reiterated:

> [A]lthough ... the Court of Justice stated emphatically in its judgment in Case 9/56 *Meroni* v *High Authority*, that the balance of powers that characterises the institutional structure of the Community constitutes a fundamental guarantee granted by the Treaty ... that statement cannot be interpreted as providing a remedy for any natural or legal person who considers that an act of a Community institution has been adopted in breach of the principle of institutional balance, regardless of whether the act in question is of direct and individual concern to that person.[20]

Emphatically, the reasoning is one of a rejection of constitutional pluralism; a refusal to equate the general legal protection of the individual furnished by the balance of powers with a comprehensive individual right – given practical shape by an expansion in individual and parliamentary rights of standing under Article 230 EC Treaty – with a comprehensive right for individuals, groups or institutions to challenge the due legislative process.

Equally, and by the same token, Europe's senior lawyers explicitly resist the temptation to themselves engage in the nomination of the plural political parties that drive the process of European integration, and appear to continue to found their jurisprudential treatment of the principle of the balance of powers within the literal faithfulness of jurisprudential interpretation. Thus, as Advocate General Geelhoed, setting aside his own preferred political preferences in favour of the strict formal application of the original meaning of the balance of powers as laid down in *Meroni*, most recently declared:

> However much it is to be regretted, from the point of view of democratic legitimacy, that the third indent of Article 202 EC has not yet been amended, those drafting the Treaty clearly chose to give the Parliament merely a modest role in establishing the requirements for the delegation of implementing powers to the Commission.[21]

With this firm statement, again made within the interminable comitology jurisprudence, and rejecting a reading of the institutional balance that would give the European Parliament a higher profile within committee proceedings, Jacqué's desire for constitutional staticism would seem to have been satisfied. All democratic temptation apart, and under the most complex of constitutional and political circumstances, the European Judiciary would seem to have avoided the pitfalls that the 1964 *Rheinland-Pfalz* Finance Court identified as having overcome its Weimar counterparts. The strict confinement of the principle of the balance of powers within the legal internal logic of *effet utile*, together with a literal formal reading of the apportionment of powers within the treaties maintains the rule of law in the troublesome face of the dynamic assault of politics.

And yet, Jacqué himself signals his alarm that the ECJ is failing to maintain staticism. Tellingly, the *critique* is one that both Courts, the ECJ and the Court of First Instance, have moved beyond their original protection logic to include the protection of 'fundamental rights' within the mechanics of their *effet utile* interpretation (Jacqué 2004: 384). Largely derived from Jacqué's disapproval of recent Court of First Instance jurisprudence (see below III.2), this *critique* nevertheless has a critical, if unintentional, importance, as it finally unveils and unravels the law-internal logic of *effet utile* to reveal European Law's entrapment within the selfsame paradigms of plural legal interventionism that challenged the *Freirechtsschule*.

Certainly, some form of formalist effort can be made to distinguish between rights that are coeval with institutional competences, as detailed within the treaties, and fundamental rights that educe from a more general canon of constitutional principle: in this light, for example, one might distinguish Geelhoed's reluctance to translate generally enunciated (in the treaties) parliamentary co-decision competences into a specific right under the institutional balance in order to challenge concrete Comitology proceedings from recent and revelatory Court of First Instance jurisprudence, which has endowed the 'region' of the Azores with a right to challenge Council regulations on the basis that regional legislative competences might otherwise be unlawfully alienated (*Azores* [2004]).[22] It might thus be argued that, whilst the former case correctly and literally interpreted the concrete provisions of the Treaty in semantic fact (Article 202 EC), the latter unduly imports into the Community legal order a general principle of legal protection under which the possession of lawful legislative competences of whatever character (supra-national, national and, now, sub-national) is coeval with a right to defend these competences within the scheme of the balance of powers.

Ultimately, however, this distinction misses the point: the legal dictum of 'no right without a remedy' may *also* be a neutral self-referential operation of legal application, but, at its core, it is still formed by an act of legal interpretation of the texts, practices and norms pertaining within a non-legal world. The interpretation of the breadth and effects of Article 202 (AG Geelhoed) and the use of fundamental principles to identify a regional right to representation within the institutional balance (*Azores*) are one and the same operation of translating fact into norm. No single treaty provision is determinate in meaning, but must also be interpreted in the light of prevailing social reality and more 'general' principles of law. If executed solely in the language of formal legal operation, *effet utile* is quite simply stated, an act of 'transcendental nonsense' (Cohen 1935): the granting of a remedy is coincidental and coeval with the identification of a competence, not in real-world practice and social interaction, but rather within an ethereal world of formal legal application; it is a simple spiritual emanation educing from the phrase 'no remedy without a right'.[23]

With this, then, we are offered an explanation for the very many (speaking in essentialist terms) inconsistencies in the jurisprudence of both the ECJ and the Court of First Instance on the institutional balance. We are also, however, offered a stern reminder that, under conditions of constitutional and political dynamism, European Law cannot simply rest upon its formalist laurels or wholly hide behind a formalist veil in its efforts to maintain constitutional or legal integrity:

> [i]n a community of law, it must be possible for anyone with the capacity to perform legal acts to assert their individual right, powers and prerogatives themselves, as and when they see fit, before the courts. That appears to me to be a general principle of law, that is to say, the expression of the fundamental right to legal protection ... .which extends ... to public authorities and institutions provided that the institutional framework allows, as it does in the European Community, conflicts regarding the distribution of powers between the institutions to be brought before the courts. (*Re Radioactive food*, paragraph 12)

Reading the text closely, the tautology is at once apparent. Advocate General van Gerven thus indulges himself in act of transcendental nonsense as, the lack of parliamentary standing under Article 230 EC (ex 173 EC) apart, Parliament's remedy for infringement of its co-decisional competence is simply deemed coeval with the existence of that competence – itself a ghostly presence invoked into being only by the language of the Advocate General. Transcendence is equally only intensified as the Court concurs with its Advocate General, allowing parliamentary standing, the 'procedural gap' in the Treaty notwithstanding, since 'it cannot prevail over the fundamental interest in the maintenance and observance of the institutional balance laid down in the Treaties [sic] (paragraph 26)'. Instead, the judgment, and European jurisprudential evolution as a whole, is only given material meaning if it is considered in the light of accompanying jurisprudence (*Re the Budget* [1986]) in which the Court itself steps outside self-referential legal logic to found parliamentary competence in the fact– norm translating and transfiguring principle that:

> The effective participation of the Parliament in the legislative process of the Community ... represents an essential factor in the institutional balance intended by the Treaty. Such power reflects the fundamental democratic impulse that the people should take part in the exercise of power through the intermediary of a representative assembly.

The judgment is lent corporeal, rather than transcendental, character by virtue of a process of norm–fact translation that has seen increasing social demands for majoritarian expression within the European Union translated and transfigured into the fundamental principles of EU law. It is this, together with other processes of fact–norm translation, that explains the readiness and willingness of Advocate Generals, such as Tesauro, curtly to dismiss Council fears that juridical expansion in the practical ability of Parliament to assert its competence entails 'alteration in the institutional balance outside the procedures and forms laid down for in the revision of the "constitutional charter"' (paragraph 20).[24] Likewise, within the realm of individual rights under the institutional balance, it is this fact–norm translation process that feeds progressive and controversial Court of First Instance jurisprudence in cases such as the *Azores*. It is also this process, however, that leaves us with various questions.

The judicial *act* of fact–norm translation is necessarily dynamic. Whilst van Gerven is one of the most open of Advocate General's, at least as regards the political conflicts lurking behind European law, the title of the most realistic must surely fall to Advocate General Mancini and, in particular, his recognition that, not only is the institutional balance 'provisional', but that, as a consequence, law must in some way be safeguarded from embroilment in political conflict (*Re the Budget*, paragraph 19). In his analysis, this is a matter of keeping the conflict out of the Courts altogether via political mechanisms such as inter-institutional agreements. Within the analysis pursued by this study, however, this is, instead, a process of identifying the real mechanics of constitutional morphogenesis that lurk behind the formalist veils of legal reasoning and that offer us the best chance of re-establishing the real-world constitutional legitimacy of constitutional staticism under conditions of political and constitutional dynamism.

In intermediary conclusion, the European legal system is confronted by exactly the same difficulties faced by the jurisprudence of the Weimar period. The European polity is dynamic and plural with its own inherent hazard of a politically compromised and politically compromising judiciary. The transcendental nonsense of *effet utile* is not the magic wand that will ensure legal integrity. Instead, law must itself step beyond self-referential operation to take a more realistic and reflexive attitude to both its position and its impact within a real world. In addition, law must develop the principled mechanics of constitutional morphogenesis that ensure the static, or enduring, *social legitimacy* of legal processes of fact–norm translation.

## III. Polity-building within the institutional balance: conflicts and consequences

The first and primary step in the identification of a principled mechanics of constitutional morphogenesis must, however, be a return to normative first principles. Certainly, the political and social forces that currently hover around what is revealed to be a forever-empty shell, awaiting constitutional meaning, are engaged in a political and social *praxis* that might and can be viewed in isolation from a normative world. Political and social forces necessarily and continuously jockey for political power. Nonetheless, the rhetoric of constitutional possession also readily reveals the fact that norm and reality are intimately associated with one another, as power positions under the institutional balance are weighed and claims to increased representation are staked in rhetorical tropes that emphasise normative visions of what the governance scheme of the European Union as a whole 'should' be.

Thus, in addition to Parliament's oft-enunciated and judicially approved claim that its prerogatives under the institutional balance must be maintained in order to safeguard 'the fundamental democratic impulse that the people should take part in the exercise of power,'[25] we sometimes find individual applicants arguing for standing under Article 230 EC (ex 230 EC), on the more individualistic basis of the *Schutznormtheorie* of Article 34 of the German Constitution, or the notion that individual liberty within a modern society must be secured by the granting of comprehensive standing in instances of flagrant abuse of governmental powers.[26] Equally, individualistic rhetoric on the purpose of the institutional balance can also be contrasted with a more communitarian attitude on the part of member states, who consistently argue that the balance must be dedicated to the defence of residual, but polity-consolidating, national sovereignty in areas of shared competence.[27] By the same token, however, the language of constitutional possession can and does also eschew all individualistic or communitarian notions of governance, to express itself in proceduralist normative terms, as (and, as we shall see below, crucially so) senior European lawyers resist greater enhancement of the European Court's position under the institutional balance, since this would 'constitute a policy of judge-made law in conflict with the constitutional logic of the Treaty'.[28]

The lesson to be learned is that public, private, national and supranational, social and political forces do not simply engage opportunistically with the vital question underlying the institutional balance: 'in the interest of whom and for what purpose is power to be balanced?' Instead, *praxis* finds reference points within existing normative notions of governance or of the legitimate polity, and seeks to read the institutional balance in their explanatory light. The lesson, however, is likewise not a simple one. Normative governance visions vary, and with this, the *sui generis* characterisation of European law again finds its limits as European jurisprudence is drawn into the selfsame process of adjudication between competing normative visions and political/social positions, which is so typical of the traditional constitutional jurisdiction.

The point is again well made by Ackerman (2000): the notion of the separation of powers is no normative monolith, but is, instead, a concept that entails a multitude of normative meanings that correspond with different and distinct positions within a real-world of social and political *praxis*. Similarly, the notion of the balance of powers is contested, not simply by virtue of political and social posturing, but also with regard to the underlying range of substantive governance visions and visions of the legitimate polity that the principle conceptually encompasses. Conflict on the nature of the institutional balance is certainly made politically and socially explicit by virtue of the uncertain *telos* of European integration. Such conflict, however, also reproduces the traditional substantive normative indeterminacy underlying all notions of constitutional settlement.

### *III.1. The separation of powers versus the balance of powers*

The apparently monolithic notion of 'legal protection' that dominates European jurisprudence on the institutional balance of powers is not set in normative stone. The truth of this statement and the key to one of the primary normative conflicts that the ambit of the institutional balance principle encompasses was revealed very early on in the process of European integration and more specifically, by the 1964 *Rheinland Pfalz* Court's reluctance to allow executive transferral of legislative powers to the EEC under the, then, Article 24 of the German Constitution.

Speaking to its own Constitution rather than to the EEC legal order as a whole, the Court nonetheless gave immediate and vivid life to a systemic problem that was always present within the national conception of a separation of powers, and was exponentially magnified within a supranational balance of powers deriving its constitutive legitimacy from national orders. Though his analysis of the European Union is flawed in the terms of this analysis, Stein clearly enunciates the enduring and underlying difficulty: democracy and internationalisation are uncomfortable bedfellows (2001). As the *Rheinland Pfalz* Court first intimated, and the German Constitutional Court forcefully underlined in its highly influential 1994 *Brunner* judgment, internationalisation or supranationalisation impacts negatively upon the national separation of powers. More particularly, the historic tension between the sovereign polity's integral or self-constituting competence to comprehensive legislative self-expression, and that same polity's interest in the efficient exercise of executive functions, is only magnified as the functional supranational interest in the practical political effectiveness of pooled national sovereignty appears to stand in an incommensurate relationship with sovereign democratic expression within the nation state.

Most often expressed in terms of the 'supremacy' conundrum,[29] and indeed also approached as such within this volume (Chapter 2), the clash between national and European constitutional jurisdictions can, nonetheless, also be recast in terms of an essential conflict between 'democratically inspired' notions of a separation of powers and the more functionally oriented concept of a balance of power.[30] The *Rheinland-Pfalz* Court was primarily concerned with the alienation of national legislative competences by a national executive: the ultimate recipient of such competences, the European legal order, was a stranger both to the German legal order, and, more importantly, to its underlying constitutional logic of the balancing of legislative and executive powers. By this same token, the substantive functional legitimacy inherent within the institutional balance of powers could never be considered as an ameliorating factor within the jurisprudence of the German Court on its own Constitution: what price supranational governmental efficiency if national democratic primacy is lost? In the efficiency-pursuing reverse scenario, that of the European legal order's functional legitimacy (Haas 1964; Ipsen 1972), the latter's formal delineation of member state and institutional competences into distinct operational areas[31] also could not pay due regard (if, indeed, any regard at all) to national concerns about the maintenance of democratic legitimacy: the logic of democracy was foreign to a functional European legal order. In short, the European balance of powers stood in a tense and uncomprehending relationship with a national separation of powers logic (Everson 1998a).

The story of the on-going tension between the national separation of powers and the supranational balance of powers is a tortuous one, which has often been told and retold, albeit mostly in the explicit terms of a sovereignty and supremacy debate (MacCormick 1995). In the terms of this analysis, however, it bears repeating, at least to the limited degree that the conflict and contradiction between national and European jurisdictions has reproduced itself within debates on the legitimate shape of an evolving European polity, and has seen the functional logic underlying the European balance of powers increasingly colonised by a separation of powers philosophy educed from normative visions of the primacy of democratic process. German Courts were once again pivotal within this colonisation process, and none more so than the Constitutional Court in *Brunner*.

Returning to this judgment with a slightly different emphasis, the issue faced by this Court can accordingly be stripped down to a further series of bare essentials: seen in this light, the core question tackled by the Court – one of whether the Treaty of European Union, and, more particularly, its provisions on monetary union, was compatible with Article 79(3) of the German

Constitution – was therefore one that hinged upon the legitimacy of a transfer by the executive under the then Article 24 of the German Constitution of national powers that were argued to be reserved to the German legislature. Though neatly sidestepping the political controversy that a negative answer to this question might produce at European level by, first, simply fudging the (insoluble) matter of the establishment of national democratic legitimation for the European exercise of a monetary competence,[32] and, second, restricting its own *Schutznormtheorie*,[33] the Court nonetheless chose to use it *obiter dicta* to send various clear political-constitutional messages to both the European constitutional jurisdiction and the evolving European polity. Amongst other things, the Justices concluded that an increasing transferral of national legislative competences to supranational level, though necessarily constrained at the time of the judgment by the integral and indispensable national interest in popular sovereignty, might be conceivable in the future, at least to the degree that the European order establishes modes of democratic legitimation of its own. The core paragraph within the judgment bears repeating:

> At the same time, with the building up of the functions and powers of the Community, it becomes increasingly necessary to allow the democratic legitimation and influence provided by way of the national parliaments to be accompanied by a representation of the peoples of the member states through a European Parliament as the source of a supplementary democratic support for the policies of the European Union. With the establishment of union citizenship by the Maastricht Treaty, a legal bond is formed between the nationals of the individual member states, which is intended to be lasting and which, although it does not have a tightness comparable to the common nationality of a single state, provides a legally binding expression of the degree of *de facto* community already in existence ... . The influence flowing from the citizens of the Union can eventually become a part of the democratic legitimation of the European institutions to the extent that the conditions necessary for this purpose are fulfilled by the peoples of Europe. (paragraph 40)

The argument pursued and the signal sent by the German Court to the European governance order is pivotal. At one level, the question addressed by the Court was an insoluble one. Simply stated: if the German Constitutional Court's assertion that the member states are the 'Masters of the Treaty' is correct, and the European Union's sovereignty is second order in nature, educing not from its own treaty sources, but flowing from national sovereignty, then any alienation of sovereignty securing national legislative competence remains an impossibility in each and every logical (liberal) analysis. In common with the individual, the sovereign national collective cannot contract away its operational autonomy: to do so is to make a slave of the individual and a tyrant of the contractual master, to make an empty shell of the national collectivity and to denude Europe's second order sovereignty of its constituent parts.[34] However, all argumentative indicators to the contrary,[35] and all unfortunate references to pre-political conditions for democratic discourse notwithstanding (Chapter 2 (IV.2)), the Court itself began to evolve various modes of escape from the sovereignty dilemma, including, among other things,[36] the implicit recasting of the sovereignty problem within the idiom of an overarching 'European' separation of powers logic (Everson 1998a),[37] with its concomitant increased role for direct democratic participation on the part of the peoples of Europe, at European, rather than national, level.

An assault upon all functional perceptions of institutional balance, as well as upon the European Council's primary legislative/representative role, the gradual augmentation of a representative (European) parliamentary competence has not only found repeated favour with the ECJ, but has also seen the balance of powers increasingly subject to the underlying logic of the separation of powers, at least to the degree that such a logic privileges the 'democratic' exercise of governance competences. Indeed, the colonisation of a European balance of powers by a separation of powers logic has now reached an apogee within a draft European constitutional treaty which – notwithstanding the European Convention's somewhat inexplicable lack of explicit consideration of the principles of the balance or separation of powers[38] – has implicitly challenged its own (diffuse) restatement of the functionally flavoured principle of institutional balance (Articles I-11(2), I-12(6) and I-45 proposed constitutional treaty, replacing Article 4 EC Treaty) through its reinforced emphasis upon the place of direct (even majoritarian[39]) democratic process within the workings of the newly re-constituted European Union (Articles I-45 to I-47).

### *III.2. Conflict, contradiction and the separation of powers*

The incremental expansion in parliamentary competences (largely in the sphere of co-decisional powers), together with the arguably schizophrenic dedication of a proposed European constitution to a functional division of competences, as well as to core democratic principles, is a key indicator of the underlying tension between various existing substantive normative visions of legitimate governance within Europe. Furthermore, the corollary role played by the ECJ and Court of First Instance in giving shape to one or other of such visions within its institutional balance jurisprudence is thus also unveiled in all its underlying material character: the name of the game of the assertion of institutional competence or individual right is not one of establishing and re-establishing *pareto* efficiency, but is instead one which entails seismic shifts in the substantive construction of the European polity, as well as the creation of the winners and losers in the political battle for the legitimate soul of the European Union.

The unusual juxtaposition of a separation of powers logic with the principle of institutional balance within the evolutive constitutionalism of the European Union thus entails a dual tension. First (just as it seeks to dissolve it[40]), it establishes an inherent contradiction between an organic member state interest in the maintenance of (legislatively expressed) national sovereignty on the one hand, and the evolution of a directly self-determining European *demos* on the other. Second, it pitches an efficiency-oriented vision of a technocratically flavoured European polity against a constitutionalising *telos* that rejects simple output legitimacy in favour of abstract principles of democratic organisation. Certainly, in the juridical European mind, individual decisions on the immediate application of the principle of the balance of powers may represent a procedural formalist operation within a constraining *effet utile* logic; at a deeper normative level, however, such decisions also have substantive consequences as they influence and mould conflict between governance and legitimate polity models, this way and that, as occasion dictates.

Equally, however, such conflict and contradiction is not limited to tension between the separation and the balance of powers. Instead, even as the European Union begins to strengthen its own separation of powers logic, it is also drawn into the traditional sophistry of historical constitutional debate. More particularly, as Ackerman demonstrates, Montesquieu's apparently monolithic separation of powers itself dissolves into a torrid series of antagonisms as its triadic structure provokes innate tensions between demands for collective legislative expression, executive professionalism or 'efficiency', and an individualistic, rights-based mode of promoting personal autonomy (Ackerman 2000). Further, casuistry is only intensified as the normative interest in democratic expression also splinters into majoritarian and dualist positions, favouring either unitary legislative self-expression, or federalist and/or functionalist divisions within the legislative competence.

The primary key to the triadic tension within a polity governed by the separation of powers is one already addressed by this analysis: Montesquieu's goal of legal protection for the individual may mean many different things to many different men. In the legal mind, it might simply be commensurate with the formal literal application of a fixed map of government powers. In the more politically philosophically attuned mind, however, the same formula converts into justification for the maintenance of particular polities. In the words of the eighteenth-century English jurist Blackstone, for example – the author upon whom Montesquieu founded his historical authority – the separation of powers, and the notion of legal protection might be used to legitimise England's 'mixed constitution', as well as the asymmetric class distinctions which it solidified and perpetuated (Kennedy 1979), in the following rhetorical terms:

> [T]he absolute rights of every Englishman (which taken in a political and extensive sense, are usually called their liberties) as they are founded on

> nature and reason, so they are coeval with our form of government (Katz and Blackstone 1979: 123).

The reference to 'nature', if not 'reason', is disingenuous: the vital argumentative turn is instead provided by the notion that the existing governance scheme within England, with its division of legislative competence between the three regal, aristocratic and plebeian estates, will furnish the wise, restrained and limited government which is, in Blackstone's philosophic purview, the best guarantee of individual liberty. In a similar vein, then, though without eighteenth-century polemics and with more direct consideration of the advantages and disadvantages of particular governance models, we find the corresponding majoritarian, dualist or, indeed, functionalist positions which extol the relative merits of majoritarianism or, alternatively, the 'mixed' constitution, in their rhetorical effort to identify the form of European governance that will be 'coeval with the liberty and rights of individual European citizens'.

On the one hand, it is thus argued that an interpretation of the European 'separation' of powers[41] in support of a greater parliamentary competence will not only allow 'stronger political leadership' and a 'more intense democratic scrutiny', but is also necessitated since the evolution of a unitary European *demos* 'is inextricably linked to the scope of the political ambitions that the European Union has assumed' (Maduro 2003: 3)[42] In stark contrast, however, other authors tend to a democratic dualism, continuing to underline the importance of member states within the institutional balance (Mancini 1998; Weiler 1998), or even slipping into a preference for executive-led governance (Majone 1998), extolling the virtues of the distribution of 'democratic' competences amongst multiple power *loci*, not only (in a very distant echo of Blackstone) in the service of the power-diluting preservation of individual liberty, but also in pursuit of the efficiency and credibility securing values of technocratic governance (Majone 1998).[43]

These are clearly arguments that both reproduce and extend the historical philosophical interchange between Hamilton and Madison on the relative merits of state versus federal governance: the contention between majoritarian and dualist visions of democratic governance, however, is no longer just confined to arguments about whether majoritarian expression is potentially destructive, rather than expressive, of personal autonomy; but has been somewhat extended to include newer dualist positions that maintain that efficiency and credibility – in short, 'standards' within government – are equally an expression of democratic as well as administrative concerns, since democracy is also all about 'effective' political action.[44] Vitally, however, they are also arguments that have found equal measures of expression or non-expression, and approval or disapproval, within the *praxis* of European governance and within the jurisprudence of the ECJ.

From inter-institutional agreements increasing parliamentary co-decisional powers, to the continued national efforts to retain integral national competences,[45] to the *ad hoc* Commission efforts to defeat the EC Treaty's non-delegation principle by careful and paced evolution of new regulatory institutions, such as agencies or committees,[46] the European polity is multi-headed in its *praxis*, simultaneously displaying a wide range of dualist, majoritarian and/or technocratic features. By the same token, ECJ jurisprudence approving and disapproving of majoritarian, dualist and/or technocratic tendencies within European governance,[47] in its turn, confirms the hydra-like character of the EU polity, the material substance of the balance of powers being turned this way and that as varied governance visions convince or fail to convince in both real and normative worlds.

However, this initial tension within the separation triad between majoritarian, dualist and efficiency-oriented perceptions of democracy and executive governance is also (importantly) heightened and added to in contemporary powers separation models, which, rejecting of Blackstone's somewhat crude evocation of the co-determinacy of liberty and existing governance schemes, place a far greater emphasis upon the notion of positive individual rights within the triadic structure. In analyses such as the *Schutznormtheorie*, the logic is not that a broad 'scheme of government' can be entrusted with the task of safeguarding individual or minority interests, but is instead the reverse, that the separation of powers must be actively directed at the protection of both individuals and minorities from the scheme of governance (or state). This modern reading of the rationale and purposes of a separation of powers is one that also has its supporters within the European Union (Maduro 2003). More importantly, however, it is one that has also seemingly found an increasing measure of support amongst a European judiciary, particularly within the Court of First Instance.

In an expression of one of the more fundamental shifts in the substantive EU governance scheme, the Court of First Instance has thus tempered a long line of ECJ case law which greatly restricted individual and group rights to challenge EU and Community action under Article 230 EC (ex 173 EC).[48] Derived from an original reading of the institutional balance principle, which emphasised the primacy of the right of EU institutions to safeguard their competences, ECJ jurisprudence has thus severely restricted individual rights to challenge Community acts with the justification that this would otherwise entail an unacceptable restriction upon legislative and executive[49] discretion. Nonetheless, as the European polity has developed, arguments that individuals should also be protected from the undue exercise of EU powers have grown in strength, and, although the Court of First Instance has joined with the ECJ in rejecting the full implications of the application of a *Schutznormtheorie* within the European constitutional framework (*Phillip Morris Inc* [2003]), the new millennium also heralded a (moderate) judicial revolution as the cases of *Alpharma* [2002] and *Pfizer* [2002] witnessed a widening of individual standing before the Court, at least as regards the ability of individual Europeans to defend themselves against the executive actions of the European Union (Ward 2005).[50]

In a certain sense, a reflection of and a reaction to an alteration within a European separation of powers which has seen functions increasingly undertaken by the executive in line with dualist/functionalist visions of the legitimate polity (see above), such jurisprudence is not, however, simply a matter of civilising technocratic governance. Instead, if read together with the *Azores* case, which allowed a(n) (sub-national) autonomous region to assert its rights under the European balance of powers, the constitutional pluralism inherent within recent Court of First Instance case law is, perhaps, the clearest indicator to date of how the European judiciary can and does take a hand in the fashioning of the material nature of an emerging European polity: to whit individual European citizens are increasingly being given (political) voice at EU level.

### *III.3. The political, administrative and constitutional functions of the institutional balance*

With this final point, it is, perhaps, useful to recall here that the principle of the separation of powers is not the only concept to suffer the pangs of triadic tension. Instead, as successive Advocates General have informed us, the principle of the institutional balance of powers can also be viewed as a contiguous political and constitutional notion,[51] as well as serving certain contemporaneous administrative purposes.[52] The constitutional pluralism inherent in a vision of a European polity which accepts the rights of a sub-national political collective to assert its presence within the supranational institutional balance, thus not only entails a vivid challenge to unitary notions of the constitutional polity (or *demos*), but also provokes simultaneous, though distinct, political conflict with visions of a European polity that place their regulative faith either in the majoritarian expressions of a representative European Parliament, or in the political balance maintained between the Union and its constituent states (rather than their sub-national units!).

In addition, however, the political and constitutional character of the institutional balance can also stand in a tense relationship with its administrative manifestation, at least to the degree that the efficiency-oriented character of an original, and sovereignty pooling, functional vision of institutional balance still lives on within the technocratic-administrative arm of the European Union. The functional division of competences between the institutions and the member states of the Union was once attuned to output legitimacy goals, largely in line with the technocratic vision. Constitutional and political pluralism, by contrast, not only appear to entail a huge potential for inefficiency within governance, but also seem to underline the dramatic shift to input legitimacy within the Union; a shift that is undermining the notion of functional efficiency-oriented competences as a whole.

### *III.4. The separation of powers versus the balance of powers versus the rule of law*

Finally, it must be asked whether these are the only tensions that European law must confront in its 'static' application of the principle of institutional balance under conditions of constitutional and political dynamism. Briefly recalling the opening argument, the mechanics of 'principled' constitutional morphogenesis demand that European Courts identify and apply legal internal principles, which are regulative and structuring of their own processes of fact–norm translation, and which will enable them to navigate the various political and social interests and substantive normative governance visions that cluster around the principle of institutional balance without fear of political prejudice. The foregoing analysis readily demonstrates that isolated acts of jurisprudential interpretation and the application of the principle of institutional balance can and, indeed, do impact strongly upon the emerging shape of the European polity, as the inherent contradictions and tensions between the principles of the institutional balance and the separation of powers, as well as between the individual triadic elements that go to make up each separation or balancing of power, necessarily embroil European Courts in the material choice of which form of polity, or, indeed, form of political process, is legitimate and when.

In addition, however, European jurisprudence is also bedevilled by a further tension within substantive normative discourse: one that is best summed up in relation to the underlying tension between the 'rule of law' and the separation and balance of powers principles. To date, this analysis has dealt with the protective function inherent within a rule of law only in its most general terms: legal certainty is maintained, and tyrannical abuse of power is guarded against by 'conservatory' acts of literal treaty interpretation. The conservatory nature of the rule of law, however, also appears in one further and distinct guise, which, at least when read in Weberian terms, might be argued to stand in a tense relationship with various normative elements that are to be found within both the principle of a separation of power and the principle of the balance of powers.

In other words, the analysis is returned full circle to the formal-legal paradox. Accordingly, we must also take care within this constitutional analysis never to forget that the primary building block within the process of European integration was, and indeed remains, the establishment of an internal market. Weber's 'formalistic' (essentialist) conception of the rule of law, it should thus be noted, was not only developed with regard to historic western European economic evolution, but was also always contrasted with (and portrayed as an uncomfortable spouse to) a western process of 'substantive' law-making educed from political and social emancipation (Weber 1967). In other words, modern constitutional states and, indeed, also supranational entities, with their notions of legislative and political self-expression, are always caught on the horns of a practical-normative dilemma: the western modern state and modern supranational entity were both born within the wealth secured by a liberal market economy – a market that was itself created and protected by a formal and non-political law that ensured the autonomy and certainty of market operations. In time, the demand for substantive democratic correction for formal market inequalities was inevitably to challenge such autonomy; but, in Weber's analysis, it could never and, indeed, should never be allowed fully to dictate market operations (and formal market law), thus undermining the wealth upon which the state or the European Union was founded (Everson 2004).

Alternatively, legislative intervention founded within majoritarian conceptions of the separation of power principle or the principle of the balance of powers should never be allowed, in their materialisation guise, to undermine the formal rationality of law. Triadic tension is, accordingly, manifold. Not only is there underlying substantive normative tension between a separation of powers logic and the principle of institutional balance, but tension also exists between the individual normative elements that go to make up both principles. Equally, the rule of law, if founded within notions of formal rationality, also stands in a tense relationship with majoritarian elements within both principles.

## IV. Conclusion: *invitatio ad offerendum* and the principled mechanics of constitutional morphogenesis

This study has encountered many different substantive views of what the current EU institutional balance entails. Thus, in various analyses, it continues to be seen as a vital fulcrum between the member states and the Union, which preserves the vital cores of both supranational *and* national interests, even as it regulates the exercise of joint and divisible competences (Joerges and Neyer 1997; Dashwood 1998). Other conceptions of institutional balance, however, also exist. For example, the neo-functionalist position, which emphasised the efficiency gains that the pooling of national sovereignty would entail, finds its echo in newer technocratic positions which not only promote effective governance, but also identify a normative character within 'effective' governance: governance, however democratic, must also be able to achieve its aims (Majone 1998). Equally, however, the current institutional balance is also beginning to show signs of development into a rights-based mechanism, increasingly being fashioned with a view to the protection of the individual European from the abusive exercise of Union power. The institutional balance, it seems, is a highly heterogeneous notion.

In addition, this chapter has also unveiled many potential and deep-seated normative ideals, into whose service the institutional balance might be pressed in future phases of European integration. Inherent triadic tension, not only between the notions of a separation of power and the concepts of the balance of power and the rule of law, but also within the notions of the balancing and the separation of powers themselves, sharpens and mirrors conflict between competing visions of the legitimate shape of the European polity and of the nature of European political process. In this regard, the social and political interests that cluster around the institutional balance are seeking to persuade the European courts to pursue a variety of polity-building aims in its jurisprudence on its application: majoritarianism, dualism, increasing technocratic efficiency, or an augmentation in rights-based individual protection. The *telos* of European integration is wholly uncertain. Only one fact is constant: the transcendental nonsense of *effet utile* logic is an insufficient basis upon which to base the integrity and enduring legitimacy of European case law on the institutional balance and the evolution of European constitutionalism. Instead, the vital task for law is now to identify the principled mechanics of constitutional morphogenesis.

But how? This study has surely offered few pointers on the evolution of a coherent and consistent *Rechtsverfassungsrecht*. Instead, it seems to have dismissed all procedural judicial endeavours to ensure constitutional consistency as a formalist veil which masks a substantive judicial role in the constituting of the European polity (however unintentional or unwanted that role might be). And indeed, its final message is one that affirms that the principled mechanics of constitutional mechanics cannot be found in pure legal analysis: that way transcendental nonsense lies. However, although extra-legal investigations are now needed to identify the factual processes that underlie fact–norm translation and the mechanics of constitutional morphogenesis, this limited abstract study, and in particular, the jurisprudence of European Courts, does contain some 'normative' reference points that might aid the systematic evolution of *Rechtsverfassungsrecht*.

Firstly, the European judiciary is adamant that it must not stray into politics or usurp the polity's constitutive role: 'judge-made law' would be in 'conflict with the constitutional logic of the Treaty'.[53] *Rechtsverfassungsrecht* is a primarily procedural, rather than a substantive, law, which legitimises itself just as it distances itself from acts and operations within a real-world. Second, however, European law, in its widest national and European ambit, is explicitly aware that the constitutive role lies with the European people. Once again, the *Brunner* Court demonstrates its genius: expansion within the direct democratic legitimation of the European Union will occur 'to the extent that the conditions necessary for this purpose are fulfilled by the peoples of Europe'. Without doubt, the German Court launches a dual 'offer to treat' and to change the contractual bases of German and European constitutionalism, to both the ECJ and to the peoples of Europe; however, this *invitatio ad offerendum* must be met by all other parties to the European constitutional contract through a clear expression of an operational reality entailing a will to engage in democratic participation. The message is clear and is reiterated by Mancini in his reliance upon the existence of (extra-legal) institutional agreements in order to found increasing parliamentary competences within European law (Mancini 1998; Weiler 1998). Politics and constitutional change occur in a real-world outside the legal internal logic of constitutional adjudication; nonetheless, courts and lawyers are always watching a real-world for signs of what facts and substantive normative visions they must include within their legal interpretative processes.

Finally, however, what of the principles of fact–norm translation? What are the exact mechanics that legitimise the recognition of extra-legal change by law? Again, whilst other non-legal methodologies will be needed in order to attempt to answer this question, the existing jurisprudence does give us some idea of where to look. In this regard, recent Court of First Instance jurisprudence, increasing the rights of individual Europeans and groups of Europeans to challenge and test EU governance, can also be cast in a less individualistic light. At least to the degree that such jurisprudence gives voice to interests excluded from the European political process, might it be that the principles of a mechanics of constitutional morphogenesis lie in Europe's ability to structure and to civilise European politics and politically constitutive action?

## Notes

1 A formal legal analysis subsequently confirmed within a sociological perspective of political-legal 'muddling' (Joerges and Neyer 1997).
2 The distinction made between 'real' and 'formal' powers is vital: certainly, for example, national parliaments might have gained a power to restrain substantive Union policy-making through their legislative powers of recall (Article 6 of the proposed constitutional treaty); the real-world impact of such a provision may nonetheless have been somewhat insubstantial given the difficulties of coordination between such a disparate set of institutions (Pinder and Bruton 1999); for details of manoeuvring in the Convention, see Shaw, Magnette, Hoffman and Verges Bausili (2003).
3 In the character of the new EU foreign minister; or, more particularly, in the character of his secretariat – will it be dominated by Commission or by Council officials?
4 More particularly, the higher normative commitment to representative (legislative) democracy and the increase in the powers of the European Parliament. See, for tensions within this majoritarian principle, Maduro (2003).
5 See, only, the widened standing for individuals under Article 230 and the Court of First Instance's implicit rejection of the divisible nature of the European polity (*Pfizer* [2002] paragraphs 166–170 and *Alpharma* [2002]).
6 On the grounds that it would unduly alienate the legislative competences of the *Bundestag*, safeguarded by Article 79(3) of the German Constitution. Note, in the meantime, Article 24(3) of the German Constitution has been amended to facilitate the transfer of competences to the European Union.

7 The decision relating to the European Economic Coal and Steel Community.
8 See, below, discussion on the *Rechtsgut* of individual rights, Section II.2.
9 The series began with '*Comitology*' [1988], denying parliamentary prerogatives to intervene in this arcane legislative mechanism, and proceeded through *Re Radioactive food* [1990] to *Commission of the European Communities* v *European Parliament and Council of the European Union* [2003], the latter cases showing more sympathy for the European Parliament. Geelhoed's statement may be found at fn. 22 of the final judgment.
10 Though, as we will see, the goal of individual protection is not sufficient to give the institutional balance within the Communities the status of an overarching common good, in which everyone is in possession of an interest, see *Phillip Morris International Inc* [2003].
11 Single European Act 1987, Treaty of European Union 1992, Amsterdam Treaty 1997 and the Treaty of Nice 2001.
12 Above all, the Comitology Decision ([1986] OJ C70/6), confirming and seeking to structure the *ad hoc* scheme of delegation of Commission powers in defiance of the non-delegation strictures of *Meroni* [1962], See, for full details of the legislative history of the Comitology Decision and its significance, Vos (1999).
13 Each treaty amendment being followed by its own surge of cases brought before the ECJ, within which institutions have sought to secure their own position within the governance structures of the European Union.
14 Once again, the Comitology Decision, is highly relevant here ([1986] OJ C70/6), since the Decision regulates the exact circumstances under which Council powers may be delegated to the Commission, and exercised, in concert with technocratic experts, to the exclusion of parliamentary co-decision competences. But, see, also, European Commission White Paper: European Governance COM (2001) 428, July 2001.
15 That is, the right to bring a legal action against other institutions under Article 230 EC Treaty.
16 See, note 9 above.
17 In the area of co-decision.
18 Minutes of the sitting of 26 October 1988 (provisional edition) pp 194–197, cited by van Gerven in *Re Radioactive Food* [1990].
19 *Phillip Morris International Inc* [2003] paragraph 87 (Court of First Instance).
20 *Federation Nationale d'Agriculture Biologique des Region de France* [2001] ECR I-3811.
21 *Commission of the European Communities* v *European Parliament and Council of the European Union* [2003].
22 *Azores (Regiăo atonóma dos Açores)* [2004], an extraordinary extension of the principle of the balance of powers (usually applying only between EU institutions and the member states) to include regions within individual states of the European Union.
23 And here, in more general terms, we find an underlying cause for the seemingly somewhat sloppy confusion of the term *effet utile* with purposive interpretation found, in particular, within common law treatises on European Law. A doctrinally pure lawyer would argue, and with some cause, that the two are strictly distinguished. *Effet utile* is a doctrinal operation, identifying the appropriate remedy for a right within the interpretative canon. Purposive reasoning privileges a political goal above the doctrinal cannon. And yet, *effet utile* cannot stand alone. In a final analysis, though doctrinally internally pure, it rests upon an interaction between law and its environment.
24 *European Parliament* v *E.U. Council* [1996].
25 *Re Generalised Tariff Preferences* [1996].

26 See, references to arguments of the applicant within Advocate General Darmon's opinion, *Industrie- en Handelssonderneming Vreugdebhil* [1994] at paragraph 38. See also *Phillip Morris International Inc* [2003].

27 An argument commonly evoked in relation to the correct legal basis for action within the treaties in matters of health, and perhaps more importantly, tax. See, for very recent example, details of the pleadings of the intervening Irish Government in *Commission of the European Communities* v *Council of the European Union* [2003], detailed in the opinion of Advocate General Albers at paragraph 43.

28 Advocate General Cosmas, *Parfums Christian Dior SA* [2002] at paragraph 10, critically rejecting a role for the ECJ in interpreting the WTO TRIPs agreement by virtue of continuing shared EU national competences in relation to WTO law: a viewpoint subsequently confirmed by the Court, at paragraph 49. See however the conflict between the ECJ and the various Federal High Courts in Germany on preferred applications of the WTO legal order within Germany in the matter of bananas (Schmid 2001).

29 And it is here that the limits to Stein's analysis become apparent: his distinction between a supremacy issue, which pitches national jurisdictions against a European jurisdiction and a balance of powers problem that requires institutional competences to be weighed up against one another, is, in a sense, a false one. The problems of balance and supremacy are merely two sides of the same coin: if the member states are included within the institutional balance, then, the core issue of supremacy relates at heart to a question of executive competence versus legislative competence. To be sure, executive and legislative competences may be found at different levels within the EU system (national versus supranational), nonetheless, the primary issue is one of the 'character', rather than the '*locus*', of European governance (2001: 521–524).

30 Moving away from a constitutional issue of the mechanics of change in the institutional balance, an original political goal of the balance was the apportionment of competences according to the ability of each institution to achieve its given aims.

31 Apportioned in neo-functionalist terms in the light of which power *locus* was best placed to perform which functions.

32 The Court's conclusion (paragraph 93) that the Bundestag retained sufficient legislative competences as a whole to maintain the sovereignty of the 'German People' is, as Joerges (1996a) has correctly pointed out, wholly unconvincing in terms of the democratic legitimation of the exercise of a specific legislative competence over monetary matters. Indeed, the judgment might ultimately be read as a residual expression within modern German constitutional jurisprudence of a post-war German constitutional tendency to restrain potentially subversive legislative power through the judicial alienation of legislative competences to technocratic institutions. Tellingly, the judgment concerned monetary competence; competences long alienated by a German judiciary from a German legislature and conferred in fact, if not in constitutional principle, upon the *Bundesbank* under the normative protection of a German theory of ordo-liberalism, or, an (informal) Economic Constitution, prizing of legally monitored financial constraint.

33 Though, under a German separation of powers principle, an individual rights-based claim to the maintenance of property might exist, 'monetary stability' was too vague a derivative of the right to property to justify an individual right of review over the conduct of monetary policy.

34 Interestingly enough, a logic also confirmed by the ECJ, at least in relation to the individual, see *Bosman* [1995].

35 At paragraph 33: more particularly, the argument that sufficient legislative competences should always be reserved to the *Bundestag* to ensure an adequate forum for the preservation of the sovereignty of the German *Volk*.

36 Thus, the Court also indicated that its human rights jurisdiction could and would be shared with the ECJ (paragraphs 12–13).

37 This plea for the creation of a common logic under which the issue of a European democratic deficit might be addressed by national and European judges alike is a key to the Court's genius and genuine efforts to further the cause of European integration. In contrast to Weiler's polemic (Chapter 2 (IV.2)) the argument made here is that the Court was very much concerned to allow for the development of European democracy seeking to provide the pivotal legal mechanical interpretational mode (i.e., shared doctrine of a separation of powers) that would overcome innate incommensurability between national and European constitutional jurisdictions.

38 Here, one can only underline the failure of the European Convention to tackle the issue of the balance of powers head on. Taken together with its utter failure to respond to the ECJ's request that the pivotal Article 234 EC mechanism of the preliminary reference also be made a part of constitutional discussion (see above, Chapter 2), the conclusion is surely one that the Convention was wholly ill-suited to consider the review of the real difficulties and issues facing European constitutionalism.

39 Article I-46 draft constitutional treaty.

40 At least in the analysis of the *Brunner* Court. In other words, whilst the German Court might have enjoyed a measure of success in creating an overarching national-European jurisdiction, it could not and cannot solve the substantive normative clash between notions of institutional balance and the separation of powers.

41 Though the argument is made in relation to existing balance of powers terminology.

42 Note, however, that this author takes a strongly dissenting position, preferring a reading of the separation of powers that privileges individual rights of personal autonomy.

43 With specific reference to the legitimising powers of the eighteenth-century balance of powers within the UK constitution.

44 Majone is explicit (2005): his technocratic governance is, in his terms and in an echo of Blackstone, an 'estate' within a system of governance that is coeval with 'good' governance.

45 More particularly, within committees of national representatives in the comitology system (reflecting the notion that their delegation to the Commission notwithstanding, Council powers should never be alienated).

46 In other words, serving the impulse to efficient technocratic governance without upsetting non-delegation principles through the concentration of additional administrative capacities within new institutions, agencies and committees, placed under the administrative umbrella of the Commission (Vos 1999: 1–10).

47 From '*Comitology*' [1988] to *Re Radioactive food* [1991], approving even of the practical expression of increased parliamentary competences, to the general tendency of the Court to approve of *ad hoc* administrative delegation, simply reviewing the actions of committees and agencies within its general jurisprudence.

48 In particular, *Plaumann* [1963], *Calpak SpA* [1980], *Cordoniu SA* [1994] *Extramet Industrie SA* [1991], *Stichting Greenpeace* [1995].

49 Particularly in the case of Article 226 EC proceedings under which the European Commission may bring actions against the member states (*Star Fruit* v *Commission* [1989], a refusal to allow a private party to force the Commission to take proceedings against a member state under Article 226 EC).

50 The transformation in jurisprudence is slight, relating to the ability of the Court to find some form of procedural 'paper right' possessed by the challenging party that would justify increased rights of standing: for example, the registering of a

request for product authorization by the party, *and only that party*, under product approval regulations.

51 Mancini in, *Re the Budget* [1986] at paragraph 19.

52 *Commission of the European Communities* v *European Parliament and Council of the European Union* [2003]; in particular, Advocate General Geelhoed's opinion, which engages in detailed consideration of the need for the maintenance for administrative efficiency.

53 *Parfums Christian Dior SA* [2000] at note 62.

Chapter 6

# The principled judicial mechanics of constitutional morphogenesis

IR: So you have faith in the idea that the creativity of judges can produce a flexible response to problems?

IE: Yes, it is one of the decision-making processes, only one of them. And so there are enough checks and balances, enough corrections if, well, an example, if the Council of Ministers tries to come to a solution, very often a compromise, and they are tired and it's already tomorrow [and] the meeting is over, or almost over. Then, they will put in a word which is subject to a lot of interpretation. And when, after, you will see that's for the Court of Justice to decide. They will say strike it from time to time, so that means that they have given a mandate to the judges. And the judges are using it. And then, later on, some may say this is a *gouvernement des juges*. But they have been asked to do it .... And moreover, if I may say ... the legislature can amend that, they can change it. That takes precedence over case law.[1]

## I. The abyss beckons

The 'community method' (*methode communuautaire*), the cumbersome procedure whereby cohesive governance within Europe is assured through a process of decision-making founded within compromise and respect for the political positions and values held and promoted by parties to the integration process, undoubtedly has much to recommend it. After all, political compromise and bargaining, if not necessarily dedicated to the identification of the 'best possible solutions', have, at the very least, ensured continuing 'voice' within a complex integration process, and have, accordingly, ensured the 'loyalty' of a diverse set of parties to this process; a process which might otherwise have alienated integral national interests to a politically unsustainable degree.[2]

Nonetheless, compromise and the need to include the full gambit of interests within a decision-making process also have detrimental affects upon the scheme of governance within Europe. A final legislative competence is sometimes exercised with greater dedication to pursuit of the integration of diverse positions within a concrete decision, and with a correspondingly less exact eye to the precision, clarity and effectiveness of substantive political action (Majone 2005). As one senior Commission official is drawn to note, the notion of 'functionality' within the Community setting is not necessarily always characterised by its more usual meaning of achieving an efficient or 'adequate' legislative result. Instead, and within the terms of a substantive understanding of the institutional balance that demands that each institution must have its own influence upon decision-making processes, functionality can give rise to 'obscure' decisions (A-04):

IR: What about the idea that the principles simply provide you with a functional approach to problem-solving? Do you think that's a guiding principle of the European Union? Or do these principles between the institutions provide you [with] checks on each other, on the exercise of power?

IE: Well, a bit of both. They do provide checks. And they do, to a certain extent, perhaps almost regrettably, impose on us a functional approach to problem-solving. Instead of saying here's a problem, how should it best be solved, and then work out who should do what, we tend to say here's a problem, we can deal with this bit, somebody else has got to deal with another bit. And then we'll try and put it all together at the end.

At one level, the negative impact of the community method should be of general concern, as a modern imperative of 'output legitimacy', or a demand for effective, efficient and economic decision-making cedes to a Byzantine complex of interest co-ordination and aggregation, which is designed to serve 'democracy', not by furnishing 'good' democratic results, but by keeping an 'EU public on board' (Identifier 88).[3] The linguistic inversion of a notion of 'functionality', however, and the underlying tension between input and output legitimacy within the European Union,[4] necessarily also raises very specific issues within the ambit of this analysis of the socially constitutive and self-constituting nature of Europe's *Rechtsverfassungsrecht*.

More particularly, the (self-proclaimed) 'mandate' afforded law to fill in the gaps left behind by the tired (compromised?[5]) legislative process, as well as the '*gouvernement des juges*', which such a mandate consequently entails, would appear to confirm the founding assertion of this volume: whilst governance within the European Union may not differ substantially from its national or international counterparts, the structures and mechanics of the process of European integration have undoubtedly exposed the simple fact that processes of government and law-making cannot simply be conceived of as encompassing a pre-determined scheme of normative government, characterised by legislative supremacy and simple acts of judicial application.

Instead, 'legal indeterminacy' takes on yet another guise, as, in addition to the inevitable incompleteness of directive linguistic tools, the indeterminacy of legal language becomes a 'political mechanism'; a mode of masking the failures inherent to compromise and a political expression of faith in the ability of judicial and legal process to flesh out the necessary final decisional contours. Seen in this light, the battle for legal materialisation, or the re-rooting of law within its social and political environment at the moment of legal application, is not simply a normative legal programme for the democratisation of inevitably indeterminate grammatical legal substance. It is not simply a choice made by European law to follow the paths trod by a *Freirechtsschule*. Instead, it is also a task directly thrust upon law by the circumstances of European integration, by the necessarily uncertain nature of the European polity and by its (democratising?) demand for the maintenance of political inclusion through processes of bargaining and decisional obscurity.

If the power of circumstances might be said to entail their own legitimating force, the political secession of decision-making powers to judicial and legal process could be argued to entail a justificatory normativity all of its own: a 'mandate', indeed.[6] Nevertheless, as we have seen (Chapters 2 (IV), 4 (III) and, below, 6 (IV)), materialisation, or the reconnection of legal process with a law-external environment, brings with it its own hazards and challenges, as law both struggles to find a suitable and adequate mirror of reality that it can digest within its own grammar, and, at the same time, seeks to maintain its own (law-internal) neutrality (methodologies). Within the seemingly 'normal' jurisdiction of legislative application,[7] such difficulties range from the inadequacy of science as an interlocutory tool for the legal recognition of reality (Chapter 3 (III)), to the danger that the 'judge-king' might, 'on the pretence of repugnancy, substitute his pleasure for that of the legislature' (*Federalist Papers* 1961: 468). The romanticism of legal organicism, the dangers posed by the recasting of law and lawyers as 'the living oracles' Blackstone and (Katz 1979: I.69) of the people, are always readily apparent within any form of adjudication. However, they are, once again, magnified as a simple 'legal' jurisdiction is left behind and an uncompromising and explicit constitutional realm is subject to 'JUDGMENT', or the purview of a law embodying the 'original constitutive will' of the people (*Federalist Papers* 1961: 468).

Within the Community and Union itself, there is little doubt that Europe's constitutional framework is still a 'moving target' (A-04). In the view of a senior Commission official, even the draft constitutional treaty retains its inevitable air of indeterminacy:

IE: Is the framework ever tested or pushed?

IR: All the time. And there are endless, endless opportunities for friction and misunderstandings because some of these things are not very clearly laid down in the law. And even the constitutional treaty, if it comes about – one of the purposes of it is to clarify these things – it will never

> do it perfectly. Maybe, in five hundred years time, everyone will understand precisely who does what. But these things are, at the moment, still moving targets. (A-04)

Even in the vital question of 'who does what', with all its underlying significance for the determination of who is accountable to whom and for what,[8] the treaties retain their air of mystery and their potential for judicial explication. Theories of adjudication founded in 'textual immanence' or 'originalism' are thus wholly defeated by the contingent nature of a European integration process whose *telos* remains subject to a multitude of competing interests, and whose final destination cannot, or dare not,[9] utter its name.

Within the explicitly (political) constitutional jurisdiction, the dangers and challenges posed by indeterminacy are only intensified as legal debate moves away from consideration of the application of, say, the intricate technical provisions of consumer protection law to concrete cases of potentially abusive preferential national treatment, in order to confront both the unveiled politics of power and the explicit political expression of power. The task remains one of identifying 'reality'. With each decision to apportion power this way or that way in the institutional balance of powers game, and with each judgment limiting or extending power with the purpose of conserving individual right or furthering collective political voice, the Court impacts directly, not only upon the power relations maintained between individual institutions, but also upon the legitimate nature of the European polity as a whole.[10] Accordingly, judicial interpretation of the constitutional jurisdiction, or the application of a constitutional principle of a balance of powers, is a socially constitutive legal act, which requires simultaneous legal appreciation of an extra-legal environment – the evolving and 'acceptable' *praxis* of a European polity – and further demands the self-constitution, or legitimation of constitutive law.

Between facts and norms, however, European law is perhaps denied as great a degree of recourse to the legitimising mechanisms of *Rechtsverfassungsrecht*, which operate at the non-authoritative limit to authoritative jurisdiction that is governed by a 234 EC preliminary reference mechanism. Argument cannot simply coalesce around the rationalising 'facts' of substantive intervention into national or European policy-making.[11] Instead, it must directly confront political and constitutive arguments, with all their underlying reference to normative imaginings, or visions of how a polity *should* be justly constructed (normative social reality constructions). At the same time, it is, in large part, required to divine its socially constitutive and self-constitutionalising force from a series of abstract 'legal principles', rather than legal facts, which themselves can no longer claim to possess an axiomatic force educed from constitution settlement.[12]

The challenge to *Rechtsverfassungsrecht* within Europe is accordingly intensified. Beyond constitutional process, the demand that law identify principles of constitutional morphogenesis to govern the evolution of the

European polity and the character of European political process, seemingly confronts Europe with the direct task of identification of Hermann Heller's, always elusive, 'moral and ethical' principles of constitutional adjudication. Alternatively, European courts must identify legal principles, or, principled mechanics of constitutional adjudication, which raise the act of judging upon indeterminate legal content to a stabilising legal act, whereby the social values evolved within an operational reality are given authoritative legal effect, or *Wirksamkeit* (Chapter 1 (IV)).

In the matter of judicial 'creativity'[13] within constitutional adjudication, the endeavour to find the 'checks and balances' which elevate judicial pronouncement from the status of potentially politically motivated intervention to that of constitutionally authoritative law-giving is, thus, a vital, yet very hazardous task. In short, where the task of constitutional adjudication involves an appreciation of social reality, together with an appraisal of proffered normative social reality constructs, as well as their dual reconfiguration within a socially constitutive and self-constitutionalising legal idiom, the influence of the 'abyss' is particularly acute. What guarantees can be identified to ensure that a 'principled' mechanics of European adjudication will not simply be infected by the ever present spectre of social irrationality?[14]

Tellingly, however, the influence of the abyss is not simply felt with regard to the act of adjudication. Instead, the methodology of research into judicial adjudication also finds itself trapped within relativist and shifting sands. Where constitutionally significant adjudication is seemingly no longer a matter of substantive judgment in intricate cases of technical legal application (instances of market regulation), the methodological difficulties accompanying the act of 'seeing into the mind of law' are predictably magnified, as vital indicators, such as alterations in argumentative style and courtroom practice, cease to have as great a potential explanatory relevance within the analysis, and investigation must instead be directly focused upon what thought and recognition patterns underlie the process of the application of legal principle.

Given such difficulties, more intricate methodological modes of examination of judicial pronouncement might initially suggest themselves for application within this study.[15] Nonetheless, given that the aim of examination is partially also one of the identification of the limits to and failings in the various social science models which offer themselves up as tools to law for the better appreciation of 'social reality', the ironic hazards of misdiagnosis of the judicial mind posed by equally 'scientifically' constructed models of academic enquiry are perhaps too great to ignore. Accordingly, and remaining firmly within a realm of sociological muddling, the simple textual and contextual evaluation of the questionnaires and Semi-structured interviews presented in the following pages cannot but be viewed as a very limited glimpse of the reality of constitutional adjudication in the absence of constitutional settlement – or, as a fleeting (potentially distorting) mirror to the potential within and limits to Europe's evolving *Rechtsverfassungsrecht*.

Nonetheless, and conscious of its limits, textual and contextual evaluation of questionnaire responses and structured interviews builds on three tranches of research:

An initial round of questionnaires sent to members of all the institutions of the European Union and the members of the European Constitutional Convention;[16]

A first set of structured interviews conducted with current employees of the institutions of the European Union;[17] and,

A second set of structured interviews conducted with past members of the Court of First Instance and the ECJ, including Judges and Advocates General, as well as, 'control' interviews conducted with practising lawyers, specialised in pleading before the ECJ and Court of First Instance.[18]

The questionnaires and the first set of interviews were designed to ascertain deep-seated appreciations of the political constellation underlying the notion of an institutional balance of powers, or the substantive meaning ascribed to it in the practice of governing Europe. Accordingly, the indicators comprised:

Degrees of co-operation and informality in the application of the balance of powers principle between institutions of the European Union and between institutions of the European Union and the member states. A large degree of informality and co-operation was presumed to be indicative either of bargaining processes between institutions, or, in contrast, of deliberative or efficient problem-solving orientations within EU governance;

The potential for reform in the institutional balance. Responses emphasising the need for the reform of the institutional balance were presumed to be indicative either of current inadequacies within the scheme of governance, or of institutional political preferences for a particular form of future European polity (for example, retention of a functionalist polity versus the creation of representative democracy).

The ranking of the services performed by an institutional balance in an effort to gain an overall picture of perceptions of the current shape of a European polity within the European Union (does the balance serve functionalist purposes, ensure citizen representation or act as a mode of ensuring checks and balances?).

Once again, the assumption made within a second series of interviews with past members of the ECJ (and the Court of First Instance) was one that a formalist legal idiom would prevail.[19] Accordingly, efforts were made to step beyond a formal legal veil through the application of indicators, such as:

An examination of the forms of legal arguments brought before the Court, as well as an examination of the evidence presented. Although the institutional balance lies within an explicit area of 'principled' constitutional application, reference to different forms of evidence and argument by the Court is nonetheless presumed to reveal legal efforts to step beyond formalist veils in the application of principles.

The concentration of the analysis upon the intersection of the institutional balance principle with the Article 230 EC judicial review mechanism, and an examination of potential differences in the treatment of applicants to the Court in line with their institutional or individual status. Stark differences in treatment are here presumed to furnish more detailed visions of the motivations underlying judicial intervention within the constitution of the evolving EU polity (for example, rights-based polity versus the preference for collective political action).

The analysis of the judicial perception of the working of the Constitutional Convention and control interviews with lawyers active before the ECJ. Both indicators were designed to tease out potential political influence within judicial process.

Various distorting factors were, however, immediately apparent within the research:

The questionnaire respondents and interviewees were self-nominating. Responses came overwhelmingly from the most 'supranationalist' institutions within the European Union, or the Commission and the Court.[20]

The response rate was generally poor, and research relevance is limited accordingly. Similarly, respondents in large part derived from northern European countries.

In the preceding and following sections, 'IR' denotes 'interviewer' and 'IE' denotes 'interviewee'. The individual questionnaire responses are identified by a numbered 'indicator'. The first set of interview data is identifiable by the prefix 'A'. The second set of interview data is identifiable by the prefix 'B'.

## II. Law and non-law: normative vision, political contention and legal principle within the institutional balance?

Between fact and norm, a constant accompanying theme within this volume is the clear disjunction between law and politics, or the misunderstanding and misconceptions within the thinking of both systems about the nature and the role of the other. Within the realm of the concept of institutional balance, this disjunction and divergence is also apparent, or, at least, seems to be so at first glance. Once again, the actions, or non-actions of a Constitutional Convention for Europe are telling. Despite its stark intervention into the political substance of the institutional balance,[21] the Constitutional Convention was true to reductionist form and gave no corresponding thought to the role that legal process would play in implementing its newly struck equilibrium. In a mirror of the Constitutional Convention's lack of interest in the significance and workings of the Article 234 EC preliminary mechanism,[22] the conclaves between Europe's putative founding fathers seemed content to relax in the political knowledge that where political will speaks, the law is not only sure to follow but also to follow faithfully.

Touching political faith in the handmaiden status of law and legal process is, however, far more nuanced within the general political culture of EU institutions. In a gentle echo of a stark founding assertion that political process within the European Union affords European law a 'mandate' to engage in the refinement of political decision-making, members of the EU institutions generally recognise the far more intricate relationship established between European politics and its 'servitor' law. Thus, as an accompaniment to questionnaire responses, which were almost evenly split on the issue of whether the institutional balance should best be viewed as a 'legal principle' or a 'political tool',[23] one member of the Commission once again stresses the political origins of the concept, but also accepts the potential tensions that might accompany the legal pursuit of political goals (A-02):

IR: Well, if such principles might be gathered under one umbrella called institutional balance, would you describe them as primarily a legal principle, for example, that might ensure that power is responsibly split between the institutions, or a political tool which facilitates solutions where there is conflict?

IE: I think it's a political principle, which takes the form of certain legal principles. But I think the objective is a political one. The objective is to say [that] the EU is about pooling sovereignty and exercising [sovereignty] jointly. But the member states don't trust each other so they need a neutral party, which is not supposed to side [with] one member state against another, but which is sort of supposed to filter the common interest of member states beyond just the multitude of national interests ... and then you have certain legal principles like the balance of power, separation of powers, *which try to give effect, which try to translate the political intention behind it into actual fact. But, I mean, as a non-lawyer, I always have the tendency to see the law as subservient to politics* (laughs; emphasis added).

Humour is, as ever, indicative. The Commission, at least, possesses its own clear substantive and political vision of the role played by institutional balance, and, more particularly, by the role which it itself plays in the protection of the institutional balance. In the common exercise of pooling sovereignty (although for what purpose remains unclear), the Commission is an honest broker, dedicated not to parochial interests, but to 'ever closer union' between member states (if not necessarily between the peoples) of Europe. Nonetheless, the substantive vision of the balance of powers, within which the Commission assumes its facilitative role,[24] for all that one might wish that it were protected by, or concretised within, 'legal principle', remains legally indeterminate. Law is not necessarily 'subservient' to politics, or better stated, subservient to any individual political vision. Instead, law can only 'try' to give effect to 'political intention'. It can only 'try' to translate political vision into 'actual fact'.

The recognition that law is not a constant, that it is not a monolithic bulwark dedicated to the service of one particular inspiring vision of the institutional balance, is again one which is reproduced, though with clear logical tensions, throughout the research data-set. Thus, whilst almost all the questionnaire respondents and all the interviewees are in complete agreement that the institutional balance should be viewed as a 'constitutional principle', presumably one with constitutive permanence, a more prosaically expressed opinion, arguing that the institutional balance 'is a bar of soap in the bath', is attributable to a political 'realism',[25] which finds stark affirmation amongst the people whose business it is to convince the ECJ (and the Court of First Instance) of its particular meaning or implications within the courtroom (B-06):

IR: Is it [the institutional balance] strictly a principle that's laid down in the treaties?

IE: No, it's a political, anthropological consequence of having creatures in the undergrowth ... some of them have prospered, some of them have not prospered. In the perpetual shifting of balance and opportunity, at any one moment, a different institution is more important. And what lawyers do, and I'm a lawyer, is help to advance their client's cause, taking account of, if it's in the pre-litigation phase, taking account of the political, the economic verities. Or, if it's actual litigation before the courts ... you argue for your client within the institutional framework that's established by the treaties and regulations.

And thus, the 'bar of soap' that is the institutional balance resolves itself into a sticky and slippery intangible mass of political contention. For all that individuals may aspire to view the notion of institutional balance as a noble constitutional principle, as a normative vision of how Europe should be governed and how its polity should be constituted, it is simply the lair 'of creatures in the undergrowth', ambitious and unconscionable beings who seize the opportunity wherever and whenever they can, in order to pursue their individual interests and gain individual power. Contrary to repeated assertions that the relations maintained between institutions are 'mostly co-operative', the institutional balance is a battlefield between ambitious institutional holders of power.[26] Far from being a momentous constitutional principle, the notion of institutional balance is simply an empty shell, guarded only by the thinnest and most hazard-prone red line of a '*gouvernement des juges*', and subject to the realist assault of the anthropological processes of

European integration, in which 'economic and political verities' or 'opportunity' dictate which interests will triumph and when. The abyss beckons us on with a vengeance.[27]

Or does it? The judges of the ECJ (and the Court of First Instance), naturally, possess their own perception of the nature and role of the institutional balance within the European Union, and of their own role, as well as the role of legal process, within its construction, oversight and application (B-05):

IR: How do you define the current notion of institutional balance? Do you see it as primarily a constitutional or a political or administrative concept?

IE: I think that there's an element of all three ... but from the Court of Justice's point of view, clearly, it is legal, and therefore, constitutional in the broad sense. It's not constitutional in the sense that we don't formally have a constitution and it doesn't look like we're going to have one. *But it is constitutional in the sense that it's a question of the legal definition of the powers of institutions.* And their rights and prerogatives as between themselves. But it is also political because the legal relationship defines the political relationship to some extent. And it's also political in the sense that even if the law isn't entirely clear, or isn't all obviously one way, nevertheless, the politicians may feel that they have to do certain things and I think that has been true, for example, over the relationship between the Council and the European Parliament (emphasis added).

Clearly, the Court is also a realist institution, recognising, for example, that a lack of clarity within European treaties on the divisions of power has often necessitated 'political', rather than 'legal', solutions. Thus, whilst it is the job of law to 'define' the legal relationships between institutions, the *lacunae* within governance schemes have often been filled, not by law, but by political agreements (inter-institutional agreements).[28] Nonetheless, the Court also has its own distinct and formalist vision of the concept of institutional balance; a vision which raises a constitutional principle of the balance of powers above the fray of anthropological political contention, and which places it firmly in a pre-political sphere of 'legal definition' – a series of rights and prerogatives to be apportioned by the Court to this or that institution in the law-internal, but politically constitutive, process of 'legal definition'.

With this, the particular difficulties of the clear identification of the meaning and importance of the notion of the institutional balance become apparent. Is it a formalistically flavoured constitutional principle of legal definition and pre-political constitution? Alternatively, is it a sphere of normative contention, within which differing visions of a European polity are presented and evaluated, and sometimes contrasted, with realistic appraisal of economic verities or political realities? Finally, is it a simple 'bar of soap', an inchoate slime of real-world power-brokering and of the promotion of individual interest? The truth of the matter is, of course, that the notion is all three things at the same time.

The legal or constitutional principle of 'institutional balance' is not quite an empty shell. Certainly, the constitutional or legal principle is a focal point for a gathering of the varied and contrasting political interests, ideas and visions of the legitimate nature of the European polity. Simultaneously, however, law and legal process makes their own, if initially wholly formalistic, claim to predate contention, in order to pre-empt the anthropological processes of European integration, and to furnish an authoritative judgment on the institutional balance (its apportionment of powers and its underlying impact upon the legitimate nature of the European polity) through processes of legal definition.

Between fact and norm, the notion of 'legal definition', or the constitutional principle of institutional balance now becomes the focus for examination. As a variety of interests, ideas and visions gather around the notion of institutional balance and clamour for substantive inclusion within it, the role of law is a socially constitutive one of the identification of the interests, ideas and visions that will prevail within the European polity. The adjudication stakes, however, are particularly high. The choice between interests, for example, is not simply a potential matter of unfairly privileging brute political power and illegitimate self-interest. Instead, interests are also always expressed with reference – rhetorical, strategic or impassioned – to the diverse visions and ideas of what particular shape the legitimate European polity should take (or be afforded by law).

Visions and ideals are not only varied, but also highly contradictory. Questionnaire respondents seem to favour an original 'functional' reading of the institutional balance. Accordingly, they lay a far greater weight upon its value in apportioning European 'competences' – as well as subjecting this division of labour to various 'checks and balances' – and are correspondingly less convinced of its ability to ensure the representation of the European citizen.[29] Nonetheless, voices might also be heard in further favour of the colonisation of the balance of powers principle by its separation of powers counterpart, and, in particular, by the majoritarian elements present within that principle (A-02): If you want to ensure acceptability, legitimacy of what we are doing, the way to go ... is to strengthen the role of the European Parliament in all this.'[30]

Equally, however, the privileging of majoritarian rule within the European Union (Maduro 2003) can also be contrasted with endeavours to give voice to individual Europeans by means of 'rights', rather than 'votes', and by the promotion of a 'conservatory' and individualistic[31] reading of the separation of powers principle. One lawyer's continuing and impassioned frustration with the predominance of policy-making over individual rights and its institutional-treaty counterpart of restricted individual standing under Article 230 EC is, thus, expressed as follows (B-04):

> [o]ne often gets the impression in many of these cases that the institutions would rather not have the individual involved – that the individual whose livelihood is put at stake is an inconvenience. And the people [who] have the gall actually to challenge some of these decisions [are] seen as an irritation.

The underlying point, however, is an obvious one. Parties and interests clustering around the notion of institutional balance may have their own particular interest in the preservation or promotion of power. At the same, time, however, they also appeal to deeper visions of a European polity. The 'stroke of genius' (A-04) attributed to a system in which the Commission acts as a 'filter' for 'the common interests of the member states' (A-02) might, at one level, be a rhetorical tool deployed in argument in order to ensure that the Commission retains its institutional powers, 'its margin of appreciation' as a negotiator (A-02). At yet another level, however, it is also an impassioned plea for the maintenance of a vision of a European polity, within which the scheme of government is so perfect as to be 'coeval with the absolute rights'[32] of every individual European (A-04):

> I personally, but perhaps you're not surprised, I must say that it's a stroke of genius to set up this system because it is probably the best one we can conceive of to do what the European Union was set out to do, i.e., you have an organisation which is responsible for discerning the general interest, making proposals in that general interest – but not responsible for legislation. The legislation is a combination of the states and the Council and the people through their directly elected represented representatives in the Parliament. And that works very well. And then you have the member states with whom there is a lot of interaction to make the system work. *Now that's the, a, political idea you can agree with it or disagree with it, it has to be written down somewhere so there's a treaty* (emphasis added).

Certainly 'we are surprised': once again, political faith in the power of law, or 'a treaty', to maintain one particular vision of the European polity is telling indeed. However, as the respondent also admits ('the' or 'a' policy?), judges are confronted with a competing cacophony of such European ideals, or normative social reality constructions, each of which is given additional flavour by economic and political 'verities', and each of which demands its promotion above all others in each and every technical decision on the apportionment of right and prerogative.[33]

The principle of the balance of powers is the focal point for constitutional morphogenesis. It is the magnet for the expression of competing visions of the 'legitimate' shape of a European polity and the legal principle within which the competing realities of the processes of European integration can be contrasted with normative visions of a European polity. It is the constitutional fulcrum within the ambit of which, European law can bend treaties, this way and that, in the effort to re-embed law within social reality, and can constantly constitute and reconstitute the European polity.

At the same time, however, the principle of the balance of powers is also the focal point for an immense challenge to law. Engaging in morphogenesis, or freeing patterns of legal observation of an extra-legal environment from a straitjacket of closed constitutional settlement and formal reasoning, European law is likewise faced with the demand that it needs must also constitutionalise itself. Between fact and norm, a socially constitutive and self-constitutionalising law, or *Rechtsverfassungsrecht* within Europe, must also identify the mechanisms and modes of 'legal interpretation', which both open a window on European integration realities, and maintain the internal coherence, or legitimacy, of European law. Alternatively, it must identify 'the checks and balances' that operate within law itself, without which even a mandated '*gouvernement des juges*' would lose any claim to legitimacy.[34]

## III. Principles and (self-) illusion within European constitutionalism

Notwithstanding the apparent failure of the draft European constitution, members of the two European Courts are confident about the constitutional status of European law. In an interesting echo of the putative role played by private law reasoning within the establishment of an initially 'private' form of European constitutionalism,[35] the origins of the constitutionalisation of European law are deemed by one Advocate General to lie in the remarkable assault made by the ECJ upon the contractual privacy maintained between the individual member states in the founding case of *van Gend & Loos*.[36] The issue of whether the concept of institutional balance is a static or dynamic concept, thus elicits its own responsive questions about the exact nature of the role played by judges in processes of European adjudication (B-01):

> What is a static and dynamic concept? To give one example, because [it is] where it all started from, *van Gend en Loos*, you could have said that [it] is a very static concept: that rights are existing between member states [which] have concluded a treaty, therefore a contract. And then, all of a sudden, the court says, yes, but third parties can also rely on that . . . . For a private lawyer to have a third party rely on a contract agreed between other parties is extremely exceptional. This is a contract between member states, so Courts said all of a sudden also third parties, citizens can rely on it. That's quite a change. And now that was a very static subject or notion and it has been made fairly dynamic by the Court.[37]

Within the judicial mind, at least, the constitutionalising consequences are clear. You do not need any form of 'political' constitutive will to found constitutionalism: '[I]f the French or the British or whoever it is, or the Dutch are voting against it, that's not a disaster for me. I think the constitution for me; more important for me is constitutionalism. And we have constitutionalism' (B-04).[38] But more significantly, dynamic judicial constitutionalism is also wholly divorced from traditional processes of constitutional 'JUDGMENT' (Chapter 3 (III)), as judicial pronouncement of the original pre-political constitutive will of the people seemingly dispenses with the textually immanent analysis of any 'static' notions and concepts within the Treaty, as well as any investigation of the will of the 'Masters of the Treaty' (originalism), to found itself instead in the intricate legal consideration of whether the private contractual autonomy of individual Europeans (sphere of unfettered economic activity under the Rome Treaty) can best be secured by the breach of one of the basic tenets of private law, privacy of contract.[39]

This apparently remarkable divorce of European law from conventional processes of interpretation finds its echo in the startled comments of a refugee common law judge on the workings of a European Court to which he had been seconded. Even common law judges are not surprised by the precedence of principles over the 'facts' within a constitutional jurisdiction, and, more particularly, over the 'facts' of the statutory expression of political will. After all, even within the common law jurisdiction, simple statutory interpretation overlaps with a distinct constitutional jurisdiction to an ever increasing degree (B-03):

> [A]nd when Parliament speaks, it speaks with precision and your job is merely to interpret and implement precisely what Parliament says. But, in constitutional law, you are supervising general *principles* on top of this totally empirical system' (emphasis added).

Nonetheless, a common lawyer who is sensitive to the socially constitutive nature of legal principles, which must, in their turn, be subject to self-constitutionalisation processes, still expresses surprise at the apparent weight laid upon principles within a European jurisdiction that is seemingly wholly divorced from a more contextual mode of common law constitutional adjudication. With reference to a lesson apparently derived from the US jurisdiction, legal principle is thus more normally to be regarded as a socially contextual instrument (B-04):

> And you found frequently you were looking to the American Federal Supreme Court [rather than] to the House of Lords as to interpreting the constitutional balance in the country. *And trying to give life and reality to general principles in the light of experience* (emphasis added).

And indeed, the ECJ seemingly also shares this much in common with its US counterpart (B-04): 'Now, when I went to Luxembourg, it wasn't a great revolution in that respect, this kind of thinking was fairly familiar to me'. However:

> What was something of a shock was that frequently, among my colleagues in Luxembourg, the facts seemed to be of almost no significance whatsoever (laughs). And it was a question of implementing the principle. You know that frequently you'd meet, you'd have a meeting of judges and [Judge X] would give you his impression of his preliminary view of the case. Very frequently, it would be a question of this case raises the principle of equality before the law. What facts do we need to ensure that we apply those principles correctly? And then we'd think up questions so that we wouldn't misapply the principle. We'd think them up and send them off to the parties. A totally different mental approach. (B-04)

Laughter in this case has a myriad of potential meanings. Does humour circumscribe common law embarrassment, the limits to common legal learning and a final inability to leave the earthy realm of common sense behind, in order fully to embrace the finely wrought grammatical, logical and intellectual intricacies of the *Code Civil* tradition?[40] Alternatively, does laughter have its roots within a far deeper and generic legal embarrassment, and an underlying awareness of the eternally contingent nature of the self-contained and self-referential foundations of law and legal principle? Is it the expression of an awareness of the illusionary and self-illusionary nature of law?[41]

'I don't see how the Court could have decided otherwise' (A-06). Thus intones one Advocate General on the imposition of supremacy and direct effect by European law. Granted, the Rome Treaty itself, being viewed by its 'masters' as little more than an international trading agreement, contained very little scope for constitutional manoeuvring of its own: '[Y]ou really didn't have any general principles, or very little except the four freedoms.' However:

> [T]here was just a need to tie this together and make sense of it .... How could [the Court] decide that national law prevails over Community law. It would have made no sense. The French Parliament could always pass any law and just forget everything that has been agreed in common. (A-06)

Equally, even though the Rome Treaty might be lacking in its own principles that would be facilitative of 'constitutional' judicial adjudication, this *lacuna* did not extend to 'more general legal principles' (A-06). European law's armoury contained more general principles that might yet play their part in achieving the imputed goals of economic community.

'General principles of law', we are thus informed, make up the oil that greases the processes of constitutional adjudication within Europe. Even *critique* from within the Court must cede to the inevitability and determinative power of general legal principle. One Advocate General's published doubts about the ever greater expansion of the notion of state liability to cover the actions of national courts and judges (van Gerven 2000)[42] is again met and overcome by the inevitable power of the bulwark of legal principle (A-06):

> [I] was astonished by all this because I can't, I mean I've said openly and in public that I can't see how we could have decided otherwise because it's a *traditional*, and also *public national law principle* that the state is responsible for the actions of all [of] the people in its courts (emphasis added).

Law simply cannot decide otherwise. Legal orders are closed systems of interpretation with internal cognitive recognition mechanisms furnished by the litany of 'shared' legal principles that each law student, regardless of national origin, learns at the mentoring knee of his or her Law School: 'to every right a remedy'; 'to every remedy a right'; 'come to law (equity) with clean hands'; 'equality before the law'; 'access to justice'; 'law (justice) is a double-edged sword'. Beyond the legitimating *Grundnorm* of finite constitutional settlement, and beyond politically constitutive will, shared 'traditional' legal principles bind *all* lawyers together in an organic and essentialist enterprise of inevitable judgment; an essentialist and inevitable process which has seen 'an ever closer union between the peoples of Europe' teased out of the stony ground of an international economic agreement concluded between member states.

Transcendental nonsense, indeed (Chapter 2 (III.2); Chapter 5 (II.1)): the futile romantic organicism of notions of 'traditional' legal principle, which are inevitably common to all jurisdictions, is matched only by the (self-) illusionary endeavour to recast poetically derived and indeterminate legal principles as rigid elements within the formalist, technical canon of legal interpretation (B-01):

> [W]hen I read the English literature, and it starts already by saying what everybody else on the continent would call a subjective right. You cannot translate it in English, you can say right, but not a subjective right. Because, of course, you have another word for objective law, that's law (both interviewer and interviewee laugh). So, we have just *recht* or right or *droit* which is both subjective and objective. But, anyway, I once read a definition in one of the judgments of the High Court, or was it the Court of Appeal[?], saying when you have a remedy, when you get a standing before a court, then you must have rights. Whereas the

> continental reasoning would be that, when you have a right, then you must have a remedy, which would force that right.

All substantive and objective doctrinal differentiation notwithstanding, and all equalising laughter apart, common and civil lawyers are undoubtedly co-conspirators in the cause of transcendental nonsense. In the constitutionally vital matters of 'access to justice' and 'equality before the law', or the question of who gains access to the ECJ under the Article 230 EC judicial review mechanism, and who might thus plead for the maintenance of their position within the institutional balance,[43] it makes no difference whatsoever if right (prerogative) forces remedy or remedy forces right (prerogative). The organic legal inevitability of right for remedy, or remedy for right is one and the same nonsensical thing. A right inevitably derives from a remedy, and a remedy inevitably derives from a right, but not in the real-world of legal application: rights and remedies are not flesh and blood beings. Instead, the inevitability of derivation occurs within the transcendental realm of legal reasoning, where principled incantation creates its own legal realities, and one and the same court identifies the existence of a right or remedy since *that selfsame court* has already identified the existence of remedy or right.[44]

## IV. Reconstructing social and political reality: legal (self-) illusion unveiled

To reiterate: judicial adjudication on the nature of the institutional balance – who has which powers and when, who might assert prerogatives (rights) and why – is not a simple game of *pareto* efficiency (Ackerman 2000). The apportionment or the division of collective power and the assertion of (individual and collective) rights is not simply a matter of identifying the most efficient form of European governance. Instead, it is a simultaneous expression of the underlying normative structure of a 'legitimate' European polity: who should decide on what for whom and when, and who is accountable to whom for what and when. Just like the concept of the European polity itself, a normative principle of institutional balance of powers is a focal point for contention in a real-world. Between facts and norms, and in the face of deep-seated polity contention, 'principled' constitutional adjudication on the balance of powers is a socially constitutive act, a concretisation of the expression of legitimate polity and a normative incursion into and influence upon the real-world of the evolving European polity.

Between facts and norms, however, adjudication upon the institutional balance must also be a self-constitutionalising act. In the interplay between formal normative self-containment and the material appreciation of real-world demands for social and political justice, law must struggle to identify its own legitimising structures. Constitutional adjudication within an evolving and contested European polity is all about the opening of a legal window onto a real-world of facts, creating influential interconnection between self-contained law and its extra-legal environment, whilst still ensuring the normative self-coherence of law. 'General principles of law' may very well constitute a necessary formalist glue of law-internal self-illusion. In a real-world, however, 'general' legal principles are meaningless: no more than a theocratic mantra of judicial self-justification. The principled mechanics of constitutional morphogenesis must instead be proximate to a real-world. Within the European jurisdiction, as within all constitutional jurisdictions, *Rechtsverfassungsrecht*, or socially constitutive/self-constitutionalising law, must also be rooted in the reflexive effort to '*try to give life and reality to general principles in the light of experience*' (B-04).

### *IV.1. Science, facts, explanation and legal reconstruction of reality*

'Giving life and reality to general principles in the light of experience', however, entails its own clear dangers. Experience, we should never forget, can be bitter:

> The most important aim of the Constitution is to avoid a repetition of the developments, which, in the Weimar Republic, led to the abolition of the separation of powers, and thus to the collapse of the rule of law. The path to the complete surrender of the doctrine of separation of powers through the *Ermächtigungsgesetz* of 1933 took its first open form in the excessively wide interpretation of Article 48(2) of the Weimar Constitution in favour of the executive.[45]

As the Rheinland-Pfalz Finance Court reminded us back in 1964, judicial assessment of 'experience' not only entails the hazard of ill-informed (amateurish) legal reconstruction of social reality, but also poses the danger that fact will simply lead norm, with the de-legitimating and dangerous consequence that law will merely descend into the instrumentalist tool of brute and brutish political power. Accordingly, potential *critique* of the ECJ's seeming aversion to 'fetishist' emphasis upon 'facts'[46] must be distinguished, at least to the degree that the Court demonstrates clear awareness that facts, as well as the scientific appreciation of facts, do have a part to play within the constitutional jurisdiction, but must likewise be strictly (normatively) circumscribed.

Thus, at the general level of constitutional adjudication, and, in particular, in the matter of the legal ability to identify instances of social injustice,[47] the Court expresses explicit awareness of the need for the introduction of interlocutory 'scientific' constructions of social reality within the Courtroom (B-05):

IE: So you wouldn't get socio-economic documents?

IR: Very little. And you know, what the Americans call the 'Brandeis Brief' ... there was [actually] very little of that kind of socio-economic explanation. In a sense, I thought that more would have been useful and I can give one particular case. There was a case about electricity nationalisation, or rather liberalisation of electricity markets. And I think it would have been greatly helpful to have had more economic explanation of how it worked and why it was important to go one way rather than the other.

In other words, in the nitty-gritty world of 'hands-on' social re-distribution, or adjudication upon the best possible organisation of socially re-distributive markets,[48] amateurish and potentially prejudiced judicial appreciation of complex social reality should be mediated against by evidence founded on the scientific appraisal of social reality.[49] Nonetheless, scientific reconstructions of reality should always also be subject to a healthy dose of judicial scepticism (B-03):

IR: What type of evidence would you have preferred to see in a judicial review case?

IE: ... in our Court of First Instance, of course, we had invariably, an extraordinary thing ... if the Commission was saying the steel industry is running a cartel ... the people, [the] businessmen in charge of the various companies never appear, never give evidence .... But you have expert testimony, say from an economist, saying he's studied the market and never has he seen evidence of such intense competition. Because all the prices move the same way .... And you find yourself caught in a conflict between experts and you haven't got the material to get at what exactly is going on .... And one often wonders whether one is really in touch with reality.

IR: What would you have preferred as evidence?

IE: Well, in those cases, being cartel cases, one would like to see the managing directors of the various companies before the court to cross examine them *as to what they were at* (emphasis added).

Frustration is telling: science or social science is not reality, merely another construction of reality, and, accordingly, another reality construct that can be contested, doubted or subverted. Nonetheless, frustration brings with it its own rewards within the parameters of this analysis, as the judicial aspiration to ascertain what 'people were really at' begins to hint at the shape of one particular socially constitutive/self-constitutionalising mirror that might operate to reflect social reality into the courtroom.

The battle for the soul of institutional balance is not, of course, merely founded within social reality: to wit, 'we, the peoples of Europe, *want* greater parliamentary prerogatives and a more representative voice within Europe'. Instead, it also entails promotion of normative reconstructions of social reality: 'we, the peoples of Europe, *should have* greater parliamentary prerogatives and a more representative voice within Europe'. To this exact extent, then, adjudication upon the institutional balance cannot merely limit itself to facts, but is also confronted with normative demands. Nonetheless, the desire 'to know what people were at', if deployed to recast and re-define the notion of 'fact' as a concept of 'explanation', has its own constitutive and constitutionalising force as law moves to submit legal, social and political processes to the disciplining effects of procedural legal standards (B-05):

> [I]n the cases coming from the national courts, what was important was to see how the national system worked, what its effect on the individual was and how the working of the national system geared with the Community treaty rule, or the rule of subordinate legislation. And so, it wasn't really evidence at all. *It was explanation* . . . . The Court of Justice is not a fact-finding tribunal, so, essentially, it was, [a question of], 'given these facts, what's the answer?' How should the law be, what is the law now? Should it be applied? That was the formal question but in order to answer it well, it was necessary to understand the national system. How did the national social security system or tax system or whatever it was, how did that work in practice? How did it come to produce this particular result for the individual? *So that wasn't really evidence, it was explanation* (emphasis added).

Within the ambit of the Article 234 EC mechanism, and even though it is not a fact-finding tribunal, the ECJ nonetheless appears to locate its considerations within 'explanation/fact', or an initial perusal of 'why' an individual might or might not be thought to be placed in a disadvantaged position. Likewise, within Article 234 EC jurisprudence, interplay between 'explanation' or 'fact' and procedural standards of law can be noted, as, to recall our insurance interface example, national legal systems are subjected to notions of administrative 'fairness'.[50] Importantly, however, procedural and explanatory interplay also play their influential role within adjudication on the institutional balance as Article 230 EC judicial review proceedings of the 'legality' of the acts of individual institutions, though, generally speaking, a legal focal point for the presentation of 'argument in a very broad sense' (B-05; presumably a politically constitutive sense) also become an adjudicative mirror on political process, and, more particularly, the facts, or factual constellation of political process.

If the vital *explanatory* distinction between *'Comitology'* and *Re-Radioactive foods* was the *fact* that, within the latter constellation,[51] 'the Commission had a different position from the Parliament' and 'therefore could not represent the Parliament properly' (B-01), the judicial strengthening of parliamentary position and power under the institutional balance is less a matter of radical alteration in the political purview of judges, and more a result of the constitutive power of the interplay between 'explanation/fact' and procedure.

IR: Specifically thinking about it [institutional balance] as a fundamental principle of European law, how do you think it relates to other leading principles of European law such as proportionality, subsidiarity, etc.?

IE: I think they're all part of the same picture. That the institutions have a defined relationship in the Treaty. Or rather, to some extent, their relationship is defined. The Treaty defines the powers of each of them and gives each of them certain powers or prerogatives in relation to particular activities. The Treaty, in a sense, does not always define what the relationship between them is. And therefore it's to that extent linked to proportionality. I suppose underlying some of the Court's jurisprudence on the powers of the Commission or powers of the Parliament is a sort of sense of '*why are you making such a fuss about this?*' Which is, in its own way, a question of proportionality (B-05; emphasis added).

The explanatory judicial key of 'why are you making such a fuss about this?', thus, finds its echo and legal rationalisation within other regulative procedural principles; principles which characterise further judicial efforts to investigate the legality of EU decision-making (B-02):

> [T]here's a margin of appreciation perhaps left to an institution when it's taking a political decision, say, on the question of subsidiarity: where can a particular objective be most effectively achieved – at national level by national measures or at Community level? The Court of Justice will not take that decision for itself, but it will simply examine the *rationality* of the decision of the institution and so allow them a margin of appreciation for judgment, [or] rational judgment (emphasis added).

Even at the level of political contention, the judiciary finds its own mode of escaping direct confrontation with individual political positions. Fact can still play a role: what has happened and why are you making such a fuss? Was political process 'proportional', and/or 'rational', and did it pay due regard to the notion of 'subsidiarity? To this measure, at least, *Rechtsverfassungsrecht* steers its socially constitutive and self-constitutionalising nature away from interventionist adjudication on the nature of the European polity. The Court is not political in the sense that it takes decisions for Community institutions; nor, is it politically constitutive, to the degree that it favours one institution above another in line with its own substantive normative vision of what the European polity should be. Instead, judicial purview of an extra-legal environment, together with the contemporaneous maintenance of internal legal coherence, is initially furnished through the interplay between explanatory fact and procedural principle. What has been going on? How can we assess what has been going on? What are the measures of sensible or rational (proportional) decision-making within Europe? By this token, adjudication is not founded in direct social or political intervention, but instead within the legal processes of the procedural structuring of political and social reality.

### *IV.2. Law and political reality: democratic experimentalism*

The notion of the procedural legal reconstruction of social and political reality is a common feature within judicial self-appraisal and the description of the workings of the ECJ. Interestingly, however, one judge is moved to make an explicit link between notions of proceduralisation, judicial impartiality and the perceived 'democratic deficit' within the European Union (B-02):

> And everybody acknowledges [that] there is a democratic deficit manifesting in various ways in Europe. Judicial review by the Court of Justice of Community measures is one method of ameliorating that democratic deficit. The Treaty requires that a measure, a directive or regulation, must state, must recite, the grounds and basis on which it has actually been adopted, including any expert reports and giving the underlying reasons and objectives. Therefore, in striking down such legislation, the Court is ensuring that the institutions exercise their legislative powers within the ambit of their constitutional functions and requirements. Allowing the Parliament to do so, because the Parliament was denied its prerogatives, is part of that *democratic constitutional balance*. So, I don't think there was anything political at all (emphasis added).

Once again, the mantra of judicial self-description is one of denial of political involvement. *Re Radioactive foods*, or its extension of protection for parliamentary prerogatives, was not a political act. Instead, the ECJ serves the principle of democracy through its review of the legality of political acts and through its perusal 'of what went on'. This perusal, which is aided and abetted by the procedural requirement that all decision-making within the European Union be accompanied by 'statements of reasons', thus furnishes the vital fulcrum by which happenings in a real-world can be explained within a legal idiom, and, at the same time, can be subsumed within the normative legal edifice in order to reconstitute social reality. Procedural principles of rationality, proportionality and subsidiarity are a contemporaneous mirror on the 'real-world' and a normative legal intrusion *into* the real-world. Through their operative counterparts of a 'statement of reasons requirement', or the demand that all decision-making be justified by reference to its 'grounds' or the various 'expert reports' relied upon, procedural principles facilitate the pragmatic legal operation of ascertaining, in the terms of judges, 'what went on'. Explanation or investigation of reality, however, is also a double-edged sword, a simultaneous act, which constitutes reality, as all decisions are likewise required by the courts to be rational and proportionate.

With this, various parallels might be drawn with reasoning exhibited by national courts within the ambit of the application of the Article 234 EC preliminary reference mechanism (Chapter 3 (III.2)). Here, too, self-constitutionalising and socially constitutive law is rooted in the process whereby political partiality is avoided, not simply through closed legal formalism, but, instead, through a reality proximate proceduralism which simultaneously opens political debate up to judicial scrutiny and disciplines it, not by means of application of substantive legal principles (for example, judicial championing of individual rights), but by means of the testing of the processes of political decision-making against their stated aims.

Importantly, however, and all the powers of proceduralisation apart, the art of *Rechtsverfassungsrecht* cannot fully escape substantive, or substantively flavoured judgment. Indeterminate law still demands a measure of 'principled' judgment that must be informed by the social and political mores which an operational social reality embodies. In a final analysis, some form of substantive adjudication has also taken place within the Court's jurisprudence. The place of the European Parliament within political negotiations has also been assured, its position at the political table confirmed by law. The substantive reading of the principle of institutional balance has been altered in favour of its majoritarian colonisation by the principle of the separation of powers, or a 'principle' of 'democratic constitutional balance'. In other words, within an explicitly constitutional jurisdiction, the problem of the judicial identification and approbation of operational social reality is a heightened one. The social and political justice demands and values which a real-world embodies must be addressed, and a procedurally conceived *Rechtsverfassungsrecht* is, therefore, exposed directly to the dangers of direct intervention within the substantive mores of the environment within which it is embedded.

All self-illusionary and nonsensical efforts to disguise substantive judicial intervention within a European polity apart, European law, or adjudication upon the institutional balance, is, therefore, and interestingly so, also engaged in its own various and varied forms of 'democratic experimentalism'. At first glance, this process of legal democratic experimentalism might be considered to be dangerous, a perverse betrayal of judicial impartiality within classical conceptions of the separation of powers. Rather than restrict its role to that of oversight over the exercise of political powers, law claims a politically constitutive prerogative for itself (B-01):

> I refuse for myself to split politics from policy, from law. For me, that's completely, that's why I would start completely different[ly] – say, of course, they are twinned and not separate notions, they are twin notions. And you cannot, as a lawyer, give a solution to something without having this policy-oriented mind. *And then again, you must try to check that – whether it remains within the legal context.* That you are not – because, after all, policy-minded means that you must find somewhere a consensus. *Now consensus is not only in the Parliament by majority, it is as well in the common law from judges, which is growing from beneath* and, it's a rather broad ideal of democracy *representative, deliberative* democracy. Everything which helps, and we should single out none of these tactics because all of that helps ... (microphone crashes; emphasis added).

Saved by the bell? Or rather, by too short a cord on the external microphone? No, because the point is remorselessly reiterated (B: 01):

> A consensus can also be present in case law. If not, a judge does not get elected. You have heard the expression the voice of '*le juge le roi*'. As Montesquieu would say the voice of the law as well as the elected representatives are ... (sentence unfinished).

Are our European judges elected? Is law a simple matter of consensus between Europe's judge-kings? Has the classical separation of powers principle, at least as it applies to a judiciary, not only been excluded from European treaties, but also been thoroughly wiped from European legal minds? What of Montesquieu? Surely, he argued that law should be raised above a fray of political consensus and election?[52] Have centuries of careful constitutional development been dispensed with? Are our judges our kings?

No. Hesitation, grammatical incoherence and incomplete expression should not be singled out as instances of revolutionary prevarication, or as an underlying and broken semantic that mirrors disintegration within the judicial function. Certainly, loss of argumentative and expressive clarity is an indication of judicial perplexity, a reaction to the clear disjunction between the demands placed upon a modern supranational law and the limits to formalist legal understandings. It is not, however, a betrayal of law and legal ideals. Quite the contrary: the vital legal function is one of 'remaining within the legal context'.

However, the challenges of law-giving within a contested supranational polity are immense. The judge is necessarily thrust into the position of the judge-king identified by the *Freirechtsschule*. He or she must make sense of the realities of a contested polity, must somehow ascertain what is growing 'from beneath'. He or she must engage in the task of legal materialisation, in the endeavour to root law within shifting social reality, including its own constructed social and political mores, such as democratic expression. Equally, however, he or she must also 'maintain legal context', must ensure the coherence of law. At this level, then, disjointed judicial pronouncement is not about the veiling of illegitimate judicial political activism. Instead, it is all about a difficult and complex effort to materialise or to 'democratise' law.[53]

In this regard, the refusal to split politics from policy or from law is thus a simple realistic appreciation of the complex realities of constitutional adjudication absent an authoritative constitution or settled *demos*. Equally, however, stuttering efforts to describe the modes of reconnection of European law to its 'democratic' environment might also be argued to be an indication of experimentalism within a substantively flavoured realm of European constitutional adjudication; or, of the readiness to test a variety of legal materialisation or legal democratisation strategies. The self-constitutionalising impulses of *Rechtsverfassungsrecht* remain prescient. Experimentalism in law must also have a firm basis within internal legal narratives and strategies. Although application of a 'traditional' cannon of legal principles may not be a convincing mode to overcome transcendental nonsense within formal jurisprudence, the demand for 'principled' (ethical and moral) adjudication remains an overwhelming one. Nonetheless, the political and social justice demands of an extra-legal environment must still be met with a degree of legal impartiality.

As a consequence, the 'principled' mechanics of constitutional morphogenesis, turn to more experimental methods to identify the social and political mores that arise within the reality of the integration process. Adjudicating upon the institutional balance, European law is also playing its direct part in the identification of the legitimate shape and nature of a European polity. Denied recourse to traditional axiomatic modes of constitutional legitimation, the ECJ must thus struggle to retain its own impartiality. Consequently, it is with an eye to this struggle that the analysis now moves on more closely to consider two potential forms of 'principled constitutional morphogenesis' within the narrative of the ECJ, or the two particular modes of legal materialisation that suggest themselves within the current data-set: 'systemic legal consensus' and 'deliberative democratic experimentalism'.

### *IV.2.1. Systemic legal consensus*

The feeling that the European Parliament 'should have its place in the sun' (B-05), is one shared by most interviewees within the data-set. Judges and Commission officials all agree that the strengthening of the position of the European Parliament is key to ensuring the legitimacy of the Union (A-02): 'If you want to ensure acceptability, legitimacy of what we are doing the way to go ... is to strengthen the role of the European Parliament in all this.'

However, could 'simple agreement' between non-elected officials and a judiciary ever be sufficient to justify an increase in parliamentary competences outside the putatively 'constitutive' deliberations of ICGs or Constitutional Conventions? Clearly, other more personal reasons may have led some European judges to promote greater protection for parliamentary prerogatives (B-05):

> At the end of the day ... yes, of course, there's a political aspect. And it's unquestionable that some judges, more than others, saw it as a point of importance that the European Parliament should have, um, should have its place in the sun, yes. However, I would also say that, in general, those judges were judges who had ... as children or young men been in a country which did not have a Parliament – and where democracy didn't work. And so I think that again, yes, it was a political point of view if you like, but it was also a *moral* point of view for many of them (emphasis added).

The appeal to 'morality' is telling. Yes, politics may play its role in judicial reasoning. But this is not the mucky politics of personal self-advancement or promotion of a political programme (B-05): 'I really do not remember any of them urging a particular point of view because of party politics'. Instead, the reality mirroring and reality forming procedural principles of *Rechtsverfassungsrecht* (proportionality, rationality, subsidiarity) are left behind and a substantive principle of 'democratic constitutional balance' (B-02) is embraced in the service of 'moral politics'.

Judicial morality: are we to be satisfied, however, that the simple personal morality of the ECJ is sufficient justification for judicially managed constitutional morphogenesis? Perhaps not: personal morality is undoubtedly a good thing, but it is also indeterminate and prone to excesses of its own. Who, after all, would really like to see the appointments to the ECJ managed with the same degree of moral horse-trading that marks appointments to the US Supreme Court? However, is there, perhaps, a degree of 'shared' historical morality within Europe and within Europe's many laws that could constitute sufficient justification for constitutional morphogenesis? More particularly, can constitutional morphogenesis be justified with reference to a shared European experience of historical constitutional failures and triumphs?

The notion of 'shared' experience can, therefore, be argued, to be a vital self-disciplining judicial key, a reality proximate principle within processes of constitutional morphogenesis. 'Consensus', or agreement that morality is shared amongst European polities, because the historical experience from which that morality derives, is also shared, should lessen the danger that principles such as 'democratic constitutional balance' are simple nonsensical expressions of formal legal reasoning, or are merely a reflection of personal historical experience and the moral peccadilloes of individual judges.

Counter-intuitively, however, such consensus and shared morality can only be divined out of diversity. One Judge's polemic against the harmonising human rights jurisdiction of the Strasbourg Court of European Human rights because it 'doesn't allow for diversity of values' is telling (B-02). The point is not simply one that a European Court has no business straying into national moral issues such as abortion,[54] but is, instead, the far deeper one that 'harmonisation for the sake of harmonisation' undermines 'national constitutional culture and tradition and competence' (B-02). Where, after all, are we to find shared history and shared morality, or points of substantial common constitutional reference if not within divergent constitutional traditions? From this vantage point, concepts of a 'shared European constitutional heritage' cease to be indistinct 'organic' or 'romantic' notions and begin to take on a 'neutral' justificatory role: the moral and ethical principles of judicial adjudication within Europe will be mined out of the pit of shared European history.

By this same token, however, moral and ethical principles of judicial interpretation remain wholly dependent upon discourse between still distinct and formally construed national legal orders. The two crucial elements within the concept of 'shared', self-constitutionalising and socially constitutive, judicial moral politics must be dialogue between distinct systems and expression of morality in 'formal' legal, rather than personal emotional, terms.

Seen in this light, the two vital signals sent to an ECJ by the German Courts begin to take on a very different significance. The 1964 Judgment delivered by the Rheinland-Pfalz Tax Court is, therefore, not simply significant for its reminder that living memory demonstrated very clearly indeed that excessive transfer of powers to an executive might lead to constitutional and moral turpitude (*Re Tax on Malt Barley*). Instead, its legal basis – the clear incompatibility of the German model of the separation of powers with the European logic of the institutional balance of powers – is a rational formal expression of shared historical experience. Translating into the underlying conversational idiom: 'certainly, Europe might be all about functionalism and the efficient management of European governance by European executives; but never forget, the separation of powers established within a German Constitution was made for very good reason'. Furthermore, its formal rational expression, confirmed by means of 50 years of constitutional jurisprudence within the Republic is a simple reflection of the judicial efforts to stay true to the founding desire of the Republic's polity never again to descend into constitutional turpitude.[55] When extending its *invitatio ad offerendum* to the ECJ to consider whether the peoples of Europe might be afforded more direct representation within European decision-making, the German Constitutional Court, in its *Brunner* judgment, was likewise making the selfsame formalist legal point: the German model of the separation of powers would set the limits to functionally conceived processes of European integration. Underlying this formal pronouncement, however, was a legal narrative of historical justification: mass democratic representation is a traditional feature within national constitutions for proven good reason – the powers of the executive must be curbed.

Formalist legal pronouncement is important: formalism reiterates the fact that the morality expressed is not simply a reflection of judicial experience, but is, instead, a mirror to the historical experiences of an entire people encapsulated within its own constitutional tradition. Judicial dialogue is also important. The ECJ cannot decide for itself which shared historical experiences should inform substantive European constitutional principles. Instead, judicial 'consensus' between Europe's laws and legal orders forms the procedural basis for substantively flavoured, or 'principled' reality recognition and, thus, for constitutional morphogenesis within Europe.

### *IV.2.2. Deliberative democratic experimentalism*

The strengthening of the position of the European Parliament within European governance is not the end of legal materialisation and legal democratisation efforts within European law. Quite the contrary: both judges and bureaucrats are explicit in their recognition of a democratic *malaise* within the European Union, and even more explicit in their expression of great doubt as to whether representative democracy, or an increase in parliamentary powers, can ever fully compensate for the democratic deficit experienced by the individual European citizen. One Commission official doubts the ability of a European Parliament, as well as Europe as a whole, ever to gain the loyalty and belief of the European Citizen (A-04):

> My mother does not know how laws are made in Westminster, but what she knows is whether she voted for the party in power or not ... and the Queen is in the palace signing them and everything is lovely. When it comes to Europe, we don't have that instinctive loyalty on the part of our citizens.

Added to this, however, another official doubts whether the Parliament can properly represent European citizens since it is too busy being flattered by national governments (A-01):

> Member states are ... discovering the European Parliament as an institution where you also can influence ... and it happens in the Parliament that you have votes where all German parliamentarians or a very large majority all [vote with] one side regards of party lines.

More importantly, however, one judge chooses to dismiss the workings of the European Parliament in its entirety (B-02):

> And they vaunt this mantra that we've increased powers to the Parliament. The Parliament is disconnected from the ordinary people.

> Their representatives are disconnected from the ordinary people. They are never elected on European policies or the positions that they take up in Parliament. People don't know what position they take up in Parliament. They never tell them what position they take up in Parliament. And they are consumed by getting more powers for the Parliament rather than exercising the ones they have. And that's my frank view.

'Frank' and unflattering: representative democratic legitimation within Europe is not simply questioned because citizens might be disconnected from their representatives, but also because their representatives are more interested in the exercise of power than in the act of representation.

Within the effort to materialise and democratise law then, whilst the parliamentary position has certainly been strengthened, judges remain open to the potential for other democratisation strategies (B-01):

> Now consensus is not only in the Parliament by majority, it is as well in the common law from judges, which is growing from beneath and it's a rather broad ideal of democracy representative, deliberative democracy. Everything which helps and we should single out none of these tactics because all of that helps ... (microphone crashes to floor).

As our perennially flustered judge reminds us, a degree of openness should always be maintained with regard to newer forms of democracy while, in particular, law and politics may form a partnership, within which law itself can be part of democratic process. Accordingly, the analysis now turns to an examination of how judges have played their part within a process of democratic experimentalism within Europe, and, more particularly, of how they have or have not sought to serve the cause of 'deliberative democratic experimentalism'.

Clearly, at one level, the pure procedural principles identified as making up a putative European *Rechtsverfassungsrecht* are, at core, also all about support for deliberative democracy. In this respect, then, proportionality, subsidiarity and rationality play their prime role in ensuring that whilst decision-making is not necessarily representative, it is, nonetheless, 'democratic', or, at least is so to the degree that the imposition of a 'rule of reason' requires that egotistic self-interest must be set aside or tested against objective 'reality-revealing' rationality criteria. Decision-making is, therefore, founded in 'arguing rather than bargaining'. Taking the analysis one level further, however, a question must also be posed as to whether European law plays any further role in encouraging deliberative experimentalism within Europe. More particularly, through the introduction of a measure of participatory democracy, or the opening up of European decision-making processes to review by other 'rationalising' forces, or 'interested' parties who might have been excluded from a legislative process.[56]

In the light of the latter question, analysis upon the institutional balance therefore intersects with more general problems of judicial review, and, more particularly, with the issue of individual standing under Article 230 EC Treaty. In other words, given the fact that the individual European citizen is poorly 'represented' within the substantive institutional balance – or rather that the representatives of the European citizen (European Parliament) are either not representative of the citizen, or have only a limited impact on European decision-making – can the individual citizen be given an alternative place within the balance by means of a right to challenge the 'rationality' of putatively 'deliberative' decision-making before the Courts? Can deliberative democracy be strengthened within the mechanics of judicial review?

As noted, individual standing under Article 230 EC Treaty is very restricted, indeed.[57] Significantly, the Court of First Instance has slightly widened individual standing to allow for the inclusion, for example, of regional governments within the circle of parties fortunate enough to be allowed to challenge EU decision-making.[58] Recent liberality, however, is more than matched by the intransigent historical jurisprudence of the ECJ. The Court does not accept the *Schutznormtheorie*,[59] whereby standing should be given to all petitioners in all cases where potential faults in decision-making are particularly grievous. In place of this judicially democratising theory, 'standing' is a formal procedural matter to be decided prior to examination of the material facts of the case. Accordingly, the explicit treaty test of 'direct and individual effect' determines that individual Europeans still have very little chance of asserting their voice within the institutional balance under the provisions of Article 230 EC.

Within the current data-set, however, judicial opinion also remains intransigent. The test of standing under Article 230 EC should not be expanded to allow for review of political decision-making. Asked whether the ECJ should allow class actions under Article 230 EC, or claims made on behalf of individuals by interest groups, one judge is adamant (B-05):

> My feeling has been that the Court itself, as opposed to some of the Advocates General, the Court itself has always been pretty strict about that aspect of judicial review. And, therefore, unless and until the treaty-makers decide that there should be class actions, there isn't scope for class actions.

Strict formalism, indeed: the Treaty has laid down a clear test and we shall follow that test until such time as it is altered (an example of textual immanence?). What, then, of the demand that Europe be democratised, that its law be materialised? Is the ECJ (rather than the Court of First Instance) wholly unwilling to try out the different forms of democratic experimentalism which might furnish an emerging European polity with an added degree of legitimacy? Has deliberative democratic experimentalism been sacrificed upon the altar of legal formalism? Perhaps not. However, the considered grounds for continuing judicial intransigence are revealing:

IE: I think this is due, in, is related, in one sense, to [notions of] Sovereignty of Parliament .... But, actually, it's to do with the practicality of legislation. There has to come a point at which various interest groups cease to have a right to interfere with the process of legislation. Because any form of legislation is bound to hurt somebody, or pretty well any form of legislation is bound to hurt somebody. And that's what legislators are supposed to take into account. They are supposed to be aware of how their legislation will affect other people. And there are, nowadays, there are all sorts of lobbies to make sure that the interests of particular groups are recognised in the pre-legislative stage. And the Community system is extraordinarily transparent to lobbying and consultation and so on. It takes so long that it is inconceivable that anybody's point of view – really, [anyone] who has taken, made any effort to make it known – has not been made known. Now if you – to the extent that you [do] allow a challenge of legislation, it means that the person who is disappointed by the political choice that's been made can then, start again in another forum ... most of the time, that actually means that, particularly the multi-nationals, will object to what is being done.

IR: So do you mean that this is a conscious decision by the Court to keep the standing narrow?

IE: No, I think, no, I don't think this is a conscious .... I think that ... any system has to say 'enough is enough, at this point we stop. We have made a political choice and that's the end of it' .... Right, two questions. Is it desirable that judges, rather than legislators, should decide that question? The second question. *What are the criteria against which judges are going to test it? Because, at the end of the day, choice is truly a political choice and not a judicial choice* (emphasis added).

A long but illuminating passage: any formalist treatment of Article 230 EC masks refined judicial understanding of democratic theory, as well as a similarly startling appreciation of social, political and legal reality. The point is not simply the abstract philosophical one that pluralist democratic conceptions are inconsistent with majoritarian government: the question is not one of the maintenance of parliamentary sovereignty or the rejection of an individually nominating political voice within the legislative process. Instead, the point is also made in full awareness of the realities of a pluralist, self-nominating European polity and the institutional and legal structures that such a polity requires.

Not only is the judicial mind aware of lobbying and plural representation at legislative stage, it also seems to approve of it as lobbying is prescribed a positive value of 'transparency'. Significantly, the Court would thus seem to be in agreement with Commission officials who feel that lobbying by interest groups, although beset by various difficulties, has, on balance, a positive impact upon the rationality and legitimacy of EU decision-making. Thus, whilst '[t]he influence of NGOs is far beyond what you would think appropriate in a democracy', and they likewise have a tendency to 'overshoot',[60] they are nonetheless an undoubted aid to 'rational' decision-making (A-07):

> Sugar is now the next reform, which we are trying to prepare and we are a bit at a loss. We don't know what proposal to make. There are several alternatives and none seems to be particularly good. So, we are listening. We are in a listening mode to everybody who wants to tell us something. Of course ... the sugar industry, the sugar farming organisations and so on, they all try to let their views be known. Plus, it's very important to do that. I think lobbying in that sense is a positive thing.

Equally, the positive rational side of 'lobbying' is not restricted to the advice and counsel given by 'organisations in the know', always potentially self-interested parties. Instead, NGOs also play their democratising role:

> [I]t's democratic ... because they do reflect, to some extent, views within the public who do not feel represented by ... [the] European Parliament. Who feel that they don't have a voice or they don't know how to influence the system (A-07).

The Court and the Commission agree. The plural self-nominating European polity is a reality, and it is a positive reality. Lobbying, or the presence of interests groups, can improve the quality of 'deliberative' decision-making. Where the Commission does not have adequate expertise, lobbying plays its useful rationalising function, ensuring that policy-making is well informed. Equally, however, the quality of deliberation is also improved as more diffuse interests, not necessarily formally represented within the institutional balance, take part in pre-legislative discussions, and present their values, ideas and opinions to the Commission.

Judicial knowledge of and sensitivity towards the Commission's reliance on the plural self-nominating European polity may itself be decried as too cosy a relationship between the 'activist' supranational institutions of European integration. As one lawyer opines (B-06): 'in my view, the court sometimes shows too much deference to the institutions'. Alternatively, the Court is simply too trusting of the Commission's ability properly to integrate all the views and values of interested parties within decision-making.[61] Nonetheless, the Court's unwillingness to extend standing seems also to derive from less cosy and more realistic factors. First, of course, constant challenge to legislative acts is time-consuming. Second, and far more significantly, however, if the Court were to intervene directly in order to decide who might challenge legislative acts before it, it would be making a clear political decision on the substantive nature of the European polity. It is one thing for the evolving European polity to nominate itself through its presence or non-presence in Brussels, it is quite another for the Court to nominate its major actors: 'at the end of the day, that choice is truly a political choice'.

Once again, the procedural contours of *Rechtsverfassungsrecht* are visible, even in relation to a substantive value of democratic expression. Law opens up its mirror to a substantive reality. It sees and approves of the process of deliberative democratic experimentalism in which the Commission is engaging. At the same time, however, it itself retreats into proceduralism and maintains its neutrality. It cannot nominate parties to deliberation without being itself embroiled in a political act: '[W]hat are the criteria against which judges are going to test it?' Instead, its politically constitutive role must be limited to review of the rationality of decision-making through procedural principles that act both to reveal the reality underlying decision-making *and* constitute that reality – the prime criteria for judicial review around the notion of institutional balance remain those of proportionality, subsidiarity and rational decision-making.

At the same time, however, rationality might also be argued to be served by one further criterion: have all parties who are affected by a political decision, been given their chance to play a part within the political process? Generally, this is a matter for the Commission. However, on a case to case basis, adjustments may be made. Accordingly, recent Court of First Instance jurisprudence may finally be argued to be procedural rather than substantive in nature. Rights of standing are not afforded to individuals or, say, to regional governments by virtue of judicial promotion of a rights discourse. Instead, individual and regional parties are allowed standing since they have been denied access to political (or executive) decision-making processes (Ward 2005).

The vital rationality criteria is therefore the judicial question – and one that is again posed in line with notions of 'explanation', or the impulse to 'see what people were at' – of, 'are you sure that all relevant interests were consulted during the decision-making process'? Rather than represent an unfortunate rights-based approach to the institutional balance, or a substantive individualistic assault on the governing principles of the Union (Jacqué 2004), cases such as *Azores* and *Pfizer*[62] seek to ensure that deliberative democracy within Europe *is* deliberative because *all* relevant interests have at least been considered.

### *IV.3. Professionalism, formalism and legal (self-) illusion re-established*

Finally, however, in an interesting parallel to findings at national level, the data-set also hints at the (self-) illusionary powers of notions of legal professionalism. Lawyers, of course, are never politically active instruments of European integration. Instead, in seeking to persuade the ECJ to apportion political power this way and that within the institutional balance, they are simply performing a service for clients (B-05): 'And what lawyers do ... is help to advance their client's cause'[63].

But (self-) illusion is also at work amongst judges, and, in particular, within their constant mantra of legal formalism (B-05):

> The Treaty is perfectly clear. The institutions have certain rights. The member states have certain rights. Other institutions, organs, bodies have certain limited rights according to the Treaty. Those who do not fall into those classes are given a right of action if it is a decision addressed to them.

The institutional balance is thus neatly wrapped up and parcelled within clear doctrinal incantations. There is no effort to locate law within reality here. Instead, law calmly steers its static abstract path through dynamic political reality.

This may be an act of transcendental nonsense. In a final analysis, however, formalism also plays a vital role. Certainly, the ECJ may not be able to widen standing under Article 230 EC, since, as one lawyer remarks, 'they are stuck with this test that has been written in the Treaty and [was] interpreted back in the 1960s. And they don't feel that they can just ignore it' (B-04).[64] However, formalism may also be argued to play a vital legitimating role within *Rechtsverfassungsrecht*; not only because formalism within European judicial dialogue furnishes a means for expression of national constitutional values but also since formalism, or rational formal adjudication on Article 230 EC, allows judges to resist the pressure to engage in the political act of the identification of the 'legitimate' European polity.

## V. Conclusion: dynamic proceduralism

The analysis finally returns to Jean-Paul Jacqué and to his seminal assertion that the principle of the 'institutional balance of powers' is a vital constitutional fulcrum which is both facilitative of 'dynamic' political development within Europe, and regulative of that dynamism, because 'static' European law both disciplines and dissipates any political conflict (Jacqué 1990: 247–360). The analysis is without doubt an inspirational one: legal formalism, or the exact apportionment of competences, prerogatives and rights by the European Treaty, is thus saved from 50 years of realist legal *critique* and recast in the role of the saviour of the contested European integration process, as austere interpretation and application of treaty strictures acts as a bulwark against unconscionable attempts to obtain power by any one European institution, member state, or, indeed, individual.

An inspirational analysis, certainly, but is it correct? Two factors in particular seem to disturb the vision. Clearly, the institutional principle of the balance of powers is 'not [simply a] separation of power' (B-01). The functional entwinement of power that it appears to envisage differs widely from Montesquieu's elegant division of state power into executive, legislative and judicial components. Nonetheless, at a deeper level of legitimation, the notion of institutional balance of power undoubtedly attracts the same conflicting normative impulses that characterise the separation of powers model. Thus, the institutional balance is also all about 'checks and balances', 'transparency in government' and even (on occasions) the 'representation of the individual'. Equally, in the course of a process of European integration, the notion of institutional balance has also come to be 'colonised' by its separation of powers counterpart. In other words, and learning the lesson taught by Bruce Ackerman (2000), the institutional balance of powers is far from being a 'neutral' normative (formal legal) instrument, subject only to occasional troublesome assault by political forces, with arguments of *pareto*-efficiency in hand, but the glint of power accumulation in their eye. Instead, the institutional balance of powers is a magnet for the promotion of, discussion on, and contest about, the nature and shape of a legitimate European polity. The principle of institutional balance is certainly a constitutional fulcrum, an expression of the changing shape of a European polity. But it is also a contested principle, a focal point for the deep-seated battle on the legitimate soul of Europe.

Equally, however, law and legal process remain indeterminate. Application of the principle in the courtroom is neither a matter of 'orthodox' adjudication (B-01), nor simple 'JUDGMENT' in the terms foreseen by Hamilton. Instead, Madison's concerns about the limits to grammatical and semantic exactness reign supreme, as judges engage in adjudicational 'ingenuity' or 'creative judgment'.[65] Additionally, however, judges also feel that they possess a 'mandate', a competence afforded to them by politicians to fill in the gaps in the European integration process and to perfect (in tandem with the Commission?) supranational European decision-making. In short, at the deeply contested interface of adjudication on institutional competences, Europe's judges and European law would seem to be engaged in a process of polity explication; a process, furthermore, that contrasts starkly with the limited oversight role apportioned to them by Montesquieu within his model of the separation of powers.

'*Le juge le roi*': 'we, the court', indeed – a nightmare scenario of judge-led European integration processes that must surely raise major concerns about the legitimacy of the European project. Or should it? After all, legal indeterminacy is a fact of life. All constitutional jurisdictions and all legal processes are necessarily marked by failings in formalism and 'JUDGMENT', by adjudicational processes carried on beyond the 'formalist veil'. European law is no exception, or rather it is *sui generis*, since the disputed integration *telos*, or even the functional requirements of the integration *telos*, intensify the problems of legal indeterminacy as the provisions of directives, regulations and even the treaties[66] remain necessarily vague, a part of the effort to keep 'everyone on board'.

*Rechtsverfassungsrecht*: between facts and norms, adjudicational struggle around an indeterminate principle of institutional balance is not an unusual judicial operation. Granted, European lawyers, judges, practitioners and academics have been thrust very forcefully into the twilight zone between legal formalism and legal materialisation. They have been thrust into the 'danger zone', within which a Max Weber, at least, felt that the task of 'democratising' law beyond formal interpretation was impossible, a simultaneous pursuit and an undermining of the necessary and civilising certainties of the rule of law. Thus, for all that the members of the ECJ may opine that, 'well, the rule of law is trying to compensate ... [the] rule of law will do that' [B-01], legal democratisation efforts are a chimera, a headlong descent into the legal and constitutional turpitude that marked the dying days of the Weimar Republic and facilitated the rise of the Third Reich. Far better the judge who demands the final settlement of Europe and the creation of a 'normal' constitutional jurisdiction (B-03):

> [n]ational courts are obliged to give precedence to European law. So what you have is national courts acting as federal courts. The public don't really appreciate that this has happened ... and it places the national judges in a very, in a very strange position because they have to overrule their own governments .... That is a division between federal power and state power that is disguised. I think that, at some stage, people are going to have to face up to the fact that if there is to be a European Community, it has to be a federal community. And it's better that the powers of the various entities be spelled out so the people know where they stand rather than relying upon judges like me to apply our creative instincts to situations (laughs).

Once again, the laughter reveals all: we really should not be doing this – we are undemocratic. By the same token, however, laughter is also indicative of the limits to formalist law (B-05): 'the facts seemed to be of almost no significance whatsoever' (laughs). Is law caught in a cleft stick, trapped between a rock and a hard place, forever called upon to fulfil a function, which it is ill-equipped to perform?

Perhaps. But there again, perhaps not. Certainly, formalist veils should be drawn aside. Judicial opinion that an institutional balance of powers should not be codified and should not be set in stone should be highlighted, together with its underlying rationale (B-05):

> And my feeling is that when you start being too prescriptive – you can do this, but you mustn't do that – there, the reality is that you

> actually cut yourself off from quite a lot of things which might have been useful.

Indeterminacy is ascribed a positive value, not for the unfortunate reason that we, in Europe, have failed to agree upon our 'constitution'. Instead, indeterminacy is also a force for positive good because it enables the vital and democratic process of legal materialisation and reception of reality within law.

> I think, on the whole, the court has managed to preserve a pretty good balance between the two extremes, the extreme of prescription to the letter and the extreme of, umm, really the letter doesn't matter, we are going to say, we're going to go for the spirit, etc. (B-05)

The tension between formal and material law-giving remains. It is a dangerous tightrope. Nonetheless, the Court has walked that tightrope and has, perhaps, also bequeathed us various concrete elements of *Rechtsverfassungsrecht*, which lend self-constitutionalising and self-constitutive legitimacy to processes of constitutional morphogenesis that focus on the institutional balance:

Core principles of *Rechtsverfassungsrecht*: Procedural principles of proportionality, rationality and subsidiarity, which, together with the legal process of explanation, both reveal reality to law and simultaneously constitute it, never once compromising law or drawing it into the political fray.

Dialogue between formal constitutional traditions: Europe's diversity remains its strength. Shared historical experiences inform common substantively flavoured constitutional principles. No one court can claim a moral high-ground. Acting together, however, Europe's individual legal orders can identify those substantive principles which should inform its overarching law.

Democratic experimentalism: Once again, Europe's democracy deficit remains its bugbear. Nonetheless, rather than pursue damaging corrective notions of individual substantive right, Europe's law can contribute to processes of democratic, and, in particular, deliberative democratic experimentalism without necessarily being drawn into brute politics.

These elements of a possible *Rechtsverfassungsrecht* will be treated in more detail in Chapter 7. Nonetheless, it should be noted here that Jean-Paul Jacqué may be right in asserting that static law is the vital constitutional fulcrum that has both facilitated *and* disciplined a process of contested European integration. Certainly, static law has nothing to do with formal legal reasoning. Instead, static law entails the far harder proceduralist effort to facilitate politics and political process, while simultaneously maintaining the internal integrity and coherence of law.

## Notes

1 Statement made by a former Attorney General of the ECJ [B-01]. Quotations are taken from questionnaires filled in by and interviews conducted with members of the European Constitutional Convention, past and present members of the ECJ (Court of First Instance) and current members of the European Commission. For full explanation of the methodology applied, and very importantly, its limits, see Section I. In the following, 'IR' denotes interviewer; 'IE' denotes interviewee.
2 Although the Single European Act of 1987 introduced a degree of majority-voting, consensus remains the major element within Community decision-making.
3 Presumably, by ensuring that the Council and Parliament (representative organs for a European public) maintain their place within the triadic institutional balance.
4 Linguistic inversion, in this case, might thus be traced to the core problem underlying the legitimation of the process of European integration. In the absence of full settlement, integration is seemingly legitimated by a variety of competing notions and theories. Thus, our classical understanding of 'functionality' (if not functionalism), or 'technocracy', whose underlying legitimating impetus derives from the ability or otherwise of a sovereignty pooling organisation 'to get the job done', and furthermore 'to get the job done well' may be classed amongst the theories prizing output legitimacy within the European Union. Nonetheless, output legitimacy is far from being the end of the legitimation story, and a corresponding demand for input legitimacy may thus yet witness the re-harnessing of the 'functionality' sobriquet to give institutional meaning to the notion that all the diverse parts of the EU polity should somehow be 'included' within decision-making, no matter how complex or obscure the legislative results may be.
5 The dangers posed by the Community method are made explicit by one Commission official (A-07): 'Now, when they find out that maybe things are not going in their direction and so on, then, they use the big cannons, you know. So either a Minister comes here on visit and expresses his views or his worries or his suggestions, or the Head of State – most active would be people like Chirac because they have a background in agriculture – will call. The President will say 'careful on this note and so on absolutely is excluded ... so you to have this. My election depends on that. You know, if you don't do this ... I'm in trouble. So, all this is a normal part of law-making in any place and here obviously as well. Now, if we don't listen, we then run into trouble'. 'Functionality' in a European law-making setting has its evident drawbacks: would Chirac's views prevail in an open democratic process? Is backroom lobbying 'normal'?
6 A mandate, moreover which is subject to legislative recall (B-01): 'That takes precedence over case law'. In other words, intergovernmentalist notions of the legitimacy of the ECJ find some support. Ultimately, case law is legitimised by the potential that it will be (legislatively) overturned. At the practical level, however, this construction can be doubted. Intergovernmental Conferences are not only rare occurrences, but may also fall victim to the self-momentum inherent to judicial law-making processes: how easy is it to deny a right once given?
7 Note, however, the doubts about the existence of a 'normal' jurisdiction within European law. See Chapter 3 (III) and Chapter 4 (III). In essence, at the non-authoritative limits to authoritative law-giving, all law is constitutional law.
8 And, thus, for the democratic construction of the European polity.
9 See Chapter 3 for a discussion of the notion of textual immanence and originalism. In short, however, theories of adjudication founded in originalism have little application within the EU constitutional setting, not simply because different interests have divergent views on the future of European integration, but also

because even a 'collective will', for example, that of the European Constitutional Convention, may be seeking to obscure the very aims it is pursuing. Thus, the views of one European lawyer on the Convention's failure to enunciate clearly a constitutional principle of institutional balance, or indeed, a separation of powers principle (B-04: lawyer): 'Yes. I think the Convention and the constitution they produced is fairly uninspiring. There is far too much detail, not enough general principles. And the fact is they could have written something general about the institutional balance. They could have described the institutions in terms of executive, legislative – in the classic way you describe governmental institutions. But they didn't probably because they didn't want to emphasise that, they want a federal government for obvious political reasons. But yes, I think they could have done a lot more, the Convention'.

10 See Chapter 5: there is no simple *pareto* efficiency here.

11 For example, which substances can safely be included within beer? See above, Chapter 2 (III.2).

12 In other words, we cannot simply assume that principles have a pre-existing legitimacy. The following pages are accordingly dedicated to the task of analysing the origins and potential legitimacy of principles.

13 A notion continually referred to in the interviews conducted.

14 In other words, a complete departure from the liberal constitutional framework and a disorientating confrontation with 'relativist' social and political views.

15 More particularly, a comprehensive 'discourse analysis' of the interviews conducted, seeking to reconstruct underlying intentions and understandings of actors through analysis of their speech mannerisms. This approach is nonetheless rejected for the reasons given. Note, however, that structured interview techniques also contain their own 'scientific', methodological premises: indicators are carefully designed to test pre-constructed propositions. Equally, contextual and textual analysis also places a certain value on speech manners. Accordingly, although the responses have been edited in order to aid comprehension, editing has been slight in order to retain primary data.

16 Of the 200 questionnaires circulated, 17 replies were received, of which 13 came from the Commission, three came from European Courts (ECJ and Court of First Instance) and one from an alternating member of the European Constitutional Convention (MEP).

17 A total of eight interviews were conducted, seven of which were with high-ranking members of the Commission. The remaining interview was conducted with an Advocate General within the Court of First Instance.

18 A total of six interviews were conducted. Past members of the Court (rather than sitting judges) were approached for obvious reasons: current members expressed unwillingness to engage in an exercise that might endanger their judicial neutrality.

19 See above, Chapter 3. Judges within the United Kingdom overwhelmingly framed their responses to interview in a formalist idiom.

20 It is nonetheless tempting also to ascribe a certain investigative value to the almost total lack of response from political institutions, above all, from the European Parliament: where, one asks, are Europe's politicians?

21 Above all, and in addition to clarification of national and EU competences, its privileging of both executive and representative functions within the balance (President of the Council; increased role for national and European parliaments within the EU legislative process), and its concomitant, if implicit, support for the colonisation of the *sui generis* EU balance of powers by a separation of powers principle (see above, Chapter 5 (I and III.1).

22 See above, Chapter 3 (II), for the restricted nature of discussions conducted between the Constitutional Convention and the ECJ.

23 Ten respondents viewed the notion of institutional balance as a primarily 'political tool', while the remainder of the respondents (seven) declared the notion to be a 'legal principle'. The respondents were given a third choice of appellation, that of 'administrative mechanism'. Interestingly, only one respondent directly felt that the balance of powers played any administrative role, and then only after the notion has been deployed as a political tool.

24 The notion of the Commission as a 'facilitator' or 'honest broker' is one reproduced throughout the data set – or is, at least, one often reproduced from the viewpoint of the Commission. In a slight alteration to triadic notions of legitimate governance, which place their faith in the ability of Courts to give authoritative judgment between warring parties, the Commission takes on the 'passive-active' role of distilling common interest out of national interest. In this guise, it is, undoubtedly, also a political animal, which must also defend its own interests under the institutional balance of powers. The institutional balance is, thus, not marked by 'tension', but rather (A-02): '[s]ometimes you also have to explain to member states, ok, the way we operate it's the Commission which is the negotiator. We do that on the basis of a mandate that the members states define, but you have to leave the margin of appreciation to the negotiator and no backseat driving, please. You don't negotiate on our behalf. We only negotiate on your behalf (laughs)'.

25 Identifier 46, interestingly, also backed up by a European judge (Identifier 135) who feels that no constitutional significance can be attached to the notion of institutional balance, 'where balance is in constant change'?

26 Interestingly, only one questionnaire respondent (a Commission 'regulator') noted any lack of co-operation in inter-institutional dealings, citing 'tense relations' with the European Parliament (Identifier 93).

27 A vision of constant struggle also noted within the Commission (A-07): 'And what happens is that each institution tries to grab power from the others. In politics, everybody wants power to lie with themselves.' Note, however, that there is inherent faith in the ability of law to regulate the battle: 'Well, there is flexibility in it, but there are also fixed rules.'

28 Between the Parliament and the Council and between the Parliament and the Commission. And, indeed, the realism of the Court is extensive: see Chapter 5 (II.2), in particular, AG Mancini's plea that friction between institutions be solved by means of inter-institutional agreement, before ever reaching the Court of Justice.

29 'Functionality' presumably once again being understood in terms of the proper representation of all institutional interests, rather than in terms of the furnishing of good and effective decision-making. The respondents were given a list of six possible functions that were played by the institutional balance (a strict division of competences, a functional approach to problem-solving, transparency in governance, representation of the citizen, checks on the exercise of power, and efficient use of resources) and asked to list the functions in order of significance. Notions of functionality, a division of competence and checks on power were overwhelmingly privileged. The representation of the citizen proved to be the poor partner within the exercise, mostly occupying place five or six on the list, alternating its lowly position with the notion of transparency in governance.

30 In the mind of this Commission official, the correct mode of ensuring greater majoritarian presence within the EU institutional balance is by means of inter-institutional agreement: 'And the way to go about it is set out in a rather formal inter-institutional, or framework, agreement'. Questionnaire respondents, by varied contrast, favour majoritarian forms of reform of the institutional balance, such as the 'extension of co-decision procedures to 95% of legislation' (Identifier 21); 'more detailed, individual control by European Parliament of

individual Commissioners' (Identifier 88); and, 'more qualified majority-voting' (Identifier 36).

31 See Ackerman's second reading of the role of the individual within the principle of the separation of powers (2000). A stark distinction must be made between a separation of powers principle that privileges legislative expression of the people's 'collective' will, and a reading of the separation of powers that emphasises the rights of individuals to protect themselves from the exercise of legislative power. See Chapter 5 (III.2).

32 See, only, Blackstone's eulogy for the mixed powers established within the post civil war English Constitution (Katz and Blackstone 1979: 123). See, also, Chapter 5 (III.2).

33 Remember, only, Ackerman (2000), there is no such thing as *pareto* efficiency in the apportionment and re-apportionment of competences, powers, prerogatives and rights between institutions, states and individuals, only deep-seated alterations in the normative governing principles that constitute society.

34 Alternatively, returning to a traditional notion of 'separation of powers', division of powers between legislature, executive and judiciary also served to control and restrain law. We are left with an uncomfortable question: which mechanisms restrain law within the institutional balance?

35 In other words, the underlying 'formalistic' reasoning that the legitimacy of European law might be founded within a non-political private sphere, where the provisions of the Rome Treaty were to be regarded as securing a non-political private economic autonomy for individual Europeans. See above, Chapter 2 (III.1).

36 *van Gend & Loos* [1963].

37 Note, though, that private law does break the notion of privacy quite often, and increasingly so in a world in which economic relationships are being reconstructed along 'associational' lines, see, for example, Teubner 2004. The vital point in private law is that bipolar contracts increasingly impact upon third parties. Those third parties should accordingly be offered some form of protection for transfer of risks, etc., from the contract to them. Seen in this light, might the breaching of the privacy of contract between member states to include citizens of Europe within it also be a matter of protection of individual Europeans from the risks of European integration?

38 Referring to the failure of French and Dutch publics to ratify the draft constitutional treaty (June 2005).

39 Referring back to the thesis propounded in Chapter 2 (II). The most important point to note here is that whilst the Court diverges from traditional or conventional methods of 'JUDGMENT', it does not necessarily diverge from 'formal' (law-internal) reasoning. Precedent exists within private law, detailing when contractual privacy might be broken. Additionally, however, contractual formalism has its own philosophical basis – the contractual (economic) autonomy of individual Europeans within the protective boundaries set by a 'public law'. Thus, the Treaty of Rome serves the economic liberalism, which, in Max Weber's view at least, was an essential 'formal' legitimating principle of a rationalising law.

40 And, within the terms of this study, likewise an indication of the potentially limited nature of the data-set applied in Chapter 3. Interviews on the application of the Article 234 EC preliminary reference procedure were exclusively conducted with common lawyers.

41 'Und Gott lachte' or 'God laughed'. Divine laughter, in some readings, signalling lack of legal substance (Teubner 1989).

42 Surely, such *critique* is correct: where the measure of the legitimacy of substantive European principles is judicial 'consensus' amongst national and European jurisdictions (see below, Section IV.2), imposition of state liability upon national

courts might appear to be an 'underhand' effort to extend the European jurisdiction beyond its 'non-authoritative' limits.

43 In particular, in relation to the European Parliament and to individual European citizens.

44 See above, in relation to the treatment of the European Parliament and individual European citizens under Article 230 EC.

45 *Re Tax on Malt Barley* [1964] paragraph 20.

46 Once again, common lawyers, with their obsession with 'facts' become the butt of European judicial amusement B-02: 'But judicial review, as its name implies, is a review of the legality of acts. So evidence in the way you put it, in the abstract, doesn't, isn't a focal point. And then, of course, as one counsel said, referring to a UK counsel with his common law fetish for facts, what have facts got to do with it?' (laughs).

47 At its core, the whole thrust of a legal materialisation movement. Formal law is 'materialised' and brought into contact with substantive reality, in order to give effect to demands for social justice (redistributive demands). See, however, Weber's dismissal of material social justice within law as a simple return to 'natural law' (Weber 1969).

48 That is, the provision of universal access to essential facilities, such as, telecommunication services.

49 For the clear link to methodologies pursued by a *Freirechtsschule*, see above, Chapter 2 (III.2).

50 At its core, the key to successful ECJ efforts within the social insurance cases to limit its intervention into socially redistributive national welfare institutions to a procedural intervention that ensures 'equality of treatment within such systems', but which likewise leaves the sovereignty of member states over social redistribution unchallenged (Everson 2003a).

51 '*Comitology*' [1988] and *Re Radioactive foods* [1991]. See, also, Chapter 5.

52 Alternatively, his was a rationalisation (fed by cultural distance?) of Blackstone's position. Judges should be independent. Not because they were in some metaphysical way 'the living oracles' of the law and the guardians of the original constitutive spirit of the people. Instead, independence was surely only a technical functional notion, designed to free judges from the worries and pressures of politics.

53 In other words, the materialisation of law, or its reconnection with its social and political environment, can also be understood as an effort to democratise law. Naturally, in this reading, 'materialisation' takes on a certain substantive value of its own. The issue is not simply one of material reconnection with fact, but also one of a normative preference for the maintenance of the supremacy (and legitimacy) of political process.

54 That is, '[y]ou take the sensitive area of abortion which is obviously sensitive in Ireland' (B-02).

55 In other words, the positive feature within formalist legal expression is uppermost – in the terms of Savigny or Jhering, the effort is one of staying true to democratic expression of political will.

56 Note, however, that this analysis places independent democratic value upon the notion of 'participation'. Instead, participation is seen as a corollary to deliberative democracy, increasing 'rationality' of democratic process through the ensuring of the consideration of the widest possible number of positions held within a society.

57 See Chapter 5 (II.2).

58 *Azores* [2004].

59 *Phillip Morris International, Inc* [2003]. See, for full details, Chapter 5.

60 Confirming Giandomenico Majone's strong critique of lobbying at EU level. In his analysis, lobbying is not a force for deliberative good. Rather, lobbying leads to an unnecessary increase in regulatory intervention (2005).

61 The cosiness of the relationship maintained between Court and Commission is confirmed by one judge (B-03): 'The judges, and the Commission, regard themselves, to a certain degree, as allies in creating a European Union'.

62 *Azores* [2004] and *Pfizer* [2002].

63 Judges, interestingly enough, are not always impressed by counsel's insistent argument (B0-6): 'And you try to invoke all declarations of human rights, including European Convention, European Union, United Nations Convention ... you just try to find ammunition everywhere. Yes, but that's a barrister .... The judge probably will be bored with it ... again he has to reply to all that. And the lawyer and since he has been a barrister, some of them have been barristers before, they know exactly what they are trying to do. And so why are you after doing it again?'

64 In other words, whilst the Justices of the ECJ may find themselves in the position of Duncan Kennedy's 'liberal lawyer', they are nonetheless constrained by precedent and unable to achieve what they would like to achieve (Kennedy 1986). Alternatively, in the RCHI analysis, they are 'locked in' to precedent.

65 Terms deployed by all interviewees.

66 In particular, the draft constitutional treaty.

Chapter 7

# Constitutionalism beyond constitutions

> The problem of the juristic philosopher, in short, is the difficult one of validating his purely formal analysis of categories for the actual world about us.
>
> Harald Laski (1935: 202)

## I. An eternity of axiom

As Harald Laski, writing in the 1930s, cogently reminds us, there is nothing new under the sun. The underlying conundrum that characterises the attempt to identify an appropriate 'constitution' for on-going European integration processes is not a novel one. The Sisyphus-like effort to distinguish the norms that might capture and effectively govern the constantly evolving institutions of post-national governance should thus not simply be understood as one final effort to establish a cosmopolitan legal (regional) order – or, as an act taken in defiance of Grotius and his ancient stipulation that, since sovereignty stems from the nation state, no higher (sovereign) order might ever (logically) be placed above national law. Instead, the troubled process of the constitutionalisation of Europe is, also, just one further manifestation of the constant historical struggle to bring transcendental law and its formal categorisations into line with an 'actual world' in which abstract ideals of human governance are very quickly superseded by the realities of social, economic and political operation. An ostensibly *sui generis* process, European integration – the taming of the international state of nature, or juridification of the 'law gap' that dominates between sovereign states – is not only characterised by, but, instead, also revealingly intensifies the age-old tension that exists between the legal imperative for abstract, self-isolating and self-legitimating categorisation (formal rationality) and the wider demand that law should be embedded within and adequately reflect the society which it purports to govern (legal materialisation).

At European level, underlying disjunction between formal legal categorisations and the real-world is aggravated by an enduring irony. On the one hand, processes of European integration are undoubtedly a product of law: after all, Europe's internal market has its undisputed genesis in legal operation, be that operation the result of judicial activism, or, alternatively, of formal legal application (Chapter 2 (III.1)). On the other hand, by encouraging – or setting in international motion – the processes of economic, social and political disaggregation that were always present at national level, Europe's law (national and European) might be argued to have simultaneously instigated the 'disintegrative' *telos*, whereby the realities of European integration would also, perforce, run away with the formal soul of European law.

Simply stated, Europe's law has itself been instrumental in the unravelling of its own abstract categories of legitimation. Both at the paradoxically non-authoritative gap between authoritative legal orders, as well as within challenging adjudicational operations on, say, the maintenance of the constitutional principle of the balance of powers, law has been explicitly divorced (or alienated itself) from its own terms of 'formal reference'. Absent categories of sovereignty or constitutional settlement, law is denied convincing recourse to its own self-proclaimed 'universality', or axiomatic claim to undisputed authoritative application.[1] As a result, it must respond directly to the facts of European integration within a new legal semantic of self-justification.

Harald Laski, a political theorist, was a man of the inter-war age. As a consequence, he was concerned primarily with counteracting the totalising state-making tendencies then manifest both on the continent and within an increasingly consolidated British Labour movement.[2] Nonetheless, he would also immediately have recognised the underlying problem faced by a post-statal and post-national European law that still clings to formal legal categorisations within its operations. Citing the pragmatically influencing thoughts of the American philosopher, William James, Laski pinpoints the essential weakness in *all* human endeavours to idealise instruments of government – or instruments of mediation between individual and collective interest – by means of the application of abstract and idealised categories of the 'state', 'sovereignty' or 'formal law'.

Just as, say, the organising ideal, or abstract category, of the post-war European welfare or social state would eventually cede ground to the factual forces of 'reform' that had sprung up outside its illusionary totalising influence, European law could never, and, indeed, can never hope to capture real-world social, economic and political processes of integration within any totalising category of abstract legal thought:

> However much may be collected, however much may report itself as present at any effective centre of consciousness something else is self-governed and absent and unreduced to unity (Laski 1917: 10).

Any effort to reduce diversity to unity by means of the application of abstract categories of thought and language (or axiom) is doomed to failure.

As Madison pragmatically notes, 'no language is so copious as to supply words and phrases for every complex idea'; to which phrase might be added the notion that no idea, no matter how intricate, can ever convincingly hope to capture an even more complex reality (*Federalist Papers* 1961: 229).

The underlying point is both a practical and a normative one. Von Jhering's heaven of infinitesimally divisible norms – or, alternatively, the derived legitimating validity of Kelsen's *Grundnorm* – is a chimera; and not simply for the reason that the process of norm derivation inexorably stumbles against its internal semantic limits as, say, the formal judicial pursuit of European Treaty competition law provisions descends into a transcendental nonsense in which formal law can no longer identify – even within its own terms of reference – the language that justifies its own application (Chapter 2 (III.2)). Instead, the pragmatic objection that no category of thought can, at its inception, convincingly claim to encompass or represent the totality of the world around it, transmutes into the normative *critique* that, once established, any totalising axiom also relentlessly offends by virtue of its exclusion of the real, or, indeed, the yet-to-become real.

To Laski, once again pre-occupied with the potential iniquities of (statal) collectivisation, the axiomatic lure of the notion of unitary statehood was, famously, a specific offence in itself:

> Hegelianwise, we cannot avoid the temptation that bids us make our state a unity. It is to be all-absorptive. All groups within itself are to be but the ministrants to its life; their reality is the outcome of its sovereignty, since, without it, they could have no existence. Their goodness is gained only through the over-shadowing power of its presence. It alone, so to speak, eternally is; while they exist but [only] to the extent to which its being implies them. (Laski 1917: 1)

Certainly, the state's axiomatic claim to universality can be argued to represent a good in itself; a necessary totalising impulse, which establishes the parameters of the *only* society in which the values both of the few and of the many can be reconciled with reference to one, abstractly established, but practically effective, authority – an authority that might and can be asserted against the particularising interests of all imputed parties, silent or otherwise, to its totality. Nonetheless, the underlying assumption that all of human 'existence' lies within the purview of an abstract state, which is, in turn, their wellspring, is disturbing indeed, and a continual affront to the notion that human existence stems not from abstract categorisation, but from real-world interaction between individuals and their environments, whether they be 'within' or 'without' the state. Certainly, whilst '[I]t would be no inapt definition of politics in our time to term it the search for social unity' (Laski 1917: 3), why must the abstract state be the sole *locus* for social unification, or, indeed, any *locus* at all?

> 'Our fellowship,' wrote Maitland, 'is no fiction, no symbol, no piece of the state's machinery, but a living organism and a real person, with body and members and will of its own'. If this be true, there are within the state enough of these monistic entities, club, trade union, church, society, town, county, university, each with a group-life, a group-will, to enrich the imagination. Their significance assuredly we may not deny. (Laski 1917: 4)

In the fashion of the true and unfettered pluralist,[3] Laski joins with Maitland and von Gierke,[4] to decry the ideal of statehood as a denial of reality, and, more importantly, to assert that the true measure of social unity within political process is to be found in a real-world of social corporations, established out of, and in response to, their own particular and tangible environments. The abstract state, by its very nature, negates the world that it seeks to totalise: it cannot engage in dialogue with the social corporations of reality, each of which, to recall Hermann Heller's terms, possess their own justice demands – expressed through group-will – which are established out of, and in response to, reality. Instead, reality, the justice demands that it reveals and entails, as well as the social corporations that give them voice are all debarred from the axiomatic body politic, until such time as the abstract state itself concedes their relevance and endows them with an existence born of further axiomatic categorisations.

The message is clear: axiomatic categorisations – in this case, that of statehood – are necessarily exclusionary. Certainly, the state may, with the passage of time, breathe abstract 'existence' into tangible living organisms, such as, say, a trade union movement established in response to real-world conditions of social disadvantage;[5] yet, recognition is contingent and delayed, forever dependent on the ponderous will and ability of the axiomatic illusions of abstraction to respond to the changing environment that they seek to totalise. The state inexorably excludes those within its boundaries – those who have yet to become 'real' by means of statal recognition. Worse still, in all its totalising personification of the abstract, the state not only creates non-entities (slaves) within its own boundaries, but also de-personifies and subjugates those outside its (territorial) borders:

> 'Rome,' writes Lord Bryce, 'sacrificed her domestic freedom that she might become the mistress of others.' Here is a Rome beyond her citizens, a woman terrible in the asceticism of her supreme sacrifice. (Laski 1917: 3)

Laski's forceful tirade against statehood reinforces all that we have learned about the 'goodness' of European integration. The ancient *res publica*, born of ideal, rather than reality, and established and reified far beyond the real lives of its own citizens (simultaneously slaves), is likewise inured against the aspirations, interests, values or, indeed, existence of those exterior to it. Updated to an inter-war age, the progeny of *res publica*, or the modern nation state, could thus take its totalising mission to its ultimate, abstractly logical, but tangibly murderous conclusion, all the while sacrificing its own citizens upon the alter of axiomatic categorisation. Processes of European integration, in contrast, though undoubtedly disfigured by their own messy realism – the creation of welfare and democratic deficits – are also founded within their own (accidental) challenge to axiom, releasing individual citizens from their absolute allegiance to states, and likewise curbing statehood, as sovereign collectivities must cede, the one to the other, in an on-going real-world process of interest and value accommodation.[6]

Given the exactness of his historical vision, Laski is clearly to be applauded as a prescient man of his own age. However, as we have seen, his analysis and critique of the state is likewise all the more remarkable and fruitful within the modern context, by virtue of the fact that it is set in a wider context of a disavowal of all categories of imputed organisation. Not only the state, but also its law (including its constitutional law), is a potentially totalising force, which, if it is to be afforded the accolade of 'juristic philosophy', must constantly struggle to 'validate' its abstractions within a real-world. And therein lies the vital rub. Between facts and norms, Laski himself dreamed of and envisaged a time when sovereign states would be strictly constrained by an 'authoritative law' that would lie far beyond statehood and its totalising axioms; a world in which 'the process of government, in a word, [would escape] from the categories in which the nation-state sought to imprison it'.

> England, for instance, may well discover that, while it may prescribe the penalties for murder, it cannot control the hours of work for miners; that while it may make its own traffic regulations, it cannot settle the scale of its tariffs (Laski 1935: 224).

And, indeed, leaving aside the (no small) matter of UK governmental intransigence on working hours, such a world has come to pass. But what of Laski's 'authoritative law' within this brave new world: how might it, and does it, differ from the totalising law of the state? More importantly, how might it, or how does it, 'validate its formal analysis of categories for the world around us?' Which are the mechanisms, which might, or do allow Europe's law to escape from the egregious errors of totalising abstraction?

## II. Europe's law beyond axiom

### *II.1. Axiom refined: a final constitutional settlement*

Paradoxically, the struggle to rid law of damaging transcendental content and to bridge the gap between abstraction and reality, might, as we have seen (Chapter 1 (IV)), be argued to have reached its apogee with the perfection of axiom. In this analysis, the post-war constitutional settlement, which saw western European nation states re-establish themselves as social or welfare states, is significant, not simply because nation states were finally to commit themselves to the project of securing the substantive welfare of their own citizens. Instead, the post-war foray made by the abstract state into a real-world of personal economic security also entailed its own act of axiomatic perfection as the notion of *inclusive* political community (and, with it, re-invigorated republican allegiance) expanded to become a vital mediating fulcrum between real and abstract worlds, taking on the pivotal on-going function of translating emerging real-world demands for social justice into authoritative state interventionism.

The *res publica*'s horizons had widened. Personal autonomy, born of the enlightenment, and secured in formal higher law, remained a guiding feature of the post-war state. Nonetheless, the powers of the political community, or the state collective, were simultaneously reinforced, as a complementary constitutional commitment to the maintenance of personal welfare raised the presumption that all citizens would be able – in fact as well as in theory – to play their material part within the life of a *polis*, which might, in its turn, claim a far greater degree of legitimacy for its redistributive intrusions into the sphere of private autonomy.

The new balance struck between personal and collective interest (the public–private divide) was thus not merely predicated upon the provision of substantive, as well as formal, justice to the individual citizen. Instead, and vitally so for the purposes of this analysis, it was also a balance which re-affirmed and re-invigorated the abstract concept of constitutional statehood by means of the incorporation of a measure of reality within the statal axiom. The empowered citizen would always be able to give effective voice to an emerging real-world, as well as to the social justice demands which that world entailed, by virtue of his or her material inclusion within a national political community. As a consequence, the political community disposed of an enhanced legitimacy and could continually adjust the reach and character of the state through authoritative acts of regulative intervention.

In other words, the writings of inter-war authors, such as Harald Laski and Hermann Heller, were not to bear fruit in the disintegration of sovereign statehood, nor yet in the admission of the positive benefits of constitutional and legal indeterminacy,[7] but rather, in their exact opposites. With the concept of the (constitutionally secured) welfare or social state, law had acquired a new *Grundnorm*, or *pouvoir constituent*, which was founded within, and reinforced by, a reality of material inclusion of the individual citizen within the political community, but which was still, at the same time, generative of (new) 'formal' legal norms of social cohesion.[8]

In all its axiomatic perfection, the post-war constitutional settlement was not to witness the death of the sovereign state and/or withdrawal from the abstract categorisations of its law. Instead, assertions of territorial sovereignty were only intensified, as nation states sought to entrench their national economies within protective barriers, so better to tailor them to meet the social needs and demands of their own polities (Majone 1994, 2005: 197). Meanwhile, welfarism and/or the social state, were likewise accompanied by a wave of technical juridification, which owed far less to the material legal endeavour to adapt legal norms to the immediate needs and demands of an evolving social reality (indeterminate application of social rights), and far more to the confident legal assumption that faithful (literal) execution of legislative and executive fiat would, of itself, give due and appropriate voice to a shared (national) vision of substantive justice founded and constantly re-founded within the national political community.[9]

The ambivalence within the post-war legal order is readily apparent: materialisation of law, or the grounding of the legal order within reality, was effected, not by means of a direct legal engagement with the social environment, but instead through ever more intense and technical processes of formal legal abstraction, or dedication of law to the literal will of the political community (Habermas 1996a).[10] At the same time, statal abstractions were only strengthened, as inclusive national communities laid claim to a heightened degree of universality that was grounded within the real-world ability of individual citizens to engage in political process. The programme to socialise law had followed the highly paradoxical route of re-invigorating formalism with purposive content, or of redirecting a still formal (in Weber's terms, 'substantively rational') law to the task of executing legislative mandates. This legal pathway was inevitably full of pitfalls and ambiguities, so that the exact measure of the ambivalence within dual processes of consolidated territorial sovereignty and intensified technical/formal adjudication was duly revealed as *critique* of the post-war welfare and social state mounted and contributed – together with practical processes of European integration – to a partial withdrawal from the full extent of the application of the welfare/social state paradigm.

Within the terms of this analysis, however, the paced retreat from the axiomatic perfection of the social constitutional settlement – whether by virtue of the (perceived) stultifying impact on society of statal intrusion into the 'life-world', or, by simple virtue of the fact that the welfare state never seemed to be able to fulfil its own normative promise ( Unger 1976: 19–22; Habermas 1996a) – only underlines the exacting nature of the self-justificatory challenges faced by Europe's law. Certainly, European law has played its own very major part in the unravelling of many of the social, political and economic complexes of norms that characterised national welfare and social states.[11] Equally, in Laski's terms, the European legal order thus established possesses its own 'higher' normative legitimacy, or, at least, does so to the exact degree that it establishes an 'authoritative' law which allows the process of government to escape from the categories in which the nation state had erroneously imprisoned it (1935: 224).

Nonetheless, the contribution made by processes of European integration to the partial retreat from welfare states and social constitutional settlements may not simply be understood as an indication that European law must learn to live without axiom, no matter how perfect that axiom may be claimed to be. Instead, the underlying ambivalence within the challenge that European law has posed to the final effort to bridge the gap between fact and norm – or ground autonomous legal reasoning within social reality – by means of abstract constructions of states and their constitutions, is one that places an even greater onus upon the European legal order to establish its own self-legitimating discourse or *Rechtsverfassungsrecht*. Alternatively, Europe's law must conceive of (re-invent) itself as a self-constitutionalising/socially constitutive law, which nonetheless pays due and guiding regard to the historical efforts of the national, social, constitutional settlement to found and continuously re-found itself within a real-world, and its very tangible demands for justice.

### *II.2. The 'free' European legal movement*

As noted (Chapter 1 (IV.1)), the clock has been turned back on Europe's law, confronting it with the self-same socialisation paradox that was faced by pre-war legal orders. Certainly, the messy realism of Europe's 'welfare' and 'democratic' deficits also stems from an overdue response to failings within European welfare states and social constitutional settlements, including, most importantly, their continuing failure to integrate the interests of 'non-citizens' within the national constitutional settlement.[12] Nonetheless, the very fact that their existence is noticed and lamented, together with more general concerns that European integration processes are sweeping away the achievements, as well as the failings, of the post-war state, is likewise an overwhelming indication of the continuing validity of the demand that, whilst practical post-war programmes of legal materialisation may have faltered, law must still continue to be embedded in its social and political environment.

Given such a situation, it is, perhaps, not surprising that Europe's law, both at national and European level, exhibits certain of the traits, or modes of legal interpretation that were argued for and suggested by the free law movement, or *Freirechtsschule*, of early twentieth-century Germany, and subsequently reproduced, albeit in differing constellations, within various other national bodies of jurisprudence and social theory.[13] Concerned that a 'seamless web of formal law' (Rotthleuthner 1988) was blind to the realities of an emerging industrial society – and, above all, could not recognise basic imbalances in individual contractual bargaining power[14] – lawyers within the free law movement relocated the emphasis of their studies of law away from the investigation of the law-internal paradigms of autonomous legal deduction to focus, instead, upon the nature of the information fed to the law by its external environment, as well as upon the particular character of the lawyer, or the ability of the legal system to process social information.

Between fact and norm: the endeavour to bridge the gap between the abstractions of a formally rational law and the emerging realities of an industrial society – or, in Herman Heller's terms, to give legal voice to *Wirksamkeit* (operational reality) and the 'achieved' societal constitution (Chapter 1 (IV)) – was grounded within a dual process of the socialisation of law. Socialisation would be effected, first, by establishing an intimate relationship between legal practice and the new 'reality-revealing' disciplines of the social sciences,[15] and, second, by again disciplining law, or guarding against the potential personal excesses of a doctrinally unfettered judiciary, by demanding that lawyers be trained in the various arts of political, economic and social analysis.[16]

The vital guiding point was thus not simply one that abstract law lacked the categories of analysis which would allow for the recognition of the social conditions prevailing within a law-external environment. Instead, a free law movement also sought to remain true to the notion of impartial law and to guard against the irrational dangers of a legal system dominated by the adjudicating presence of Ehrlich's negatively characterised 'judge-king' (Chapters 1 (IV) and 2 (III.2)). Notions of legal organicism were to be wholly eschewed. Instead, any potential air of romanticism would be dispelled, as lawyers themselves would be required to be trained in the methodologies and modes of thought prevalent within the sciences and social sciences.

In Harald Laski's parallel analysis, the guiding feature of a socially responsive law remained its mechanical or 'scientific' character. 'The mechanism for the discovery of necessary legal change' was not one that might be 'discrete or casual'; instead, legal change, the adaptation of the abstract categories of law to social reality, should be 'organised and continuous in nature' (Laski 1958: 545). The socialisation of law undoubtedly demanded the socialisation of lawyers themselves, or the development of a 'moral insight into the law' (Laski 1958: 571). Nonetheless, such moral insight was to be organised with reference to scientific principles, with lawyers being required to develop an 'intimate acquaintance' with the notion of 'political economy', as well as with a 'critical jurisprudence', which would not only furnish them with a 'healthy scepticism' of the instrument of formal law, but which might likewise give 'the law its insight into the environment of which it is the expression' (Laski 1958: 26–27).

Progressive law was to be encouraged: lawyers were to be the engines of social evolution, adapting the fixed categories of formal law to meet the justice demands of a real-world that they were conditioned not to recognise (Kennedy 1997). At the same time, however, the quasi-scientific formalism of, say, von Jhering's heaven of infinitesimally divisible norms, should not simply be abandoned in favour of the personal moral peccadilloes of individual judges. Instead, the quasi-science of formal legal method should cede to the social insights of 'real' scientific methodologies; or, a scientific method, which would always guard against the potential romanticism or simple prejudices of the judge-king. Science would be the law's window upon social reality, and, at the same time, its bulwark against social irrationalism. Max Weber's often stated concerns that a free law movement was courting disaster, exposing the vital regulative certainties of a rule of law to the potential 'value irrationalism' of doctrinally unfettered adjudication, would be countered by the re-invention of the law (and lawyers) as an engine of socially sensitive scientific method.

Turning to a modern European law, and, above all, a European law lacking in any form of axiomatic constitutional settlement, both the potential and the actual value of the re-invention of law as a scientific methodology is hard to doubt. Judges working within European law do occasionally bemoan the lack of scientific studies within their courtrooms and, above all, highlight the vital role that science (or social science) could, but does not yet, play in shedding light upon the redistributive consequences of European legal adjudication.[17] However, the wistful judicial concern that 'there was [actually] very little of that kind of socio-economic explanation' within courtroom proceedings before the ECJ (Chapter 6 (IV.1)), cannot detract from that fact that, whilst scientific methodologies may not yet have been fully utilised to cast a legal mirror on the wider social impact of European law, scientific or social scientific studies still play their more tangential part in furnishing European law with a (politically) neutral tool with which to delineate a European jurisdiction.

In other words, the materialising value of science within Europe's law, or its ability to afford European and national law with a reality-adequate portal on incremental processes of European integration, became most apparent as the formal legal expression of European jurisdiction and the integrative European interest faltered in the face of the inability of a socially autonomous European law to justify and, more importantly, to delimit, its constant unravelling intrusions into national complexes of market regulation (Chapter 2 (III.2)). Above all, the wedding of economic theory and scientific study with the legal principle of proportionality was to prove to be a marriage made in heaven, as, say, studies on the potential ill-effects, or otherwise, of drinking additive-laden beer allowed a European judiciary to set aside national, 'culturally conditioned' regulation, not with simple recourse to the abstract categorisations of a law dedicated to European market integration, but instead, with reference to the reality-adequate argument that additives within beer were not, in fact, harmful to the health of European consumers.

Within this scientifically flavoured adjudication scenario, the benefits of the integration of scientific method within law were twofold: not only had science allowed law to set the polemics of entrenched national regulatory discourses aside following a forensic investigation of their validity; instead, the elevation of the procedural principle of proportionality to the status of a higher legal check upon regulatory (political) justifications had also preserved the aloof autonomy of law – European law need not judge directly upon the quality or validity of national regulatory discourse, but merely subject it to certain, scientifically determined and reality-revealing, rationality criteria (Joerges 2002b).

In other words, European law is engaged in its own materialisation efforts, making effective use of scientific disciplines, both as a mirror on an extra-legal world, and as bulwark against its own embroilment within potentially partisan adjudication. However, the rationalising impact of science (social science) within European law, and, above all, its ability to shield law from socially derived 'value irrationalism', would also appear to have its limits. Both at national and at European level, judges and lawyers engaged in the application of the European legal order, also display a large measure of scepticism about the use of science within the courtroom. Whether the concern be one that science can be distorted to meet the particular needs of one client (Chapter 4 (II.3)), or one that law cannot communicatively converse with science, or whether, by contrast, it relates to the perennial lack of agreement between individual scientists and scientific studies (Chapter 6 (IV.1)), the modern European legal order itself doubts whether science can, in fact, act as an adequate mirror to a real-world: '[A]nd one often wonders whether one is really in touch with reality' (Chapter 6 (IV.1)).

In part, such healthy legal reservations are a necessary corollary of the coming of age of scientific, and, above all, of social scientific disciplines. In the first half of the twentieth century, authors within the free law movement were able to invest much faith in the revelatory powers of what were still relatively young disciplines: somewhat naïvely, studies in political economy and sociology retained full confidence in their innate ability to portray the 'truths' of the world around them, without any degree of distortion from their own discipline-internal (normative) premises. Nonetheless, in the modern age, an increasing awareness of the existence of methodological relativism determines that any scientific claim to unveil the existence of the 'facts' of a real-world will always be treated with a degree of caution. More importantly, however, the modern relationship between law and science, and especially so within a European setting, is also inevitably tempered by the realisation, albeit largely unstated, that the introduction of an 'organised' and 'continuous' post-formalist methodology within the law cannot be limited to the simple deployment of science in order to reconstruct the facts of a law-external environment within the courtroom, but must, instead, also entail the establishment of a far more complex degree of interaction between an autonomous legal method, scientific or organised modes of reality construction and the various modes in which social values are created and presented within a real-world.

In short, the noted oscillation between the formal and material legal methods within the supposedly 'activist' jurisprudence of the ECJ is not simply an indication of continuing controversy over which particular forms of economic rationality should guide the process of the integration of European markets. Instead, the occasional retreat of the Court into the transcendental nonsense of formal method – particularly in the face of such national cultural barriers to economic advance as a ban upon abortion or a refusal to allow Sunday trading – is likewise confirmation of the inability of science to furnish law with rationality criteria in situations in which Europe's law stumbles against competing rationalities and/or social values, which can no longer be appraised within a neutrally organised (scientific) framework of reality recognition.

Herman Heller's underlying exhortation to the law to identify an 'ethical' and 'moral' basis for the legal appraisal and constitution of *Wirksamkeit*, or the achieved societal constitution, still hangs heavy over the head of the law, re-awaking the fears, most powerfully enunciated by Max Weber, that a material legal order would inexorably succumb to value irrationalism, and, more cogently, prompting the European legal order to retreat once again into its own axiomatic and abstract categorisations, no matter how incoherent its pronouncements might appear within a real-world environment of European integration.[18]

### *II.3. Europe's reflexive legal order*

The vital lesson for a legal order seeking to root its pronouncements within a real-world is thus a threefold one. First, the endeavour to reconstruct reality within the legal order must extend far beyond the simple rebirth of law as a scientific methodology. Certainly, in Harald Laski's terms, material law, or a law which pays due regard to its own non-legal environment, must be continuous and organised in nature. Nonetheless, such organisation cannot be founded in a mere synthesis of, say, legal and economic methodologies: law may not become the handmaiden of any one, potentially value-laden, scientific methodology. Instead, science (social science) plays its appropriate part within a post-formalist legal order when it is deployed as a rationality criterion to act, on the one hand, as a restraining yardstick upon autonomous legal methodologies and, on the other, as a constraint upon hidden self-interest.

As our wistful judge reminds us, adjudication on the liberalisation of national electricity market impacts upon redistributive policies throughout the European Union, determining the prices that advantaged and less advantaged consumers will pay for power and heat. Seen in this light, the legal extrapolation of an individual right to supply market services across national boundaries should be taken in full cognisance of the social impacts of judicial decision-making. As Laski likewise notes, a vital part of the effort to bring the abstract categorisations of law into a relationship with real-world social, economic and political processes must be the evolution of a 'critical jurisprudence' which is prepared to evaluate its own categorisations in the light of their real-world impact; an impact that science can help to reveal.[19]

By the same token, however, critical jurisprudence can make further use of science, not simply to delimit and discipline its own actions, but also to order or to constrain the world around it: in tandem with legal principles, such as proportionality, rationality or subsidiarity (Chapter 6 (IV.1)), the forensic powers of science may be harnessed by law in order to subject political, economic or social processes to closer scrutiny and, thus, to reveal and/or censure cloaked and partisan motivations that subvert, rather than promote, the stated purposes behind legislative or regulatory intervention.

Second, however, for all that law may deploy science in a manner, which is constitutive and evaluative, both of its own autonomous reasoning and of the 'truth-claims' made in the world around it, the limits to and weaknesses within scientific method must always be recognised. Above all, the scientific search for real-world truths necessarily falters, not simply because scientific methodologies may be contaminated by their own methodological (normative) relativism, but also because the justice claims manifest within a real-world may likewise be legitimated by their own subjective value systems, which are not necessarily amenable to, or compatible with, objective categorisation. Substantive justice, after all, remains an act of faith, or, to deploy Roberto Unger's formulation, the 'social expression of love', an inchoate power that is impossible to capture within any one axiomatic framework of legal expression (1976: 19–22).[20] To adapt and apply the thinking of Max Weber: value irrationalism is a natural feature of the social environment of law. More importantly, and to underline once more the achievement of the post-war welfare state and social constitutional settlement, value irrationalism possesses its own social legitimacy, or, at the very least, does so to the degree that it gives voice to the justice demands that are prevalent within a real-world. Nonetheless, value irrationalism is an anathema within law itself, and it is here that the third lesson to be learned by the legal order that seeks to found itself in the real-world becomes most apparent.

Hermann Heller's plea, it should be recalled, was one that the law should develop its own ethical and moral character, in order that it might transform the curse of legal indeterminacy into its constructive opposite; more particularly, that it might translate the challenging lack of definitive content within legal provisions into an engine of social evolution – an engine that could, and indeed would, be responsive to the emerging justice demands of an extra-legal environment. In no small part comparable with Laski's demand that law should always seek to adapt its abstract categorisations to the demands of an actual world, Heller's value-laden exhortation to law, nonetheless, leaves one vital question open: which are the mechanisms which ensure that the moral and ethical character evolved by law is an appropriate or socially legitimate one?

In Heller's age, one still marked by nationalism and cultural consolidation, the notion that an underlying degree of 'social and political homogeneity' within the polity would allow the legal order to draw upon a shared and immutable set of cultural and social values might perhaps still have claimed a measure of applicability (Heller 1927,1928b). Above all, a national and culturally homogenous community confronted with the wide-ranging and socially destabilising inequities of mass industrialisation would surely be dedicated to the same goal of the amelioration of the poverty and inequality, which threatened the common enjoyment of national life. Nonetheless, in a post-national age, marked most tellingly by the desire – given permanent expression in European law's commitment to the principle of (national) non-discrimination – to overcome cultural and national schism, the call to cultural homogeneity is surely far too crude a mechanism to ensure that the ethics and morals expressed within law are those of the society that it seeks to sustain, rather than those of its own wholly fallible and potentially partisan servants.[21]

If the greatest reality-revealing strength within Heller's treatment of the legal order is to be found in his recognition that legal indeterminacy is not an enemy of legal authority, or a challenge to the certainty of formal legal reasoning, but, is, instead, law's portal on social reality, its vital key to the adaptation of law to meet the justice demands which a real-world reveals and entails, then, by the same token, legal indeterminacy within a modern world, or inevitable *lacunae* within the legal semantic, can no longer be addressed by means of a simple appeal to notions of social and political homogeneity and the shared values, to which it supposedly gives rise. Instead, the real-world of European integration is characterised by the exact opposite of homogeneity. A plurality of views, opinions, interests and values is the defining characteristic of a post-statal (post-modern?) era. A reality-adequate law, which takes its mission to adapt abstract categorisations to an 'actual' world seriously, must, as a consequence, and fully in accord with Heller's underlying concerns about the necessary recognition of real-world justice demands, remain open to plural visions of social need, social value and social legitimacy (see the next section).

And therein lies a further rub: if society is marked by plural value relativism, law's defining ethics and morality cannot be drawn directly from its external environment: which values would it draw upon, and which values would it dismiss? Instead, the materialisation of law, the adaptation of its abstract categories to an external environment and the justice demands that it entails, must, much in the manner of the formally rational legal order, be governed by a socially autonomous morality; a law-internal ethic which supports and orders law-external processes of social contestation, but which, at the same time, leaves law the master of its own integrity.

In the terms of modern legal theory, the task of legal materialisation, and the dedication of law to the needs of the society in which it is embedded, has become a matter of redesigning the legal order as a reflexive system of norms which is responsive to the ever changing external demands made of it, but constant in the law-internal values which it espouses. Expressed either in the value neutral terms of systems theory, or, alternatively, laden with ideals derived from liberal philosophy,[22] the unitary modern legal theoretical concern is, thus, one of identifying the norms (values) which constitute an autonomous and authoritative legal order, and which, at the same time, allow for the appropriate translation of the justice demands made within a real or actual world into binding (integrative) law.

## III. Europe's *Rechtsverfassungsrecht*

Within the context of the process of European integration, the notion of reflexive law might accordingly be argued to have reached its logical apogee in the dual process whereby a European legal order (national and European) is simultaneously forced to 'constitutionalise' itself and the world around it. On the one hand, the lack of conventional constitutional settlement continues to determine that law is denied recourse to the axiomatic legitimating powers of a *pouvoir constituent*, the revolutionary abstraction, which seeks to totalise the world of social organisation, and, thus, establishes its own final and authoritative legal order. By the same token, however, the failure to impose the totalising abstractions of social organisation upon a real-world of European integration also leaves Europe law with the problem of confronting and managing a plurality of tangible, rather than imputed, social values, interests and opinions.

At theoretical level, the inevitable consequence of this constellation of (constitutional) non-settlement is thus the evolution of a radical and reflexive proceduralism within law itself. Still in thrall to all the concerns of the settled constitutional state, including the demand that an authoritative legal order should also take steps to ensure social and personal justice (welfare), a European legal system must seek its own and its environmental *raison d'être* within 'neutral' norms of legal and social organisation. That is, within norms that are free from totalising (substantive) content, but, which, at the same time, fulfil a reflexive and socialising legal function by promoting and fostering both the plural processes of social contestation that mark the European polity, as well as the means of their reconciliation, without once implicating legal method within real-world conflict.

The proceduralism suggested is undoubtedly radical in nature: the vital distinction to be drawn is one between the final act of the 'constituting' of the polity and the on-going dual process of the 'constitutionalisation' of law and society. The core paradigms of a radical proceduralism necessarily differ, both in meaning and impact, from the advanced technical proceduralism of the welfare state. Law is not a(n) (substantively rational) automaton, which is simply free to wield all of the maxims found within the established proceduralist canon, without thought about, or reflection on, their real-world impact. Thus, for example, the notion of 'equality of bargaining power' cannot be safely and unthinkingly assumed to serve the totalising aims of an abstract commitment to the maintenance of a social market economy (Unger 1976). Instead, the legal order must always ask itself whether the imposition of an equality of bargaining power necessarily brings with it immediate gains in terms of support for ordered social contestation within a real-world and, thus, for the legitimacy of law itself.

In the absence of constitutional settlement, and in the absence of totalising axioms of legal authority, the application of proceduralist legal method remains conditional upon its constructive reflexive impact in each and every case of adjudication. The revolution has yet to be brought to a final conclusion (Chapter 3 (I)): the polity is neither settled nor constituted. Instead, the sole legitimate 'purposive' function of law is surely only one of giving voice to revolution, one of fostering, ordering and facilitating social contestation (together with the real-world justice demands that it reveals and entails), all the while drawing its own 'constitutional' authority from its (socially autonomous) radical and reflexive vigour.

Law without axiom, Amen: within the messily realist context of European integration processes, the existence and evolution of a legal order which is 'organised' and 'continuous' in nature, and which grounds its (post-settlement) authority within a radical and reflexive proceduralism, may not be immediately apparent. On the contrary, the often tortuous mixture of formal and material legal reasoning, the occasional descent into transcendental nonsense, as well as the permanent hint of 'judicial activism', seem only to underline the validity of Harald Laski's concern that post-axiomatic law might itself cede to 'discrete' or 'casual' reasoning – or, indeed, to confirm Max Weber's warning maxim that the legal order that eschews formal rationality will inevitably descend into value irrationalism.

Nonetheless, Europe's law (national and European) is a law in fact, rather than in theory, and, above all, in its efforts to constitutionalise on-going and uncertain processes of European integration seems to offer us one of the most significant laboratories for the evolution of a post-axiomatic law that is rooted in reality rather than abstraction. Seen in this light, the stumbling efforts of judges and lawyers throughout Europe to adapt their abstract categorisations, however haltingly, to an 'actual' process of integration, undoubtedly furnish valuable lessons for the theoretical attempt to elucidate the exact procedural mechanisms of legal reasoning that might usefully characterise a post-statal and post-national law. Between fact and norm, the establishment of a reflexive and constitutionalising relationship between law and its extra-legal environment inevitably remains a messy process. Beyond axiom, theoretical perfection or logical coherence is hard to achieve. In this regard, processes of constitutional morphogenesis within Europe – or the pragmatic efforts of law and lawyers to defy existing legal logic and to furnish Europe with a constitutional status beyond the broken paradigm of the closed constitutional settlement (Chapters 1 (VI) and 2 (V)) – prove their full worth, offering prescient lessons on both the achievements and the pitfalls of a legal order which has been forced to function without axiom.

### III.1. European legal formalism revisited

The notion of formally rational law inevitably remains an anathema to any theory of law that seeks to establish a meaningful and evolutionary relationship between law and its extra-legal environment. The moral and ethical status of formally rational orders must inexorably be doubted: with origins to be found either within the *pouvoir constituent* (constitutive *Grundnorm*), which gives birth to the (constitutional) statal axiom, or, alternatively, within a Weberian commitment to the principles of legal certainty that secure the autonomous exchange values of the face-to-face marketplace across the whole of an advanced and complex society, formally rational legal orders are value compromised. In other words, whether dedicated to the consolidation of the revolution and the abstract totalisations of the revolutionary polity, or, by contrast, wedded with the autonomous exchange logic of the liberal market economy, formal law is closed to the influence and demands of the real-world events, interests and values, which conflict with the understandings encapsulated within its founding act or guiding theology. By this same token, the abstract categorisations of the formal juristic philosopher reign supreme, building an autonomous system of norms that brooks no congress with the process of the materialisation or socialisation of law. Between facts and norms, formal rationality errs on the side of norm autonomy and coherence; a failing that is only compounded by the inability of formal reasoning to fulfil its promise of the provision of infinite interpretational permutations – the shadow of transcendental nonsense hangs heavy over formal law (Chapters 2 (III.1), 5 (II.2) and 6 (III)).

Nonetheless, just as surely as the seamless web of formally rational norms closes the legal order, making it deaf to the emerging justice demands of a real-world, it just as certainly secures the immediate environmental impartiality of law. Social and political autonomy is clearly also won either at the underlying cost of the legal promotion of potentially inappropriate social abstractions (legal dedication to autonomous exchanges logic), or at the immediate cost of simple logical incoherence (transcendental nonsense). Nonetheless, legal autonomy retains an undoubted value within any reflexive and proceduralist theory of law, and it is in this light that the very particular recidivistic formalism to which a European legal order would appear to be prone should be re-assessed.

Granted, the formalism pursued by an original ECJ which allowed it to begin to establish a life for European law beyond the immediate will of the contracting member state governments, may have been rooted within a Weberian conception of autonomous exchange logic, which, with time, became increasingly difficult to reconcile with interventionist national efforts to secure the real-world welfare of European polities. Nonetheless, the formalist stance adopted by the ECJ in the 1960s similarly allowed European law to weave its authoritative path between conflicting, contrasting, and potentially law compromising, federalist and more nationalistically flavoured visions of the shape and nature of the legitimate European polity.[23]

Formalism continues to protect the legal order from too direct an involvement within social conflict. Alternatively, legal formalism retains a value within a modern legal order to the exact degree that it allows for a delimitation of the authoritative jurisdiction of law (Schauer 1988): the final disposition of the shape of a legitimate polity is not one for the legal order to make. Law, as a ECJ reminds us, has its own limits and should not fall prey to any form of instrumentalism in the matter of the 'constituting' of a 'legitimate' European polity. A rights-based reading of the standing to be imparted to individual European citizens under Article 230 of the European Treaty must, for example, be resisted, no matter how nonsensical such a decision may initially appear: '[W]hat are the criteria against which judges are going to test it? [A]t the end of the day, [such a] choice is truly a political choice and not a judicial choice'.[24]

Is formalism still to be justified as the final defensive bulwark of law? Can the nonsensical retreat into mantras of uncritical literal legal interpretation be legitimated if and when plural political pressures threaten to undermine the immediate neutrality of law? In Laski's terms, such a legal trade-off is potentially 'discrete and casual', and is always disconcerting. Nonetheless, it may also, be occasionally justified. Certainly, formalism always entails the imposition of certain pre-conceived values on the extra-legal environment (autonomous exchange logic or pursuit of the goals of the constituted revolutionary polity). Equally, it is difficult to conceive of any particular set of circumstances that would justify legal retreat into formal bunkers in the abstract: immediate threats of political contamination cannot be conceived of in an 'organised' and 'methodological' manner. Nonetheless, the 'judicial choice' to take steps to prevent the embroilment of law within immediate political conflict, or, indeed, to avoid determinative adjudication on the legitimate shape of the polity, is one which must always be left open, and, likewise, is also one which may be cast in a more constructive light.

Thus, it should be recalled, the legal tool of appeal to established, formalised, legal orders has not simply been wielded in order to protect a

European legal system from immediate political contamination. Instead, where European judges have not been able to circumvent demands that the European legal order should give voice to substantive values, and, more particularly, the values enshrined within the notion of the inviolate nature of parliamentary democracy, legal authority for principle-laden adjudication has been established with reference to the shared constitutional traditions of the member states, or to the historically validated experiences of constituted European polities which are to be found within national constitutional settlements: '[A]nd so I think again, yes it was a political point of view, if you like, but it was also a moral point of view for many of them' (Chapter 6 (IV.2)).

Alternatively, Harald Laski's 'critical jurisprudence', or critical legal ability to cast the inexorable nature of formal legal categorisations into doubt, may, quite perversely find its most important instance of application, at the point where the legal order consciously and knowingly decides to withdraw into itself, and to return to the formulae and incantations of settled (formal) jurisdictions. Certainly, judicial 'choice' and judicial 'morality', always potentially irrational, lie at the core of formalist withdrawal. Nonetheless, and at least to the degree that the current conditions of legal plurality (existence of a variety of equally authoritative legal orders) are maintained within Europe (Chapter 6 (IV.2)), choices are surely made and morality surely imposed in full cognisance of the meaning and the impact of the decisions taken.

As a prescient ECJ judge once again reminds us, the decision made by the Court to enhance the powers of the European Parliament may have been a 'political' one. At the same time, however, the decision was also rooted in the 'morality' of individual judges; a morality, which, in its turn, could be traced to history and historical lessons, and more importantly, to 'common' European historical lessons incorporated and encapsulated within several settled (axiomatic) national constitutional traditions. Conscious, detailed and critical dialogue and interaction between European judiciaries (systemic consensus), it can be argued, may yet justify translation of historically validated morality into the European legal order.[25]

### *III.2. The real-world of European adjudication*

'Its trying to make it work rather than interpret exactly what it is' (Chapter 4 (III.4)). As a UK Barrister prompts us to remember, Europe's law continues to defy comprehensive logical analysis. It remains imperfect, a product of reality rather than design. To this exact degree, underlying incongruity within Europe's *Rechtsverfassungsrecht* is, perhaps, unavoidable. The effort to identify the emerging structures of radical and reflexive proceduralism must also learn to live with incongruity or an incoherence, which views the occasional retreat into formal reasoning, not as a threat to methodological coherence, but, instead, as a conformation that a law that seeks to establish its own adequacy in the face of a complex reality will always struggle to adapt its thinking to the demands placed upon it in a real-world.

Sociological muddling: the mechanical operations of *Rechtsverfassungsrecht* retain an air of mystery, a lack of final definition, which reflects the ever changing demands made upon European law within a dynamic rather than static European polity. However, by this same token, and behind its formalist façade, Europe's *Rechtsverfassungsrecht*, in all its self-constitutionalising and socially constitutive splendour, makes ready use of a variety of mechanisms to cross the gap between facts and norms, and to root itself within real-world happenings rather than contrived axioms. 'It is trying to make it work, rather than interpret exactly what it is': the quest of European law to achieve 'workablility', to find real-world solutions for the 'actual' problems that cannot be solved within the individual and immutable axiomatic logics of Europe's many interlocking legal orders, furnishes it with a reflexive reality-revealing power all of its own; a power that is no longer constrained by abstract categorisation, but which, instead, seeks justification for the application of norms in the series of legal 'invitations' that are made to a real-world to enunciate its own immediate (non-abstract), rather than axiomatically pre-conditioned, justice demands.

The search for Herman Heller's *Wirksamkeit*, 'operational reality', or achieved societal constitution, is thus, once again, brought one step closer to conclusion. Faced with problems that defy the referential landmarks of conventional, sovereign legal orders, Europe's law is forced into a process of dialogue both between legal orders and between law and society. The ancient self-proclaimed 'universality' of law, or axiomatic claim to undisputed authoritative application has been superseded. By the same token, Europe's law is furnished with the power to seek new solutions to real-world problems within the framework of a new legal universality, or the recognition that legal authority no longer derives from axiom or from the philosophical dictates of the *res publica*, but rather from its exact opposite: the social reality that the *res publica* has always obscured and repressed.

The exact measure of this new legal universality, or wedding of law with social reality, is to be found at all levels of European adjudication: first, within the national legal self-internalisation of principles of (national) non-discrimination, and a willingness to assess the real-world impact of national adjudication upon other national polities;[26] second, within the German Constitutional Court's preparedness to ameliorate the effects of its once-inexorable constitutional logic in the light of European integration realities (Chapters 2 (IV.2) and 5 (III.1)); and third, within the ECJ's re-dedication of its day-to-day jurisprudence to the effort to answer the vital reality-revealing questions of 'what are you at' and 'why are you making such a fuss about this?' (Chapter 6 (IV.1)) Fact has trumped axiom, and law revels in the potentially universal freedoms of reality-adequate adjudication. More importantly, however, fact has also trumped axiom in a wholly reflexive process whereby law's efforts to root itself within an extra-legal environment cannot be determinative, but are, instead, always located within the discursive legal impulses, or contractual offers, which are sent out by the law to its own social and plural legal environments – impulses that stress the organisational parity of legal and non-legal worlds.

Beyond axiom, law cannot dictate to its non-legal environment, or, indeed, to any other legal order that is founded within its own autonomous rationality. Instead, command is replaced by dialogue, or, at the very least, is replaced by dialogue to the exact degree that adjustments between the (formally) autonomous legal systems that make up an overarching European legal order, as well as between Europe's law and a European society, are made on the basis of the discursive *invitatio ad offerendum*. For all its (overstated) flaws, the *Brunner* judgment of the German Constitutional Court must be identified as a defining moment within the process of the constitutionalisation of European integration; not, however, by virtue of the explicit challenge laid down by a national constitutional order to the ECJ, but rather by reason of the Constitutional Court's recognition of the relative (restricted) authority of its own legal (constitutional) order – an authority that is constrained both by the nature of the dynamic social and political processes of a European integration reality, and also by the particular degree of recognition that could, or would ever, be afforded to its decision-making by a supranational legal order that is grounded within its own very distinct legal rationality.

Vitally, the core of the Court's judgment, as well as the proposed course of future jurisprudence, was formed by an enhanced understanding of the notion of 'operational reality': legal orders and social reality are conjoined as *equal* partners within a waltz of developmental constitutionalism. Accordingly, all legal dictates were dispensed with. Instead, a very particular legal signal and impulse was given, an 'offer to treat' was made: the *Bundesverfassungsgericht* would withdraw from full application of the principle of popular sovereignty within a German jurisdiction (*Volkssouveranität*), but would do so only to the degree that a European jurisdiction had established, or was prepared to establish, its own structures of democratic representation. German norm (axiom) would cede to European fact. However, the Court would not itself pass judgment upon the (legitimate) existence or otherwise of a European polity. Instead, the invitation was made, both to a European public, and to a ECJ, for they themselves to consider, reflect and, vitally, act upon the realities of European political integration (Chapters 2 (IV.2) and 5 (III.1)).

### *III.3. Revolution, politics and deliberation*

In short, and in further explanation, both the occasional retreat into formalism and the radical effort to engage in reflexive (non-determinative) dialogue with social reality can be argued to be two sides to the same coin: two complementary, if sometimes imperfect, elements of a European *Rechtsverfassungsrecht*, which, confronted by the state of permanent revolution within the European polity, seeks to eschew the reproduction of the errors of abstraction and refuses to determine the course of the revolution through application of substantive legal visions of a European *finalité*.

It is not law but forces exterior to law which should determine substantive changes in the shape and the nature of the European polity. More particularly, however, the forces of 'politics', both at national and at European level, instead of any one law or legal order, should be the guiding force within the processes of social contestation that determine the day-to-day *telos* of European integration. In contrast, constitutional morphogenesis, or the translation of the facts of European integration into the norms of European law should be facilitative, rather than determinative in nature; at whichever level (be it national or European), Europe's law cannot pre-empt reality, must not accede to the temptation to become a political tool in its own right, but must instead await upon the pleasure of the politics of social contestation.[27] By this same token, recidivistic retreat into formalism thus also equates with a clear renunciation of a political jurisdiction for the law, whilst reflexive dialogue between legal and social orders preserves the developmental constitutional prerogatives of political process and social contestation.

Between fact and norm: law cannot create reality, cannot rest secure in any assumption that social contestation can simply be directly absorbed into and ameliorated by legal rationality. Instead, the constitutionalising relationship between legal order and social contestation is of a more complex and subtle character. The politics of social contestation must be allowed to run their course. More particularly, however, legal authority, or the vital, self-constitutionalising and socially constitutive, fulcrum within Europe's *Rechtsverfassungsrecht*, is established *only* to the degree that law enables the politics of social contestation to run its course, and, more importantly, to run its course *within* the structured and ordered idiom of European legal process.

'I refuse for myself to split politics from policy, from law' (Chapter 6 (IV.2)). This stark judicial assertion of political and legal congruity should not be viewed as an unfortunate admission of legal political partiality, as a manifesto for the politicisation of law. Instead, it is a simple recognition that law cannot function without politics, and, equally, an assertion that politics cannot function without law. Politics furnishes law with its vital mirror on social reality. Politics or political contestation alone can legitimately determine which of the plural and competing social values, interests and opinions that cluster around European law might prevail in any one instance. Equally, however, politics within the revolutionary (unsettled) polity must be secured and sustained by law. If revolution is not to descend into meaningless expressions of power and violence, or – potentially far worse within the pluralist vision of social organisation enunciated in Chapter 3 – to determine its own end by means of the imposition of the closed and foreclosing constitutive act, it must itself be sustained by a framework of law, which draws its sole constitutionalising authority from its own ability to check and order, and also to sustain the political forces of permanent revolution.

Seen in this somewhat dramatic light, the altogether more prosaic efforts of national judges and the justices of the ECJ to encourage workable decision-making within Europe and to succour a *telos* of European integration beyond the broken axioms of national (and European) constitutional settlement nonetheless assume their own self-constitutionalising and socially constitutive vitality. The science (social science) that was so beloved of a free law movement thus takes on a new significance within the post-national and post-statal constellation of European integration; not because it can itself act directly as the law's mirror on a real-world, but because it can be harnessed together with the principles of 'proportionality' and 'rationality' found within the socially autonomous logic of a radically proceduralist legal order, in order to ensure – albeit only ever imperfectly – that the only appropriate conduit between legal and extra-legal environments, 'politics', functions in an open, honest and transparent manner. Are the arguments brought to justify social or political action truly dedicated to their stated aims?

Equally, however, the distant, but unqualified, approval which Europe's law affords the institutions of European integration (more specifically, the Commission) in their intense efforts to nurture, self-nominating and self-defining, extra-statal interest and interest groups – a distant approval that is, importantly, sometimes backed up by direct judicial intervention[28] – functions to ensure that political processes within Europe remain, as far as is ever possible, open to all emerging political interests, and, most importantly of all, remain open to the emerging (or yet-to-emerge) real-world interests of the evolving post-national and post-statal European polity.

European mechanisms of 'legal politicisation' are experimental in nature, potentially imperfect and developed piecemeal as the circumstances of adjudication and creativity of European justices and European institutions dictate. Nonetheless, they appear to share one major advantage. Being founded within the processual notion which equates 'deliberative politics' with 'good politics', legal endeavours to politicise the process of European constitutional morphogenesis eschew any efforts to legitimate political process within Europe, as well as the outcomes that trail in its wake, with reference to pre-conceived notions of what the polity should be, or what it should be directed towards. Notions of proportionality and rationality are measures of immediate, rather than axiomatic, 'democratic' legitimation, which judge political process in terms of its conduct rather than its genesis. By the same token, tolerance of interest-based political expression leaves the final question of the legitimate character of the European polity open and constantly amenable to a process of self-nomination and self-determination in the most universal of real-world terms. The character and purpose of permanent revolution, together with its ability to reveal yet-to-be discovered real-world justice demands, is thus assured and never foreclosed by the application of abstract totalisations.

Democratic deliberative experimentalism: the efforts of the European legal order to facilitate, nurture and order a structured political process of decision-making within a realm of European integration that has escaped the confines and limitations of our traditional national democratic polities is, undoubtedly, its greatest strength. Yet, it also remains its greatest weakness. The stumbling process whereby Europe's law struggles to ensure that the European integration *telos* is of an emerging European polity's *own* making, rather than an axiomatic imposition, is, without doubt, a vital step towards the achieved societal constitution. Absent the axioms of constitutional settlement, law's authority is not to be found in any illusionary form of totalising legal 'universality'. Instead, the reflexive procedural mechanisms of the European legal order seek to secure a new form of universality, within which social reality, rather than illusionary totality, determines the evolutionary course of normative social organisation, and, with regard to which, law assumes a mantle of authority through its ability to translate fact into norms, or social justice demands into institutions of European governance, precisely by virtue of its refusal to adopt any final constituting role within the European polity – or, alternatively, by reason of its constant endeavour to ensure that real-world constitutional advance is made by real-world political forces.

Nonetheless, the readiness of European law to engage in democratic experimentalism cannot but raise concerns about the sustainability of Europe's *Rechtsverfassungsrecht*. Just as certainly as law seeks its own *proprium* in its own socially autonomous morality or ethic, so, too, must the forces of political contestation find their *raison d'être* and self-legitimising force in their own autonomous rationality and justice-revealing function. However, and as noted in Chapter 1, Europe's post-statal and post-national constellation leaves us with no room for recourse to the traditional democratically legitimating mechanism of the republican polity and its majoritarian politics. Regardless of the rights and wrongs of pluralist disavowal of the traditional republican polity and axiomatic illusions of universality, European integration processes have, in simple fact, sprung the confines of the traditional closed polity with its determinative democratic majorities, thereby dictating that we seek elsewhere for our final arbiter of democratic legitimacy within political process.

It is in this regard that Europe's law is dependent, rather than socially autonomous. Its forays into democratic experimentalism and the structuring of political process are wholly contingent upon the sustainability of a notion of 'democratic deliberation', which has, in its turn, liberated the concept of democratically legitimated political process from the axiomatic closure forced upon it by political majorities, pairing it down instead to its core processual elements: political contestation and political process are legitimated by 'arguing' rather than 'bargaining' (Fossum 2004). But which has, likewise, dispensed with all the legitimating props of the constitutionally settled polity – its notion of political community, its public–private divide, its constitutively crafted individual rights, its clear apportionment of individual and political responsibilities, as well as its emotional appeal to Habermasian notions of 'constitutional patriotism'.

## IV. The constitutional imperative

Therein lies the final rub: born out of the liberal constitutional settlement, can a notion of deliberative democracy function without its complex sustaining framework of rights, social or political solidarity, and (totalising) authoritative constitutional axiom? Possibly not: recourse to theories of deliberative democracy at European level is often tentative in nature and highly aware of its specific limits.

Thus, as a reiterating example, the concept of deliberative supranationalism conspicuously eschews all claim to be establishing any form of overarching European democracy, and, instead, roots its assertion of 'democratic legitimacy' precisely within the constitutionally settled national polity (Joerges 2002a). Seen in this light, the norms of rationality and proportionality imposed by European law are not themselves directly sustaining of a new and uniquely European political process, but, instead, act indirectly, seeking to ensure that traditional democratic process within all national polities is duly respected by and is respectful, not only of the imperatives of European integration, but also of the justice demands made by other democratically legitimated national polities. By the same token, however, the final democratic sustainability of rationality and proportionality criteria might also be doubted, more especially, at the point where national and European political interests are simply incommensurate with one another, or, alternatively, are 'irrationally' irreconcilable.[29]

Equally, however, theories founded within the notion of a 'directly deliberative polyarchy', for all that they might revel in the positive nature of their potential illiberality – or their ability to give voice to social groups which do not necessarily share all (if any) of the sentiments of liberal constitutional settlement[30] – are likewise aware that the effort to identify the norms that might effectively arbitrate between the interests of self-nominating polities remains an experimental one, and wholly dependent upon the development of the mechanisms that will ensure social cohesion within a self-nominating, diverse and plural 'polity'.[31]

Theory is confounded and experimentalism reigns supreme. More importantly, however, academic concerns about the theoretical limits to deliberative democratic experimentalism are also echoed within a real-world of

European integration: first, at the critical limit to European market integration, where economically integrative rationalities meet socially redistributive logics that cannot simply be set aside with recourse to rationality criteria which can reveal and unveil, but can never trump, a solidaristic (irrational) national interest in social justice (Chapter 2 (IV.1)); and second, within the realms of a self-nominating European polity, which must also always remain vulnerable to the accusatory interrogative of 'why should this interest be represented above all others'.[32]

Deliberative notions of democracy within the post-statal and post-national constellation are far from perfect, and the law that espouses them is still contingent upon on-going endeavours to ensure, or to circumnavigate the need for perfection. Additionally, the mirror to theoretical imperfection is to be found in the logical incoherence of Europe's *Rechtsverfassungsrecht*: its recidivistic retreat into formalist reasoning where the *proprium* of deliberative democracy has yet to evolve to allow for the resolution of 'essential' or organic conflict between the plural interests of a European polity, where the axioms of the national social constitutional settlement (state) must still delimit the application of European competition law,[33] and where literal application of formal European legal provision furnishes the European legal order with the means to escape any politically flavoured pronouncement on the legitimate shape of the European polity.

Europe's *Rechtsverfassungsrecht* currently atones, at least within its own realm, for any potential experimental weakness in the political organisation of social contestation, still finding its own higher, though perhaps logically incoherent, 'authority' in such cases, in its refusal to assume any determinative political jurisdiction. Nonetheless, if political contestation is not simply to descend into political violence, the quest for a political *proprium*, or autonomous (and socially reflexive) political authority cannot be restricted to a European legal order, but must extend to European political theory and, most importantly, to a real-world of European politics. Seen from the viewpoint of European politics, rather than European law, which are the exact mechanisms that will ensure the sustainability of political deliberation beyond the traditional constitutional settlement, and which are the forms of political discourse and exchange that will ensure a substantive and real-world political solidarity beyond the axiomatic powers of the constitutive act? The question is not one which law alone can decide. As we have seen, the legal order, in all its radically reflexive and proceduralist guise, can serve the dual causes of legal self-legitimation and the stabilisation of deliberative rather than determinative politics. But one final question inevitably remains: can politics reinvent itself, can it project itself beyond narrow historical expressions of personal, national, statal, or, indeed, self-interest, in order to attain a universality that is founded within a real-world response to real-world problems, rather than any pre-conceived and closed notion of political community?

The messy realism of political, economic and social processes of European integration has presented the law of Europe (national and European) with a constitutional imperative. In the absence of axioms of constitutional settlement, law is denied recourse to its traditional universality, or, to an authority that was founded within the totalising axioms of the constitutional nation state. In its efforts to fulfil its traditional function of furnishing an extra-legal environment with stable and authoritative structures of social ordering, law has accordingly been forced to move far beyond the traditional canons of constitutional theory, in order to identify the mechanisms of *Rechtsverfassungsrecht* that might substitute for the lack of a constitutional settlement.

This, the voyage of discovery upon which European law was launched, was a simple response to the realities of a real-word of social, political and economic organisation. Moreover, it has proven to be a voyage of rediscovery, in which constitutional morphogenesis, or the process of constitutionalising European integration beyond the broken axioms of the traditional constitutional settlement, has relocated the focus of juridical concern within the formal-material paradox which characterised the legal theory of the inter-war era.

The evolution of constitutionalism beyond constitutions as simple *fait accompli*: for law, the constitutional imperative has been one of relocating its own autonomous legitimacy within its ability to give voice to its own extra-legal environment, to engage in a radically reflexive relationship with a real-world. The constitutional imperative is a highly uncomfortable one, implicating Europe's self-constitutionalising/socially constitutive legal order in the constant oscillation between material and formal jurisprudence, as well as the occasional inadequacy of its own procedural mechanisms of reality recognition. Nonetheless, the substitution of 'reality' for axiom, the on-going effort to bridge the gap between facts and norms and to adapt the abstract categorisation of juristic philosophy for the 'actual' world around law, has also brought with it renewed awareness of a higher normative imperative; a normative imperative, which likewise determines that, whilst the experimental endeavour to establish a post-settlement politics that is governed by its own authoritative law is one that is full of pitfalls and potential catastrophe, it is one that cannot and must not end.

The lesson is there to be learned, both in Europe's past and in Europe's future. Settled constitutional closure of a European 'community' would entail an inevitable and unacceptable act of exclusion. The social theorists of an inter-war age, most particularly Harald Laski and Hermann Heller, were concerned to free Europe's slaves: the 'non-citizens' who were victims of notions of national self-determination; the 'national' citizens who were victims of their own nation's industrial success; as well as the entire citizenry and non-citizenry of all European nations, who could so easily be sacrificed on the aesthetic altar of statal abstraction. At this, one, 'European' level, the lesson has perhaps been well learned: although flawed, the continuing European concern with the securing of individual welfare, as well as the determining European principle of (national) non-discrimination, at least herald the willingness to attempt to solve the core failing in the putative 'universalism' of a European tradition of constitutional settlement – its entrapment of the whole of European existence within national axioms of closed community, which cannot but exclude the realities of a shared European life.

Nonetheless, the pasts and futures of Europe are also many. Harald Laski may have been concerned to liberate the real-world social corporations of his age and political purview; equally, Hermann Heller may have been preoccupied with giving voice to the social demands for justice, which were, in his experience and social temperament, in most pressing need of a mode of expression. In the meantime, however, we have learned far more: we have learned that not only European nationalism, but also Europe's very core, its central claim to 'civilisation', its liberal sentiment and abstract historical mission to ensure 'universality', have claimed and still continue to claim a multitude of victims in a real-world.

It is in this sense that the establishment of an overarching European *res publica*, or closed constitutional settlement must be resisted. From the past victims of European colonial expansion, to the current ('extra-European') victims of Europe's economic efforts to secure its own (closed) wealth and welfare, from the past victims of Europe's imposition of a culturally and homogenous vision of acceptable human behaviour, to the current ethical, gendered or subjective victims of the objectively constructed (liberal) notion of the human subject – not only the territorial concept of Europe, but also the abstract philosophy within which it is founded, is one that creates slaves and sacrifices itself on its own myriad alters of self-projection. A closed and constitutionally settled Europe would undoubtedly remain deaf to the emerging justice demands of a 'non-European' world.

This, then, is the final justification for continuing our stumbling and flawed efforts to identify the politics and its supporting authoritative law that might rid human organisation of its slaves. If a European philosophical legacy, or European 'civilisation', is to retain its legitimacy in an increasingly global and globally localised context of 'actual' human life, then it must attain a measure of 'real-world' universality. Not the axiomatic fiction of universality, which currently finds its potentially most repressive expression in the promulgation of global human rights regimes: what are 'rights', but preconceived constructs of false human personality that mask, just as surely as they secure, (western) strategies of global domination? But, rather, in the, yet-to-be identified real-world politics of universal solidarity (founded within the recognition of the 'other'?), which is forever open to the emerging justice demands of an 'actual' world, and which is governed by its own, socially sensitive and socially responsive, law.

'Rome was a terrible mistress'. 'Europe' traduces just as it seduces; but it might yet redeem itself, at last fulfilling its own universal philosophical promise by means of its preparedness to continue to engage with real-world economic, social, political and legal processes – even though these processes might also end in European dissolution.

## Notes

1 Or, as Laski opines in relation to the state (1935), 'it is a universality simply of formal reference'.
2 Primarily directed to the establishment of a people's 'collectivity', which might justify the imposition of the large-scale governmental instrumentalism that would be necessary in order to effect economic redistribution (Everson 2003b).
3 Seemingly even arguing outside the categories of plural political expression within a federal constitution that were established by Madison.
4 Note, Maitland's status as the progenitor of English pluralist thought is established by virtue of his translation of and commentary on the definitive work of the German political philosopher (von Gierke and Maitland 1987).
5 For example, a Trade Union becomes a tangible being within the purview of the state, once, and only once, it has been recognised and delineated by formal labour regulation.
6 Alternatively, the process whereby a higher legal commitment to notions of national non-discrimination translates into a political norm, whereby each national polity must take the interests of other polities into account within its decision making processes (Joerges 2002a).
7 See above, Chapter 1 (IV), on Hermann Heller's plea in favour of a constitutional indeterminacy that would allow the transcendental structures of the constitution to be bent to meet the justice demands inherent within a constantly evolving social reality. See, also, Dyzenhaus (1999: 204).
8 Alternatively, in Dahrendorf's famous normative re-evaluation of T.H. Marshall's descriptive sociological account of the establishment of the UK welfare state (post-war constitutional moment), the circle of constitutionally guaranteed rights, with civic rights at its centre, political rights around them and welfare rights at its periphery, was an abstract axiom of constitutional government, with reality at its core. Individual empowerment remained the primary organising feature of the modern state and its constitution. However, political collectivity, with its commitment to welfare would continually act to renew individual empowerment, in practice as in theory, as the individual citizen would be guaranteed a sufficient level of material comfort to allow him or her to engage fully with and within the body politic (Marshall 1953; Dahrendorf 1990).
9 Returning to Max Weber's terms, one of the vital characteristics of the law of the welfare/social state is its reliance upon the legal reasoning category of 'substantive rationality' (Teubner 1983: 267). The modern law of the welfare state was, without doubt a 'purposive law'. However, the programme of social renewal was dictated by a legislature, whilst law continued with its traditional role of deduction of norms from a legislatively established code – a modern formalism, displaying all the ambiguities of its traditional predecessor.
10 The irony of post-war material law, is thus one of a legal order that was finally to be undermined by its excessive degree of formalisation – a degree of formalisation that likewise facilitated the transfer of traditional legal functions, at least within an area of wealth redistribution, to the administration (Harlow and

Rawlings 1997: 9), and resulted in the bureaucratic alienation of the individual citizen. Note, however, that the formalism, if not excessive formalism, of the post-war welfare state was also a chronicle of a story long foretold: simple review of the most conservative of the cases of the pre-New Deal US Supreme Court, thus reveal that it is not the seemingly intransigent majority, which engages in acts of wilful formalism, when refusing to allow the fourteenth amendment of the US Constitution (freedom of contract) to be trumped by regulative state provisions (restricting hours of work or enforcing labour rights). Such acts were merely a denial of judicial choice in relation to interpretation of the constitutional norm – a cloak for reactionary personal judgments (Schauer 1988). Instead, formalism, or literal application of the constitution in the light of police powers afforded to individual states is the preserve of the liberal minority within the Court, in particular, Justice Holmes: see, only, *Lochner* v *New York* (1905). Formalism, it should never be forgotten, also serves the aims of (legislatively driven) reform.

11 See above, Chapter 2, especially Sections III.4 and IV.1. Above all, European law played a major part in undermining the 'corporatist' confusion of social and welfare aims within much national legislation.

12 See, once again, the dictum of Joerges, that the major practical-normative achievement of European integration processes is the fact that they have forced all national polities to take the interests of other polities into account in their decision-making processes, (Joerges and Neyer 1997) or, indeed, their more prosaic inability to ensure the sustained economic growth needed to satisfy normative promises of economic welfare made to their own national addressees (Majone 1996), more particularly, the observation that corporatist states were also damp ening of economic progress.

13 Above all, within the critical legal studies movement within the United States (including authors such as Felix Cohen and Duncan Kennedy), but also within English political and social theory; most remarkably in the works of Harald Laski.

14 Or, indeed, recognise the modes in which society itself was compensating for contractual imbalances through collectivisation of labour within the workplace (Sinzheimer 1977).

15 Hence, the modern appellation of law as 'sociological jurisprudence', see Teubner (2004).

16 See, Ehrlich (1987), and, for details of the general movement towards social sciences, Rottleuthner (1988), above all his characterisation of Sinzheimer's objections about the nature of formal law. See, also, for the reproduction of such ideas within American legal theory and UK political theory, Cohen (1935) and Laski (1958: Chapter 10).

17 See Chapter 6 (IV.1), 'And you know, what the Americans call the 'Brandeis Brief' . . . there was [actually] very little of that kind of socio-economic explanation. In a sense, I thought that more would have been useful and I can give one particular case. There was a case about electricity nationalisation, or rather liberalisation of electricity markets. And I think it would have been greatly helpful to have had more economic explanation of how it worked and why it was important to go one way rather than the other'.

18 See Chapter 1 (IV) for details of the interaction between the views of Max Weber and Hermann Heller. See, also, Chapter 2 (III.2) for the incoherence of the ECJ's formalist jurisprudence on cultural issues.

19 The reference to the *Brandeis Brief* is particularly telling.

20 The core of Unger's reluctant critique of the law of the welfare state is, thus, its inevitable inability to translate morally spontaneous expressions of community into a coherent legal framework. Law, it seems, is able only to pay lip service to

the social face of love through procedural (and sometimes counter-productive) maxims such as 'equality of bargaining power'.

21 And here Weiler's critique of the formulations deployed by the *Bundesverfassungsgericht* does have validity (Weiler 1995).

22 Alternatively, a distinction must be made between the sociological investigations of Niklas Luhmann, which simply reveal the manner in which a legal order receives impulses (irritations) from its external environment and translates them into its own rationality, and the more philosophical approach of Jürgen Habermas, which lays a far greater emphasis upon the ability of legal mechanisms of norm–fact translation to furnish a constant and constitutive legitimating power, both within law itself and within a wider society. See Chapter 2 (V).

23 See, only, Chapter 2 (III.1), and the efforts of the ECJ in the 1960s simultaneously to tread an impartial path between the conflicting political interests of federally minded and more 'nationalistic' member state governments and imbue EU law with a life and purpose of its own.

24 See only, Chapter 6 (IV.2), and the ECJ's praiseworthy unwillingness to extend individual standing under Article 230 EC. See, also, below, Section III.3.

25 See Chapter 6 (IV.2). The critical moment within such adjudication is thus supplied by the process of conscious interaction between equally legitimated legal orders.

26 See Chapter 4 (III.1), with reference to the preparedness of national justices to refer cases under the 234 mechanism, which they feel 'will be of importance to other jurisdictions'.

27 And here, the maintenance of a plurality of legal orders, as well as dialogue between legal orders, once again gains vital significance: national orders are the best placed to assess the separable political commitments to European integration of member state polities; the European legal order is the best placed to evaluate the evolution of a European political process.

28 See Chapters 5 (II.2) and 6 (IV.2): thus the vital key to understanding recent increases in the breadth of individual standing under Article 230 EC Treaty is not the sudden evolution of a right-based approach to the safeguarding of the interest of individual Europeans, but, rather, the desire of the European Courts (in this case, the Court of First Instance) to ensure the proper representation of all relevant interests within the European decision-making process.

29 In other words, where a final decision must be made as to which politically legitimated interest must be allowed to prevail: at this point, whilst notions of proportionality and rationality can do much to reveal the true nature of the interests presented, they lack the status of morally imperative norms and may even court the danger of skewing the political process in favour of technocratic rather than democratic decision-making – notions of rationality and proportionality are close in their nature to broader utilitarian notions of governance, which might be tempted to decide the final issue in light of the maxim that the greatest possible gains must be brought to the greatest possible constituency.

30 Sharing much in common with the underlying normative efforts of Laski to free the republic's slaves, see, Cohen (2002).

31 In other words, constitutive 'liberal' individual rights cannot simply be dispensed with; instead, other means of formalised social recognition must be found (Cohen and Sabel 1997).

32 In other words, are we really content to allow politicisation processes within the European polity to be led by interest groups, over which traditional national polities have little or no control.

33 See, only, the various social insurance cases heard by the ECJ, Chapter 2 (IV.1). Although the Court may have taken jurisdiction over national social insurance

provision, and may likewise have sought to bring various elements of its rational proceduralism into play within the national social constitutional settlement (i.e., its exhortation to national administrative law that all relevant interests should be allowed to challenge – potentially abusive – collective bargaining processes), the final decision not to apply Articles 80 and 82 EC Treaty to national insurance schemes was likewise founded within judicial 'choice' and judicial 'morality' – or the recognition that the shared constitutional traditions of the members states supported such socially redistributive insurance arrangements.

# Bibliography


Ackerman, B, 'The new separation of powers', *The Harvard Law Review*, 2000, 113(3), pp 633–792.

Ackerman, B, 'The rise of world constitutionalism', *The Virginia Law Review*, 1997, 83, pp 771–797.

Ackerman, B, 'Rooted cosmopolitanism', *Ethics*, 1994, 104(3), pp 516–535.

Ackerman, B, *The Future of Liberal Revolution*, 1992, New Haven, CT: Yale University Press.

Ackerman, B, *We the People Transformations*, Vol 1, 1991, Harvard, MA: Harvard University Press.

Ackerman, B, 'Constitutional politics/constitutional law', *The Yale Law Journal*, 1989, 99(3), pp 1–96.

Ackerman, B, 'The Storrs lectures discovering the constitution', *The Yale Law Journal*, 1984, 93, pp 1013–1072.

Alexy, R, 'Basic rights and democracy in Jürgen Habermas' procedural paradigm of the law', *Ratio Juris,* 1994, 72, pp 227–238.

Amstutz, M (ed), *Die vernetzte Wirtschaft: Netzwerke als Rechtsproblem*, 2004, Zürich: Schultheiss.

Armstrong, K, 'Legal integration: theorizing the legal dimension of European integration', *Journal of Common Market Studies*, 1998, 36(2), pp 155–174.

Benedict, ML, 'Constitutional history and constitutional theory reflections on Ackerman, reconstruction and the transformation of the American Constitution', *The Yale Law Journal*, 1999, 108, pp 2011–2038.

Brüggermeir, G (ed), *Verfassung für ein Ziviles Europa*, 1994, Baden-Baden: Nomos.

Burley, A-M and Mattli, W, 'Europe before the Court: a political theory of legal integration', *International Organization*, 1993, 47, pp 41–76.

Carter, SL, 'Constitutional adjudication and the indeterminate text: a preliminary defence of an imperfect muddle', *The Yale Law Journal*, 1985, 94, pp 821–840.

Chalmers, D, 'The dynamics of judicial authority and the constitutional treaty', in Weiler, J and Eisgruber, Ch (eds), *Altneuland: The EU Constitution in a Contextual Perspective*, 2004, Jean Monnet Working Paper 5/04, NYU, [http//www.jeanmonnetprogram.org/papers/04/040501-14.html].

Chalmers, D, 'The reconstitution of European public spheres', *European Law Journal*, 2003, 9(2), pp 127–189.

Chalmers, D, 'Repackaging the internal market – the ramifications of the Keck judgment', *European Law Review*, 1994, 19, pp 385–407.

Christiansen, Th, 'Intra-institutional politics and inter-institutional relations in the EU towards coherent government?', *Journal of European Public Policy*, 2001, 8, pp 747–767.
Cohen, F, 'Transcendental nonsense and the functional approach', *Columbia Law Review*, 1935, 35, pp 809–849.
Cohen, J, 'For a Democratic Society', in Freeman, S (ed), *A Cambridge Companion to Rawles*, 2002, Cambridge: Cambridge University Press.
Cohen, J and Sabel, Ch, 'Directly deliberative polyarchy', *European Law Journal*, 1997, 34, pp 313–342.
Coppel, J and O'Neill, A, 'The European Court of Justice: taking rights seriously?', *Common Market Law Review*, 1992, 29, pp 669–692.
Cram, L, 'Introduction to special issue on the institutional balance and the future of EU governance: the future of the Union and the trap of the "nirvana fallacy"', *Governance – An International Journal of Policy Administration and Institutions*, 2002, 153, pp 309–324.
Dahrendorf, R, *The Modern Social Contract: An Essay on the Politics of Liberty*, 1990, Berkeley, CA: University of California Press.
Dashwood, A, 'States in the European Union', *European Law Review*, 1998, 23(3), pp 201–216.
Dervin, B and Melvin, JV (eds), *Progress in Communication Sciences*, 1984, Norwood: Ablex.
Dicey, VS, *Law & Opinion in England*, 1930, Edinburgh: R. & R. Clarke.
Dicey, VS, *The Law of the Constitution*, 8th edn, 1926, London: Macmillan.
Dyzenhaus, D, *Legality and Legitimacy: Carl Schmitt, Hans Kelsen and Hermann Heller in Weimar*, 1999, Oxford: Oxford University Press.
Ehrlich, E, *Freie Rechtsfindung und freie Rechtswissenschaft,* 1987 (reprint from 1903), Aalen: Scientia.
Elftheriadis, P, 'Begging the constitutional question', *Journal of Common Market Studies*, 1998, 36(2), pp 255–272.
European Court of Justice (ECJ), *The Future of the Judicial System of the European Union* (submission of the ECJ to the Nice IGC), 1999, Luxembourg: European Court of Justice.
Everson, M, 'Legal constructions of the consumer', in Haupt, G and Trentmann, F (eds), *Legal Constructions of the Consumer, The Making of the Consumer*, 2005, London: Berg Publishing, pp 99–124.
Everson, M, 'Accountability and law in Europe: towards a new public legal order?', *The Modern Law Review*, 2004, 67(1), pp 124–138.
Everson, M, 'A court between a rock and a hard place: social pluralism and the European Court of Justice', *The Journal of Legislative Studies*, 2003a, 8(4), pp 98–116.
Everson, M, '"Subjects" or "citizens" of "Erewhon?": law and non-law in the development of a "British citizenship"', *Citizenship Studies*, 2003b, 71, pp 57–84.
Everson, M, 'Beyond the *Bundesverfassungsgericht*: on the necessary cunning of constitutional law', *European Law Journal*, 1998a, 4, pp 389–410.
Everson, M, 'Administering Europe', *Journal of Common Market Studies*, 1998b. 36(2), pp 195–216.
Everson, M, 'The legacy of the market citizen', in Shaw, J and More, G (eds), *New Legal Dynamics of European Union*, 1995, Oxford: Clarendon, pp 73–89.

*Federalist Papers,* Hamilton, A., Madison, J and Jay, J, *The Federalist Papers*, in Clinton, R (ed), 1961, New York: The Mentor Library.

Flood, ET, 'Fact construction and judgment in constitutional adjudication', *The Yale Law Journal*, 1991, 100, pp 1795–1881.

Fossum, JE, 'Still a Union of deep diversity?', in Eriksen, EO, Fossum, JE and Menéndez, AJ (eds), *Developing a Constitution for Europe*, 2004, London: Routledge, pp 226–248.

Garrett, G, 'International cooperation and institutional choice in the European community's internal market', *International Organisation*, 1992, 462, pp 533–560.

Gough, JW, *Fundamental Law in English Constitutional History*, 1955, Oxford: Clarendon.

Graber, MA, 'Asking better questions – the problems of constitutional theory', *Political Science and Politics*, 1993, 262, pp 216–222.

Grey, JS, *Liberalisms Essays in Political Philosophy*, 1989, London: Routledge.

Griffin, SM, 'Constitutional theory transformed', *The Yale Law Journal*, 1999, 108, p 2115.

Grimm, D, 'Integration durch Verfassung', *Leviathan*, 2004, 32, pp 448–463.

Grosswald-Curran, V, 'The politics of memory/Errinerungspolitik and the use and propriety of laws in the process of memory conservation', *Law and Critique*, 2003, 14(3), pp 309–323.

Gumbrecht, H-U and Ludwig Pfeiffer, K (eds), *Paradoxien, Dissonanzen, Zusammenbrüche Situationen offener Epistemologie*, 1991, Frankfurt a.M: Suhrkamp.

Haas, EB, *Beyond the Nation State*, 1964, Stamford, CA: Stamford University Press.

Habermas, J, *Zwischen Naturalismus und Religion*, 2005a, Frankfurt: Suhrkamp.

Habermas, J, 'Europa ist uns über die Köpfe gerollt', *Suddeitsche Zeitung*, May 2005b, p 3.

Habermas, J, 'A constitution for Europe', *New Left Review*, 2001, 11, pp 5–26.

Habermas, J, 'Paradigms of law', *Cardozo Law Review*, 1996a, 17, pp 771–784.

Habermas, J, *Between Facts and Norms,* William Rehg (trans), 1996b, London: Polity Press.

Habermas, J, 'Über den internen Zusammenhang von Rechstaat und Demokratie', in Preuß, UK (ed), *Zum Begriff der Verfassung*, 1994, Frankfurt a.M: Fischer.

Habermas, J, *Zwischen Faktizität und Geltung: Beiträge zur Diskurstheorie des Rechts und des demokratischen Rechtsstaats*, 1992, Frankfurt a.M: Suhrkamp.

Hamilton, A, Madison, J and Jay, J, *The Federalist Papers*, Clinton, R (ed), 1961, New York: The Mentor Library.

Hanafin, P, *Constituting Identity: Political Identity Formation and the Constitution in Post-Independence Ireland*, 2001, Aldershot: Ashgate.

Harlow, C and Rawlings, R, *Law and Administration*, 2nd edn, 1997, London: Butterworths.

Heller, H, 'Die Krise der Staatslehre', 1934, reproduced in *Gesammelte Schriften,* 1992, Tübingen: Mohr-Siebeck.

Heller, H, 'Veröffentlichungen der Vereinigung der Deutschen Staatsrechtslehrer', 1928a, reproduced in *Gesammelte Schriften*, 1992, Tübingen: Mohr-Siebeck.

Heller, H, 'Politische Demokratie and Soziale Homogenität', 1928b, reproduced in *Gesammelte Schriften*, 1992, Tübingen: Mohr-Siebeck.

Heller, H, 'Der Begriff des Gestezes in der Reichsverfassung', 1927, reproduced in *Gesammelte Schriften*, 1992, Tübingen: Mohr-Siebeck.
Hirst, P, *The Pluralist Theory of the State*, 1993, Oxford: Routledge.
Holmes, S, 'Verfassungsförmige Vorentscheidungen und das Paradox der Demokratie', in Preuß, UK (ed), *Zum Begriff der Verfassung Die Ordnung der Politischen Suhrkamp*, 1994, Frankfurt a.M: Fischer.
Ipsen, H-P, *Europäisches Gemeinschaftsrecht*, 1972, Tübingen: J.C.B.Mohr.
Jacqué, J-P, 'The principle of institutional balance', *Common Market Law Review*, 2004, 4(1), pp 383–391.
Jacqué, J-P, 'Cours Général de Droit Communautaire', in Clapham, A (ed), *Collected Courses of the Academy of European Law*, Vol 1, book.1, 1990, Dordrecht: Martinus Nijhoff.
Joerges, Ch, 'Deliberative supranationalism: two defences', *European Law Journal*, 2002a, 8(1), pp 133–151.
Joerges, Ch, '"Good Governance" in the European internal market: two competing legal conceptualisation of European integration and their synthesis', in von Bogdandy, A, Mavroides, PC and Mény, Y (eds), *European Integration and International Co-ordination. Studies in Transnational Economic Law in Honour of Claus-Dieter Ehlermann*, 2002b, Den Haag: Kluwer.
Joerges, Ch, 'Taking the law seriously: on political science and the role of law in the process of European integration', *European Law Journal*, 1996a, 2, pp 105–135.
Joerges, Ch, 'The market without a state', EUI Working Papers in Law (1996/2), 1996b, Florence: European University Institute.
Joerges, Ch and Everson, M, 'Re-conceptualising Europeanisation as a public law of collisions: comitology, agencies and an interactive public adjudication', in Hoffmann, H and Turk, A (eds), *Administrative Governance*, 2005, London: Edward Elgar.
Joerges, Ch and Everson, M, 'Law, economics and politics in the constitutionalisation of Europe', in Eriksen, EO, Fossum, JE and Menendez, AJ (eds), *Developing a Constitution for Europe*, 2004, London: Routledge.
Joerges, Ch and Neyer, J, 'From intergovernmental bargaining to deliberative political processes: the constitutionalisation of comitology', *European Law Journal*, 1997, 3, pp 273–299.
Joerges, Ch and Trubek, D (eds), *Critical Legal Thought: An American–German Debate*, 1988, Baden-Baden: Nomos.
Kahn, R, 'Rethinking constitutional theory, method, practice and doctrinal change', *The Journal of Politics*, 1995, 57(1), pp 229–242.
Katz, SN and Blackstone, W, *Commentaries on the Laws of England*, 1979, Chicago: Chicago University Press.
Kennedy, D, *A Critique of Adjudication fin de siècle*, 1997, Cambridge, MA: Harvard University Press.
Kennedy, D, 'American constitutionalism as civil religion: notes of an atheist', *Nova Law Review*, 1994, 19, pp 909–922.
Kennedy, D, (1988) 'Comment on Rudolf Wiethölters "Materialisation and proceduralisation in modern law"', in Joerges, Ch and Trubek, D (eds), *Critical Legal Thought: An American–German Debate*, 1988, Baden-Baden: Nomos, pp 511–524.
Kennedy, D, 'Freedom and constraint in adjudication: a critical phenomenology', *Journal of Legal Education*, 1986, 36, pp 518–562.

Kennedy, D, 'The structure of Blackstone's Commentaries', *Buffalo Law Review*, 1979, 28, pp 205–379.

Keohane, R, *Neo-Realism and its Critics*, 1986, New York: Columbia University Press.

Kirchhoff, P, 'Das Kooperationsverhältnis zwischen Bundesverfassungsgericht und Europäischem Gerichtshof', in Müller-Graff, P-Ch (ed), *Perspektiven des Rechts in der Europäischen Union*, 1988, Heidelberger Forum für Europäisches Recht Band 1, pp 163–182.

Klare, KE, 'Legal culture and transformative constitutionalism', *South African Journal on Human Rights*, 1998, 14, pp 146–167.

Kleinhenz, G, *Zur politischen Ökonomie des Konsums*, 1978, Berlin: Dunker & Humblot.

Krippendorff, K, 'Paradox and information', in Dervin, B and Voigt, MJ (eds), *Progress in Communication Sciences*, 1984, Norwood: Ablex.

Kuhn, TS, *The Structure of Scientific Revolutions*, 1970, Chicago: University of Chicago Press.

Laduer, K-H, 'Towards a legal theory of supranationality: the viability of the network concept', *European Law Journal*, 1997, 3(1), pp 33–54.

Laenerts, K, 'Some thoughts about the interaction between judges and politicians', *University of Chicago Legal Forum*, 1992, 9(3), pp 93–133.

Laski, HS, *A Grammar of Politics*, 4th edn, 1958, London: Allen & Unwin.

Laski, H, (1935) 'Law and the state' (*Studies in Law and Politics*), 1935, reproduced in Hirst, P (ed), *The Pluralist Theory of the State*, 1993, London: Routledge.

Laski, H, *Studies in the Problem of Sovereignty*, 1917, Cambridge, MA: Yale University Press (reprint 1968).

Lepsius, MR, 'Die Europäische Gemeinschaft: Rationalitätskriterien der Regimebildung', in Zapf, W (ed), *25te Deutschen Soziologentage,* 1991, Baden-Baden: Nomos.

Lepsius, MR, *Interessen, Ideen und Institutionen*, 1990, Opladen: Westdeutscher Verlag.

Luhmann, N, *Das Recht der Gesellschaft*, 1993, Frankfurt: Suhrkamp.

Luhmann, N, 'Sthenographie und Euryalistik', in Gumbrecht, H-U and Pfeiffer, KL (eds), *Paradoxien, Dissonanzen, Zusammenbrüche Situationen offener Epistemologie*, 1991, Frankfurt a.M: Suhrkamp.

Luhmann, N, *Grundrechte als Institution: Ein Beitrag zur politischen Soziologie*, 1965, Berlin: Duncker & Humblot.

MacCormick, N, 'Risking constitutional collision in Europe?', *Oxford Journal of Legal Studies*, 1998, 18, pp 517–532.

MacCormick, N, 'The Maastricht-Urteil, sovereignty now', *European Law Journal*, 1995, 1, pp 259–266.

Maduro, MP, 'The new form of Majoritarianism from the EU', *European Law Review*, 2003, 28(6), pp 900–904.

Maduro, MP, 'Reforming the state or the market, Article 30 and the European constitution economic freedom and political rights', *European Law Journal*, 1997, 3(1), pp 55–82.

Magnette, P, 'Does the process really matter? Some reflections on the "legitimating effect" of the European Convention', 2003, CES Working Papers, Harvard, no.102.

Marshall, TH, *Citizenship and Social Class*, 1953, London: Pluto Press, 1992.

Majone, G, *Dilemmas of European Integration: The Ambiguities & Pitfalls of Integration by Stealth*, 2005, Oxford: Oxford University Press.
Majone, G, 'Delegation of regulatory powers in a mixed polity', *European Law Journal*, 2002, 8(3), pp 319–339.
Majone, G, 'Europe's "democratic deficit": the question of standards', *European Law Journal*, 1998, 4(1), pp 5–28.
Majone, G, *Regulating Europe*, 1996, Oxford: Routledge.
Majone, G, 'The European Community as a fourth branch of government', in Brüggermeir, G (ed), *Verfassung für ein Ziviles Europa*, 1994, Baden-Baden: Nomos.
Mancini, GF, 'Europe: the Case for statehood', *European Law Journal*, 1998, 4(1), pp 29–42.
Marks, G, Hooghe, L and Blank, K, 'European integration since the 1980s: state centric versus multi-level governance', *Journal of Common Market Studies*, 1996, 34, p 341.
Marshall, TH, *Citizenship and Social Class*, 1953, London: Pluto Press, 1992.
McCormick, J, *Carl Schmitt's Critique of Liberalism against Technology*, 1997, New York: Cambridge University Press.
McCowan, M, 'The European Parliament before the bench: ECJ precedent and EP litigation strategies', *Journal of European Public Policy*, 2003, 10(6), pp 974–995.
Mestmäcker, E-J, *Wirtschaft und Verfassung in der Europäischen Union: Beiträge zu Recht, Theorie und Politik der europäischen Integration*, 2003, Baden-Baden: Nomos.
Mestmäcker, E-J, 'On the legitimacy of European law', *Rabels Zeitschrift*, 1994, 54, pp 614–635.
Mestmäcker, E-J, *Die Vermittlung von europäischem und nationalen Recht im System unverfälschten Wettbewerbs*, 1969, Bad Homburg: Gehlen.
Micklitz, H and Reich, N, *Verbraucherschutzrecht in der Bundesrepublik Deutschland*, 1980, New York: Van Nostrand Reinhold.
Milward, A, *The Rescue of the European Nation State*, 1996, Oxford: Routledge.
Moravscik, A, 'Preferences and power in the European Union: a liberal intergovernmental approach', *Journal of Common Market Studies*, 1993, 31(4), pp 473–524.
Müller-Graf, P-Ch (ed), *Perspektiven des Rechts in der Europäischen Union*, 1998, Heidelberger Forum für Europäisches Recht Heildelberg, Band 1.
Offe, C, 'Ausdifferenzierung oder Integration', in G. Fleischmann, G (ed), *Der Kritische Verbraucher*, 1981, Frankfurt: Campus.
Perez, O and Teubner, G (eds), *On Paradoxes and Inconsistencies in the Law*, 2005, Oxford: Hart Publishing.
Pernice, I, 'Multilevel constitutionalism in the European Union', *European Law Review*, 2002, 27(5), pp 511–529.
Pinder, J and Bruton, J, *Steps towards a Federal Parliament*, 1999, The Federal Trust: European Essays.
Pollack, MA, 'Representing diffuse interests in EC policy-making', *Journal of European Public Policy*, 1997, 4, pp 572–590.
Posner, R, 'Against constitutional theory', *New York University Law Review*, 1998, 73, p 1.

Preuß, UK (ed), *Zum Begriff der Verfassung: Die Ordnung der Politischen*, 1994a, Frankfurt a.M: Fischer.

Preuß, UK, 'Der Begriff der Verfassung und ihre Beziehung zur Politik', in *ibidem, Zum Begriff der Verfassung: Die Ordnung des Politischen*, 1994b, Frankfurt a.M: Fischer, pp 7–36.

Rasmussen, H, 'Remedying the crumbling EC judicial system', *Common Market Law Review*, 2000, 37, pp 1071–2000.

Reich, N, 'The November revolution of the European Court of Justice', *Common Market Law Review*, 1994, 31, pp 459–492.

Riesenberg, P, *Citizenship in the Western Tradition: Plato to Rousseau*, 1992, Chapel Hill: University of North Carolina Press.

Rotthleuthner, H, 'Three legal Sociologies – Eugen Ehrlich, Hugo Sinzheimer, Max Weber', *European Yearbook of Legal Sociology*, 1988, pp 227–259.

Salmond, JW, 'Citizenship and allegiance' (Part II), *Law Quarterly Review*, 1902, 17, pp 49–63.

Sand, I-J, 'Understanding the new forms of governance mutually interdependent reflexive destabilised and competing institutions', *European Law Journal*, 1998, 4(3), pp 271–293.

Schauer, F, 'Formalism', *The Yale Law Journal*, 1988, 97, pp 509–548.

Schepel, H and Wesseling, Rh, (1997) 'The legal community judges, lawyers, officials and clerks in the writing of Europe', *European Law Journal*, 1997, 3(2), pp 165–188.

Schmid, Ch, *Multi-level constitutionalism and constitutional conflicts interconnecting the National, European and international economic constitutions in the Banana dispute*, 2001, PhD Thesis, European University Institute, Florence.

Shapiro, Martin, 'Judicial independence the English experience', *North Carolina Law Review*, 1976, pp 577–652.

Shaw, J, 'What's in a Convention? Process and substance in the project of European constitution-building' in Michalowitz, I (ed), *Reihe Politikwissenschaft/Political Science Series 89*, 2003, Vienna: Institute for Advanced Studies.

Shaw, J, *Law of the European Union*, 3rd edn, 1996, Oxford: Palgrave.

Shaw, J, '*The Birth, Life and Death of a Proposal The Ill-Fated Services Draft*', Paper presented at the meeting of the European Community Studies Association, 11–14 May 1995, Charleston, South Carolina, cited in Slaughter, A-M and Mattli, W, 'Revisiting the European Court of Justice', *International Organisation*, 1998, 52(1), pp 177–209.

Shaw, J, Magnette, P, Hoffman, L and Verges Bausili, A, *Convention on the Future of Europe*, 2003, London: IB Tauris.

Simpson, AWB, *Legal Theory and Legal History Essays on the Common Law*, 1987, London: Hambledon.

Sinzheimer, H, *Ein Arbeitstarifgesetz: Die Idee der sozialen Selbstbestimmung im Recht*, 1977, Berlin: Duncker & Humblot.

Slaughter, A-M and Mattli, W, 'Revisiting the European Court of Justice', *International Organisation*, 1998, 52(1), pp 177–209.

Slynn, G, 'The Court of Justice of the European Communities', *International Law and Competition Law Quarterly*, 1984, 33, pp 409–429.

St Clair Bradley, K, 'Sense and sensibility – Parliament v Council continued', *European Law Review*, 1991, 16(3), pp 245–257.

Stein, E, 'International integration and democracy: no love at first sight', *American Journal of International Law*, 2001, 95, pp 489–543.

Stein, E, 'Lawyers, judges and the making of a transnational constitution', *American Journal of International Law*, 1981, 75, pp 1–27.

Stone Sweet, A, 'Constitutional courts and parliamentary democracy', *West European Politics*, 2002, 25(1), pp 77–100.

Sunstein, C, 'Judge Scalia's democratic formalism', *The Yale Law Journal*, 1997, 107, p 529.

Sunstein, C, 'Social norms and social roles', *Columbia Law Review*, 1996, 96, p 903.

Sunstein, C, *The Partial Constitution*, 1993, Cambridge, MA: Harvard University Press.

Sunstein, C, 'Cost–benefit analysis and the separation of powers', *Arizona Law Review*, 1981, 23, p 1281.

Talberg, J, 'Supranational influence in EU enforcement the ECJ and the Principle of state liability', *Journal of European Public Policy*, 2000, 7(1), pp 104–121.

Teubner, G, 'Dealing with paradoxes of law – Derrida, Luhmann, Wiethölter', in Perez, O and Teubner, G (eds), *On Paradoxes and Inconsistencies in the Law*, 2005, Oxford: Hart Publishing.

Teubner, G, 'Coincidentia oppositorum das Recht der Netzwerke Jenseits vom Vertrag und Organisation', in Amstutz, M (ed), *Die vernetzte Wirtschaft Netzwerke als Rechtsproblem*, 2004, Zürich: Schultheiss, pp 7–38.

Teubner, G, *Law as Autopoietic System*, 1993, London: Blackwell Publishing.

Teubner, Gunther, *Recht als autopoietisches System*, 1989, Frankfurt a.M: Suhrkamp.

Teubner, Gunther, 'Substantive and reflexive elements in modern law', *Law & Society Review*, 1983, 17, pp 241–285.

Teubner, G (ed), *Dilemmas of Law in the Welfare State*, 1985, Berlin, New York: De Gruyter.

Tridimas, T and Nebbia, P (eds), *European Union Law for the Twenty-First Century*, 2005, Oxford: Hart Publishing.

Trubek, D, 'Max Weber on law and the rise of capitalism', *Wisconsin Law Review*, 1972, 3, pp 720–753.

Unger, R, *Law in Modern Society*, 1976, New York, London: Free Press.

van Gerven, W, 'Of rights, remedies and procedures', *Common Market Law Review*, 2000, 37, pp 501–536.

von Bogdandy, A, Mavroides, PC and Mény, Y (eds), *European Integration and International Co-ordination. Studies in Transnational Economic Law in Honour of Claus-Dieter Ehlermann*, 2002, Den Haag: Kluwer.

Von Gierke, O and Maitland, FW, *Political Theories of the Middle Age*, 1900, Cambridge: Cambridge University Press, 1987.

Vos, E, *Institutional Frameworks of Community Health and Safety Legislation: Committees, Agencies, and Private Bodies*, 1999, Oxford: Hart Publishing.

Walker, N, 'The idea of constitutional pluralism', *The Modern Law Review*, 2002, 65(3), pp 317–359.

Ward, A, 'The draft EU constitution and private party access to judicial review of EU measures', in Tridimas, T and Nebbia, P (eds), *European Union Law for the Twenty-First Century*, 2005, Oxford: Hart Publishing.

Weatherill, S, 'Consumer safety legislation in the United Kingdom and Article 30 EEC', *European Law Review*, 1988, 13(2), pp 87–105.

Weber, M, *Economy and Society*, Vol 2, 1969, in Roth, G and Wittig, C (eds), Berkeley, CA, Los Angeles, London: University of Berkeley Press.

Weiler, JHH, 'Europe – the case against the case for statehood', *European Law Journal*, 1998, 4(1), pp 43–62.

Weiler, JHH, 'Does Europe need a constitution? Demos, telos and the German Maastricht decision', *European Law Journal*, 1995, 1, p 217.

Weiler, JHH, 'A quiet revolution – the European Court of Justice and its interlocutors', *Comparative Political Studies*, 1994, 26, pp 510–534.

Weiler, JHH, 'Journey into an unknown destination – a retrospective and prospective of the European Court of Justice in the arena of political integration', *Journal of Common Market Studies*, 1993, 31(4), pp 417–445.

Weiler, JHH, 'The Transformation of Europe', *The Yale Law Journal*, 1991, 100, pp 2403–2480.

Weiler, JHH, 'The community system – the dual character of supranationalism', *Yearbook of European Law*, 1981, p 267.

Wiethölter, R, 'Recht-Fertigungen eines Gesellschafts-Rechts', in Joerges, Ch and Teubner, G (eds), *Rechtsverfassungsrecht*, 2003, Baden-Baden: Nomos.

Wiethölter, R, 'Materialization and proceduralization in modern law', in Teubner, G (ed), *Dilemmas of Law in the Welfare State*, 1985, Berlin, New York: de Gruyter, pp 221–249.

Wincott, D, 'The role of law or the rule of the Court of Justice? An institutional account of judicial politics in the European Community', *Journal of European Public Policy*, 1995, 2, pp 583–602.

# Index